Simon Jenkins is the author of the bestselling *England's Thousand Best Churches* and *England's Thousand Best Houses*, the former editor of *The Times* and *Evening Standard* and a columnist for the *Guardian*. He is also chairman of the National Trust.

Also by Simon Jenkins

England's Thousand Best Churches
England's Thousand Best Houses

A SHORT HISTORY OF ENGLAND

SIMON JENKINS

In association with National Trust

P

PROFILE BOOKS

This paperback edition published in 2012

First published in Great Britain in 2011 by
PROFILE BOOKS LTD
3A Exmouth House
Pine Street
London EC1R 0JH
www.profilebooks.com

10 9 8 7 6 5 4 3 2

Book design by James Alexander
www.jadedesign.co.uk

Printed and bound by CPI Group (UK) Ltd,
Croydon, CR0 4YY

A CIP catalogue record for this book is available
from the British Library.

ISBN 978 184 668 463 0
eISBN 978 184765 756 5

Contents

~

Introduction

~

I HAVE ROAMED ENGLAND all my life. I have climbed Cornwall's cliffs, wandered Norfolk's marshes and walked the Pennine Way. I know England's cities and towns, churches and houses. For all that, until recently I did not really know England, for I was not aware of how it came to be. My England was a geographical stage set, a backdrop for events and characters familiar from my childhood: Alfred the Great, the Norman conquest, Magna Carta, Agincourt, Henry VIII's wives, Good Queen Bess, Cromwell, Gladstone, Disraeli, the Great War, Winston Churchill. Each stood as a magnificent moment in time, but they did not join up. They lacked a narrative.

I set out here to tell that narrative as simply as possible. I was helped by finding it exhilarating. England's history, its triumphs and disasters, must be the most consistently eventful of any nation on earth. Its origins lie in the Dark Ages, and possibly before, in the occupation of the eastern shores of the British Isles by Germanic tribes from the continent. They brought with them the name of Anglii, probably from the 'angle' of the coasts of Germany and Denmark. Their settlement on the north-east coast was named Angle-land and later England. These newcomers quickly drove the earlier inhabitants, so-called 'ancient Britons', to the west and north, to beyond Hadrian's Wall, the Welsh uplands and the Irish Sea, forming boundaries of England that have remained roughly constant ever since.

The English were themselves invaded by Vikings and by Normans. But while they had obliterated their British predecessors, they kept their Anglo-Saxon culture and language through all subsequent incursions. They were astonishingly resilient, aided by the security of an insular geography and the seafaring enterprise often shown by island peoples. They quickly evolved a common language, common laws and a common system of government, rooted in a tension between the Saxon autonomy of 'kith and kin' and the Norman tradition of central authority. That tension is a leitmotif of my story. England was a nation forged between the hammer of kingship and the anvil of popular consent, a consent regularly withheld, not least by the Celtic half of the British Isles which came to form the first 'English empire'. The result was such conflicts as led to Magna Carta, the baronial wars of Henry III and the Peasants' Revolt, culminating in the religious and political revolutions of the Tudors and Stuarts. These revolutions resolved into a constitutional monarchy subject to a parliamentary democracy that was to prove the most stable in Europe.

The story was not always happy. Relations with France, the land of the Norman conquerors, were mostly dreadful, with conflict throughout the Middle Ages and again in the eighteenth century. Most British rulers understood the need for a defensive rather than aggressive stance towards the outside world. Yet from the Plantagenets to the elder and younger Pitts, the craving for overseas domain rarely dimmed. It led Britain to amass the largest empire the world had ever seen. It brought much glory and helped bind together the peoples of the British Isles in a 'united kingdom' of shared endeavour, whose legacy continues to this day. But the British empire came at a price and lasted barely two hundred years. In the twentieth century Britain's global dominance passed to its offspring, America, leaving behind as a tidemark the extent of spoken English. Britain then declined, to become a relic of its former greatness and something of a poseur as a world power, its sovereignty compromised by European government and by the disciplines of a global economy. I return to these themes in my epilogue.

This is specifically a book about England. I regard Wales, Scotland and Ireland as countries with their own histories. They have spent less than half their existence as components of a union of 'Great Britain and Ireland', an embrace that tends to subordinate them in conventional histories of Britain. But England is a country in its own right, different from its neighbours and with a people who call themselves English in differentiation from Scots, Welsh and Irish. Only when referring to all these collectively do I use the terms Britain and Britons. Indeed England is now part of two confederacies, of the United Kingdom and of the European Union, with separate assemblies and variable tiers of sovereignty. To be British and to be European is to be a legal member of one of those unions, and to become British is to sign a piece of paper. To be English is more a matter of self-definition, identifying with a distinctive culture and outlook as well as geography. To become English is a matter of assimilation, which can take a few years or a few generations. The genius of Englishness is that it encompasses all origins and races, but in a culture specific to the territory defined by the original Anglo-Saxon occupation.

The English have never been good at describing themselves. In the age of imperial confidence they did not feel the need. Today most of them dislike seeing themselves as Europeans, but they are no better at defining themselves as against their Celtic neighbours. They waged wars of suppression against Wales, Scotland and, with peculiar brutality, Ireland. At the start of the twenty-first century they find themselves with Ireland mostly detached and Scotland and Wales semi-detached, politically as well as culturally. The English component of the United Kingdom is thus left in a strangely anaemic limbo. It has no parliament or distinctive political institutions of its own. To refer to England and the English as distinct from Britain and the British is often treated as hostile to the cosmopolitanism implied by the union, even as racist. The English flag of St George has acquired a tinge of chauvinism and xenophobia and been adopted by the far right. I find this absurd. England is a country entitled to define itself and take pride in doing so. I believe that definition should begin with a narrative of its history.

To some, history is a matter of chance, to others it is fashioned by heroes and villains, and to others it is buried in geography, economics, even anthropology. There are many ways of a telling a nation's story, with a current fashion for the personal and controversial. There are histories social, cultural, 'popular' and, in England's case, imperial. But a short history can only be selective, and the selection will be mostly devoted to politics. A nation is a political entity and its birth and development form a narrative of those who deployed power within it, be they monarchs, soldiers, politicians, the mob in the street or, more recently, the mass of voters. I regard history as more than a straight chronology but as links in a chain of cause and effect. It is this chain that holds the secret of how England came to be where it is today.

Saxon Dawn

~

410 – 600

IN THE YEAR 410 a letter was sent from the embattled Roman emperor, Honorius, to colonists in his province of Britannia. They had already lost the protection of the legions, withdrawn from Britannia during the past half century to defend the empire, and had written pleading for help against Saxon raids from across the North Sea. The emperor was beset by Visigoths, and a distant colony at the extremity of the known world was strategically unimportant. The civilisations of the Mediterranean, supreme for a millennium, were in retreat. Honorius cursorily advised the colonists to 'take steps to defend yourselves'.

The fifth and sixth centuries in the British Isles were truly dark ages. Iron Age Celts, so-called ancient Britons, had migrated from the continent between a thousand and six hundred years BC, and had intermarried with Roman invaders in the three centuries after the birth of Christ. But the retreat of the legions left them too weak to defend themselves or their legacy of Roman villas, temples and theatres. They lay vulnerable to the raiders against whom they had pleaded for help.

From where did these new invaders come? Historians seeking 'the birth of England' are soon enveloped in controversy. Two theories are advanced for what happened at this time in the eastern half of the British Isles. One is that Germanic tribes moving south towards France were balked by the Franks under Emperor Clovis and diverted across the North Sea. Their invasion, perhaps assisted by Roman mercenaries already resident in Britain, was essentially genocidal. They massacred or wholly subjugated the indigenous British tribes of eastern England, such as the Iceni and Trinovantes, and obliterated their culture.

This thesis is supported by the few witnesses who survived the period. The only contemporary source, a sixth-century Welsh (or west country) monk named Gildas, graphically laments the fiery invasion of 'impious men ... that did not cease after it had been kindled, until it burnt nearly the whole surface of the island, and licked the western ocean with its red and savage tongue'. He quoted a fifth-century document, the Groan of the British, telling of a Britain bereft of Roman protection: 'The barbarians drive us to the sea and the sea throws us back on the barbarians.' By the late seventh century the 'Father of English History', the Venerable Bede, took the genocide thesis as given in his *Ecclesiastical History of the English People*. He wrote of the Anglii invading in such force as to leave their Germanic settlements deserted. Little or no trace of any preceding British culture remained. The British, or Brythonic, language and Romano-Christian religion disappeared. So-called Romano-British villas and towns fell into decay or were burned.

Another theory is that there was no external invasion, rather an internal expansion, since the eastern parts of Britain had long been settled by Germanic and Belgic peoples, trading and raiding the shores of the North Sea. Recent DNA archaeology reinforces a view of the sea round the British Isles as navigable 'territory', while interior land forms a less permeable barrier. Thus the culture of the British Isles at the time of the Roman retreat was divided between the North Sea coast, settled over the centuries by Germanic tribes, and the Irish Sea and Atlantic coasts, which were Celtic in language and culture. The theory suggests that there were few 'ancient Britons', or Celts, in eastern parts and therefore none to eradicate. This explains the paucity of Brythonic language traces and place names, though it does not explain the references to an overseas invasion and the overwhelming Celtic belief in one. The possible resolution of these divergent theories is that both were true in part, with new waves of Germanic settlers arriving after the Romans left, adding to longer-standing Germanic enclaves.

Either way it seems clear that over the course of the fifth and sixth centuries a people whose language and society derived from the continent of Europe moved aggressively westward across Roman Britannia, overwhelming the indigenous British. According to Bede this movement comprised Jutes, Frisians, Angles and Saxons. 'Saeson', 'Sassenach' and 'Sawsnek' are the old Welsh, Gaelic and Cornish words for the English. In *c.*450 Jutes under the brothers Hengist and Horsa, possibly once hired as mercenaries by a Romano-British ruler, Vortigern, landed in Kent and spread as far as the Isle of Wight. At the same time Angles arrived from the 'angle' of Germany in Schleswig-Holstein, lending their name to East Anglia and eventually to England itself. Saxons from north Germany settled along the south coast and penetrated the Thames basin, forming territories known to this day as Essex (east Saxon), Middlesex, Wessex and Sussex. These peoples are referred to as Saxons and their language as Anglo-Saxon. A strong argument deployed by the invasion theorists is that all trace of Roman Christianity appears to have been eradicated from land occupied by the pagan Saxons. In contrast, Wales at this time was seeing a fervently Christian 'age of saints'. Dozens of Welsh churches date from the sixth and even fifth centuries and the oldest cathedral in Britain was begun by Deiniol in Bangor in 525. At much the same time St Petroc was preaching in Cornwall, and St Columba was travelling from Ireland to the Scottish island of Iona, founding a monastery there in *c.*563.

Gildas told not only of the misery inflicted by the Saxons on the British but of resistance. In the 540s he wrote of living in what appears to have been the Severn valley in a period of peace, the Saxon advance having stalled in the west country. He attributed this to a British leader who defeated the Saxons at the turn of the sixth century at a place called Mount Badon, possibly near the fort of South Cadbury in Somerset. The only commander he mentions by name was Ambrosius Aurelianus, a Romano-Briton born in the late fifth century who 'won some battles and lost others'. His nickname may have been 'Bear', the skin of his military tunic. Bear is *artos* in Celtic.

This glint of light in the darkness is the nearest history gets to 'Arthur'. On it was based a giant edifice of legend. From Gildas was derived the Arthur of the ninth-century propagandist Nennius, and of the twelfth-century fantasist Geoffrey of Monmouth, responsible for much of the imagery of north European chivalric culture. This led to the bestseller by Thomas Malory in the fifteenth century, *Morte d'Arthur*. Following Malory came Tennyson, the pre-Raphaelites, Hollywood and the 'Holy Grail', conjecturing a mystic pre-Saxon paradise called Camelot, with a wizard called Merlin, and many a knightly deed, heartbreak and tragedy. Britons, Saxons, Normans and Tudors were all to claim Arthur as their own, as if driven by some desperate magnetism towards a pure and noble past.

If Gildas's period of peace existed, it did not last. Towards the end of the sixth century Saxons had settled along the length of the River Severn, where a Welsh saint, Beuno, reported on 'strange-tongued men whose voices I heard across the river'. He feared that one day they would 'obtain possession of this place and it will be theirs'. Yet while Saxons occupied the great valleys draining into the North Sea, Britons were left in occupation of Scotland, Ireland, Wales, Cornwall, Cumbria and the Hen Ogledd ('Old North' in Welsh) of the Scottish borders. The Celtic tongue had by now divided into two groups, Goedelic (Irish and Scots Gaelic and Manx) and Brythonic (Cumbric, Welsh and Cornish). At this time or earlier a migration took place from Cornwall across the Channel to Armorica in France. Here Roman Britannia was recreated as Brittany, and the language as Breton, distantly related to modern Welsh.

By the end of the seventh century, the Saxons were combining into larger groupings under early kings. The first to emerge with any distinction was Ethelbert of Kent, who reigned from *c.*580 until his death in 616, a pagan who cemented an alliance with the cross-Channel Franks by marrying Bertha, granddaughter of King Clovis of France, subject to the condition that she retain her Christian faith. She brought her own chaplain and is said to have worshipped at the old Roman church of St Martin in Canterbury. It was probably for this reason that Pope Gregory was later to send his first Christian missionaries to Kent under St Augustine.

At the same time in the north, Northumbria was cohering under a great warrior, Ethelfrith, king of Bernicia (593–616), who was to entrench the boundaries of Saxon settlement against British resistance. The north-British Gododdin tribe, possibly based on the rock of Edinburgh, had their deeds recorded by a bard named Aneurin in *The Gododdin*, the first great work of British (as opposed to English) literature. His saga tells how an army of 300 warriors marched south under their leader Mynyddog, sometime about 600, meeting Ethelfrith near Catterick in Yorkshire. Of one British soldier Aneurin wrote:

> In might a man, a youth in years,
> Of boisterous valour …
> Quicker to a field of blood
> Than to a wedding
> Quicker to the ravens' feast
> Than to a burial.

Yet the Gododdin were wiped out, with only Aneurin escaping to tell the tale. His poem is known in a transcription into medieval Welsh, but scholars believe the original to have been in the Cumbric language of the north British tribes and similar to Welsh (in which case present-day signs at Edinburgh airport in Gaelic should be in Welsh).

Worse was to follow for the British. In 603 a Scots-Irish army from Dalriada, a kingdom stretching across the Irish Sea from Argyll to Antrim, met the same Ethelfrith in battle at Degsastan, believed to be near Roxburgh. The Northumbrians were again victorious. They then carried their supremacy south along the west coast to confront the Welsh. In c.615 Ethelfrith encountered 1,200 Welsh Christian monks near the old Roman town of Chester, and slaughtered them 'for opposing him with their prayers'. He went on to defeat the main Welsh army and bring his domain to the banks of the Dee. To the Anglo-Saxon Bede, writing a century later, Ethelfrith was the true founder of Northumbria, who 'ravaged the Britons more than all the great men of the English, insomuch that he might be compared to Saul, once king of the Israelites, excepting only this, that he was ignorant of the true religion'.

The area of Saxon England was beginning to take shape, south of Hadrian's wall and east of the Severn and the Devon border. Pockets of ancient Britain appear to have survived in the Pennine uplands and in places such as Elmet in west Yorkshire (which was overrun in 627). But the surrounding England was in no sense a nation. No authority, king or church had replaced the Romans. People were ruled, if at all, by Saxon warlords regarded by the Christian Celts in the west as marauding, illiterate pagans. Saxons were people of lowland rather than upland, accustomed to fight and farm across the great plains of northern Europe. They could fell trees and use ploughs that cut deep into alluvial soil, but they stopped when they reached higher land. Here the country was less fertile and the Britons perhaps less easy to overcome. The zest for conquest seemed to evaporate as it moved west.

Saxons were rooted in loyalty to family, settlement and clan, embodied in the Anglo-Saxon phrase 'kith and kin', derived from 'couth [hence uncouth] and known'. Their focus was not a distant king and court but a communal hall in the centre of each settlement, where communities of free farmers (ceorls) would swear allegiance to their chiefs. These elders – or ealdormen – and subordinate thanes were owed hospitality and military service in return for the defence of the subjects' lives and land. The oaths Saxons swore bound them to those whose lineage they shared and with whom they tilled the earth. This contractual 'consent to power', as distinct from ancient British tribalism and Norman ducal authority, was described by later law-givers as habitual 'since time out of mind'. It found its apogee in the representation of leading citizens on the king's 'witengemot' or witan, most primitive precursor of parliament. To Victorian romantics all this was a dim Saxon echo of what the Greeks called democracy.

The Birth of England

~

600 – 800

IN 596 POPE GREGORY NOTICED two blond-haired slaves in a
Roman market place and asked where they were from. On being
told they were 'Angli' he is reported by Bede as replying, 'Non
Angli sed angeli,' not Angles but angels of God. Britain was a
forgotten colony on the distant border of the Frankish empire,
then covering much of modern France and Germany. Gregory
was an ardent missionary and sent a bishop, Augustine, to the
court of Ethelbert of Kent and his wife, the Frankish Christian
Bertha. On landing at Thanet in 597, Augustine's party of forty
Benedictines was ordered to meet in the open air, for fear of
what the pagans regarded as their sorcery.

The success of Augustine's mission was confirmed in the
Christianising of Ethelbert and his donation, in 602, of a
site in Canterbury for a new cathedral. Augustine became
Canterbury's first archbishop while Ethelbert drew up England's
first legal code of ninety clauses, granting privileges to the new
church. It is also the first document in the 'English' or Anglo-
Saxon language. The following year Ethelbert and Augustine
boldly sought reconciliation at a meeting in the Severn valley
with Welsh church leaders from Bangor and elsewhere. The
latter practised a Celtic liturgy inherited from Rome, but were
monastic rather than evangelical, following their own calendar,
penitent customs and form of tonsure, shaving the front rather
than the crown of their heads. The two parties could not agree,

not least over the authority of Rome. An angry Augustine allegedly threatened the British that, 'If you will not have peace with your friends, you shall have war from your foes.' He returned to Kent empty handed.

Meanwhile King Redwald of East Anglia (*c*.600–24), was expanding his domain across the heart of England to form what became the central kingdom of Mercia. He is little known except as probable occupant of the Sutton Hoo ship burial in Suffolk, found in 1939 and now in the British Museum. It includes plate and gems from the Mediterranean and Byzantium, swords and a splendid helmet from the Rhine. Sutton Hoo offers a window on a cosmopolitan civilisation that remains tantalisingly obscure.

In Northumbria Ethelfrith, scourge of the Gododdin, had been succeeded by Edwin (616–33), a king with an army potent enough to sweep south through Mercia as far as Kent. On defeating the West Saxons he carried back to York not only Ethelbert's Christian daughter Ethelburga, but a Roman monk, Paulinus, who in 627 baptised him and his thanes, and founded York Minster. One converted thane spoke to Edwin of a sparrow in a wintry hall at dinner time, which 'flies in at one door and tarries for a moment in the light and heat of the hearth, then flying out of the other, vanishes ... So tarries for a moment the life of man in our sight, but what is before it, and what after it, we do not know. If this new teaching tells us anything certain of these things, let us follow it.' Edwin's pagan high priest was less reflective. He hurled a spear into his own temple and ordered its conflagration.

Edwin's supremacy did not last long. He was challenged by the powerful Penda of Mercia, a pagan allied to the Welsh ruler Cadwallon of Gwynedd. In 633 these leaders met and killed Edwin at the battle of Hatfield Chase in Yorkshire, putting much of Northumbria to fire and the sword. The Christian cause in the north briefly collapsed, but a year later another Christian Saxon, Oswald, occupied Northumbria from his asylum on Iona. He brought with him a monk named Aidan, with whom he founded a monastery in 635 at Lindisfarne off the Northumbrian coast. England appears to have taken to Christianity with speed. Even Penda allowed his children to be baptised and asserted that 'they were contemptible and wretched who did not obey their god, in whom they believed'. When he was finally defeated in 655 by Oswald's brother, Oswy, the last pagan ruler of England died. The Saxon animist and warrior gods Tiw, Woden, Thunor and Freya survived only as days of the week.

What sort of Christianity England should espouse remained open. Lindisfarne practised the Ionan rite, reinforced in 657 when Oswald's brother and successor, Oswy, founded a new monastery at Whitby. But many at the Northumbrian court followed the Roman rite introduced to York by Paulinus. What began as a domestic dispute over when to fast and celebrate Easter soon extended to disputes within the Northumbrian church, Ionan traditionalists confronting Canterbury modernists. In 664 Oswy summoned church leaders from Canterbury to a synod at Whitby, where battle was joined between Colman of Northumbria and Wilfrid of Ripon. Wilfrid, who had visited Rome and strongly supported its cause, represented Canterbury because he spoke Anglo-Saxon. To him, the authority of the pope and the expansive Roman liturgy outshone the backwardness of the Celts. He swayed the synod, and, more important, Oswy, preaching that St Peter was 'the rock of the church' and holder of the keys to life hereafter. The Ionans under Colman retired in dudgeon to Ireland, itself the scene of liturgical divisions. Wilfrid became bishop of York.

Rome swiftly exploited its triumph. A new papal emissary arrived in 669, Theodore of Tarsus, born in Asia Minor and versed in Greek, Roman and Byzantine scholarship. By the time of his death in 690 he had established fourteen territorial bishoprics under Canterbury. The kings of Kent and Wessex were encouraged to write new legal codes based on those throughout the papal domains, exempting the church from civil duties and laying down rules for social and marital conduct. Penalties for theft, violence and trespass recognised a hierarchy under the king, where bishops ranked with thanes and clergymen with ceorls.

England might still have been disunited politically at the end of the seventh century but the synod of Whitby saw it join the mainstream of Europe's ecclesiastical culture. The church now began a period of wealth and influence that was to last until the Reformation. In a country often at war with itself, Theodore's church ministered to all English people, educating them and offering them welfare and public administration. It instigated, on the bleak coast of Northumbria at Lindisfarne, a flowering of scholarship that was to become as rich as any in Europe. To produce great illuminated codices and gospels required an industry of scribes and materials. The gospel produced at Lindisfarne in 698 and now in the British Library displays a marriage of Celtic and continental motifs as rich as anything yet seen in the civilisation of northern Europe. It would have taken years of labour and is estimated to have used the skins of 1,500 calves.

In 674 a new monastery was founded on the Tyne at Jarrow by Bishop Biscop, a churchman of the new era who had been on five pilgrimages to Rome, returning each time with craftsmen, musicians, manuscripts and donations for his churches. The Jarrow monastery was host to the Venerable Bede, whose *Ecclesiastical History of the English People* was published in 731. Bede saw Britain over the previous two centuries as a pagan land brought to a state of grace by Saxon Christianity, a highly coloured thesis since in most of the British Isles, the reverse was the case. None the less Bede was a unique witness to England's earliest years and the first to show a sense of Englishness. He was the earliest to use the word Angle-land and the first to apply some chronology to the country's birth and growth.

By the eighth century what was termed 'ascendancy' in England was passing from Northumbria to Mercia. Here in 757 arose Offa, the first English king whose dominance was recognised across Europe. Offa (757–96) was a monarch in perpetual movement, administering justice and exacting tribute across his domain. He had his own coins minted – including, uniquely, one with the head of his consort Queen Cynethryth – and in 785 marked England's boundary with Wales with a rampart, Offa's Dyke, from the Dee to the Severn. The dyke was more a border demarcation than a defence, and there is evidence it was located so as to give some fertile land to the Welsh, as in a treaty. In 786 the pope sent ambassadors to Offa's court, with papal demands on both canon and secular law. That the Mercians should entertain such demands is a measure of the reach of Roman jurisdiction. Offa obtained a new archbishopric, at Lichfield, in return for an annual gift of gold, and agreed to 'consecrate' his son Egfrith as heir to his throne. This secular contract between the English state and the Roman church was significant and was to cause Saxon and Norman monarchs no end of trouble.

Towards the end of Offa's reign a Northumbrian monk, Alcuin of York, the leading scholar at the court of Charlemagne, was able to refer to him as 'a glory to Britain [Britannia] and a sword against foes, shield against enemies'. But Offa's personal ambition exceeded his power. When Charlemagne proposed that his son might marry the Mercian king's daughter, Offa agreed on condition that Charlemagne's daughter married his son. The emperor was reportedly enraged by such implied equality and broke off relations, even banning trade with Mercia for a period.

After Offa's death a weak line of successors led to another shift of ascendancy, this time south to Wessex. Lichfield was demoted in favour of Canterbury and in 814 Egbert of Wessex (802–39) invaded Cornwall, bringing it under Saxon sovereignty. This invasion was not occupation or assimilation as in regions to the east. The Saxons called the region West Wales, and it retained its language and local rulers. To this day, the Cornish regard inhabitants east of the Tamar as 'English' and outsiders. Egbert then moved against Mercia, consulting his elders over whether to fight the Mercians or sue for peace. The Anglo-Saxon chronicles record that 'they thought it more honourable to have their heads cut off than to lay their free necks beneath the yoke'. In the end, they had to do neither. The Wessex victory at the battle of Ellandun, near Swindon, in 825 moved the centre of English power emphatically south, where it has resided ever since. Egbert went on to attack East Anglia and Northumbria and unite the land that was England.

After two centuries of what Milton called 'the wars of kites and crows, flocking and fighting in the air', the English people under Egbert and his successors could contemplate a Saxon peace. The temporary ascendancy of Wessex was acknowledged and its capital of Winchester became the seat of England's kings. But a nemesis was at hand. As the Saxons had threatened the ancient Britons from the east so now, wrote an Anglo-Saxon chronicler, 'whirlwinds, lightning storms and fiery dragons were seen flying in the sky'. Alcuin reported to Charlemagne: 'Never before has such terror appeared ... as we have now suffered from a pagan race.' The Vikings were coming.

The Danes

~

800 – 1066

THE SAXONS WERE PEOPLE of the land. Their Scandinavian neighbours, the Vikings, were people of the sea. Those from Norway had long raided Scotland and the coastal settlements round the Irish Sea, while the Danes had raided down the North Sea and deep into France. Their weapon was the longship, a fighting machine that could sail fifty miles in a day and draw less than three feet with sixty men aboard. Blond-haired 'berserk' warriors crowded its decks and pagan gods adorned its prow. One contemporary usage of their name was as a verb, 'to go viking' or raiding. Fleets of longships crossed the Atlantic to Iceland and Greenland. They rounded the coast of France, sailed upriver to raid Paris and headed south into the Mediterranean. They reached Constantinople, where the patriarch's guard was composed of Vikings. Longships penetrated the rivers of Russia, founding Kiev. Like the Spanish conquistadors, they initially sought only booty but increasingly they set up colonies, creating a 'norseman', or Norman, culture round the coasts of Europe.

In 790, three longships landed on the Wessex shore. A Saxon official from Dorchester rode to greet them and ask their business. They killed him on the spot. Three years later Northumbria was appalled by the sacking of Lindisfarne, with the loss of hundreds of manuscripts and illuminated books. The chronicles reported that 'the heathens poured out the blood of saints around the altar, and trampled on the bodies of saints in the temple of God like dung in the streets'. Monks who escaped the sword were taken as slaves. In 806 came a similar horror, the destruction of St Columba's 200-year-old monastery on Iona, mother church of Celtic Christianity and burial place of Scottish kings. Its ruination was so severe the site was later abandoned, to be re-established in the thirteenth century.

By the early years of the ninth century Viking raids had become regular. The largest, apparently concerted, assault on England came with a landing on Sheppey in Kent in 835. Then in 845 the red-bearded marauder Ragnar Lodbrok was wrecked off the coast of Northumbria, whose king threw him into a dungeon filled with vipers. He is said to have died calling for revenge from his sons, Halfdan and Ivar the Boneless. They needed no encouragement. Ivar was already ruler of Dublin.

In 865 what the chronicles called a 'great heathen army' arrived in East Anglia and carried all before it. A Northumbrian king was executed by having his lungs extracted through his back as a 'blood eagle'. York fell and became a Viking trading post, Yorvik. The Danes then proceeded against Mercia and Wessex. Any who resisted were murdered, such as Edmund of East Anglia, whose body was used for archery practice, to be commemorated in Bury St Edmunds. The invaders reached Reading in 871 and Wareham in 876.

By now the invasion was becoming an occupation. The newcomers began to settle, dividing their conquered territory north and south of the Humber. They intermarried and their language mixed with that of the local population. Danish law arrived, as did place names ending in -thorpe, -by and -gill. Land was divided into ridings and weapontakes instead of Saxon hundreds. Five new boroughs were established at Lincoln, Stamford, Nottingham, Derby and Leicester, and England from the Tees to the Thames became known as the Danelaw. Only when the Danes reached Wessex did they encounter serious opposition from two kings, Ethelred and his brother Alfred

(871–99). Fighting continued throughout the 870s until the 'year of battles', 877, after which Alfred fled to Athelney in the Somerset Levels. Here in the legendary land of King Arthur he planned guerrilla warfare, earning reported fame by burning a poor woman's cakes on a fire while lost in thought.

Alfred returned a year later to lead Wessex to victory over the Danish commander Guthrum at the battle of Edington outside Chippenham. This victory was crucial to English history. Had the Danes won, Guthrum would have extended the Danelaw and paganism throughout the now dominant kingdom of Wessex. England would have been occupied in its entirety by a new power and become part of a Scandinavian confederacy, which in turn might have resisted the Norman conquest. As it was, the defeated Guthrum was baptised a Christian, with Alfred as his godfather. The Danes abandoned Wessex but remained in occupation of the Danelaw, embracing probably a third of England's population. Despite Guthrum's defeat, Danish raids continued in Kent, Devon and elsewhere throughout Alfred's reign. London remained a Viking town until 886.

Alfred is the first English monarch of whom we possess a rounded picture. He reorganised the Wessex army as a standing force, supplemented by a territorial tribute of one soldier from each 'hide' or freeman's farm. Across Wessex he built fortresses, or burghs, with ramparts to render them immune to future Danish attack. He planned a navy, designing its ships as longships and hiring Danish mercenaries to man them. This led to a rare series of naval victories over Viking raiders, including the defeat of a reported armada of 250 ships off Kent in 892. This fleet came not from Denmark but ominously from the mouth of the Seine in France, where Vikings under Rollo were soon to be granted the land of Normandy by the French king. The future Normans were not French but Viking to the core.

Alfred replanned his capital at Winchester on a Roman grid pattern that survives to this day. After decades of Viking desecration of monasteries, he bemoaned the fact that in all Wessex there was no clerk who could speak Latin. Scholars were invited from the continent and half the royal revenues went to church schools, with the intention that the English should be literate and that Winchester should rival the great courts of Europe. Latin texts were translated into Anglo-Saxon, including one by Alfred himself of the sixth-century humanist Boethius. In about 890 Alfred commissioned the Anglo-Saxon chronicles, basis of almost all our knowledge of the period after Bede. 'I know nothing worse of a man,' said Alfred, 'than that he should not know.'

A new legal code, based on those of Ethelbert of Kent and Offa of Mercia, collated an emerging English law on a basis of Saxon precedent. Alfred approved 'those laws which our forefathers observed which I liked ... many which I did not like I rejected with the advice of my councillors.' One thoughtful statute held that if a man is killed by a falling tree, the tree should belong to his family. Kings were to be protected from treason, but in return had to ensure law was enforced and security maintained. As Offa had made kings subject to the church, so Alfred made them subject to the law. It was the early stirrings of a concept of consent to rule, to which later generations of lawyers frequently referred.

After Alfred died in 899 he was succeeded by his son Edward ('the Elder') and grandson Athelstan (924–39). Learned, pious, 'golden-haired', Athelstan 'the Glorious' was the first English king known to have remained unmarried. He secured his throne by marrying his sisters to the kings of the Saxons, Franks and Burgundians. In return he received the sword of Constantine and the lance of Charlemagne as gifts. Yet even Athelstan could not rule without challenge. In 937 he faced a major attack from an Irish Sea confederacy, an alliance of Welsh, Scots and Dublin Vikings. After a battle at Brunanburh (possibly in Cheshire) 'five kings lay dead on the field' in what the chronicles called 'the greatest battle won by the edge of the sword' on English soil.

Athelstan was not among them, though he died shortly afterwards and the Wessex supremacy degenerated into family feuding until it passed to Edgar (959–75). He succeeded in uniting England at peace and, in a grand conference held in Cheshire in 973, is said to have been rowed on the Dee in homage by the kings of Wales, Cumbria, Strathclyde, Scotland and Norse Ireland. But no early monarch could ensure his legacy and Athelstan's death returned the country to dynastic squabbles. These culminated in the disastrous thirty-eight-year reign of Ethelred 'the Unready' (978–1016), who came to the throne at the bidding of his mother at the age of ten. His nickname referred not to his youth but to his incompetence. Edgar's chief minister, the elderly Archbishop Dunstan, predicted at his coronation that 'such evils shall come upon the English nation as it hath never suffered from since the time it came to England'. The reference to the English still as newcomers is intriguing.

Ethelred ruled in exceptionally difficult times and his reputation suffered from accounts written during the anarchy soon after his death. In 991 the Danes staged an eighty-ship attack on Essex, to which the young Ethelred could only respond by paying blackmail money, or 'Danegeld'. This sent a message that every Viking understood: booty was to be had in England by merely threatening to fight. For a decade the Vikings relieved England of quantities of gold and silver, involving the ransacking of churches and monasteries and the imposition of penal taxes. In 1002 Ethelred reacted to an attack by Svein 'Forkbeard' of Denmark by ordering the slaughter of all Danes across eastern England, the so-called St Brice's Day massacre. Svein's own sister, in the Danish enclave in London, pleaded for her life with Ethelred but she too was killed.

The consequence was predictable. Svein returned in a fury and Ethelred had to scour England for Danegeld, estimated at four times what passed for the nation's cash income. Annual attacks meant that by 1013 the Danes were sufficiently in control of England to force Ethelred to flee to Normandy. There he married Emma, sister of the Duke of Normandy, by whom he had a son who would become king of England, the future Edward the Confessor. On Svein's death in 1014, the witan (the Anglo-Saxon parliament) requested Ethelred's return on a strict promise of 'good government', the first such recorded contract between an English king and his subjects.

The result was a resumed Danish invasion in 1015 by Svein's son, Cnut (Canute), bringing with him an army of 20,000 from across northern Europe in 200 longships. A chronicle reported that 'there were so many kinds of shields, that you could have believed that troops of all nations were present ... Who could look upon the bulls on the ships threatening death, their horns shining with gold, without feeling any fear for the king of such a force? Furthermore, in this great expedition there was present no slave, no man freed from slavery, no low-born man, no man weakened by age. All were nobles.' There followed a year of sustained war by Cnut's army against Ethelred's effective son, Edmund Ironside. The walled city of London fell, as did all of Wessex, Mercia and Northumbria. Although Cnut could not conquer all of England, the deaths of Ethelred and Edmund ensured that he became king. Cnut (1016–35) was crowned in London at Christmas 1016. Alfred's great kingdom had been reduced to a wasteland of marauding bands. Six months later Cnut married Ethelred's widow, Emma of Normandy, partly legitimising his succession and embracing England in a Viking empire that eventually extended from Wessex through Denmark to the north of Norway. This, and not 1066 half a century later, marked the true demise of Saxon England.

Cnut was said by the Norse sagas to be exceptionally tall and strong, and 'the handsomest of men, all except for his nose, that was thin, high-set, and rather hooked'. He was constantly on the move between his realms of England, Denmark and Norway. He received the homage of the Scottish ruler, Malcolm (nemesis of Macbeth), and went on pilgrimage to Rome, bringing Christianity back to Scandinavia. He was ruler of more territory than any English king before Henry II. Of his character we know nothing except a strangely corrupted legend. When, according to a twelfth-century chronicle, he set his chair in the sea to bid the tide turn back, it was not, as children used to be told, a show of folly but the opposite. As he leapt back he cried, 'Let all men know how empty and worthless is the power of kings.'

On Cnut's death in 1035, his sons feuded over the succession, enabling an Anglo-Danish courtier, Godwin of Wessex, to acquire the position of kingmaker. Extrovert and ruthless, he secured the throne for Ethelred's son, the forty-one-year-old Edward the Confessor (1042–66), who thus began his reign as Godwin's puppet, marrying his daughter despite having reputedly taken a vow of celibacy. Edward surrounded himself with French-speaking courtiers and was, in practice, the first Norman ruler of England. It was from Edward's day, not from the Norman conquest, that English state documents were written in French. He began the great Norman abbey at Westminster and extended the shire reeves, or king's sheriffs, to form a parallel structure of kingly authority to that of the local Saxon earldoms. This dualism between monarch and territorial ruler was to be a sometimes explosive, sometimes creative feature of England's medieval constitution.

At court there arose another dualism, between Godwin's Anglo-Danes and Edward's French-speaking Normans. Amid growing tension at court, Edward was supported against Godwin by such prominent Saxons as Earl Leofric of Wessex, husband of Godgifu (God's gift, or Godiva). It was she who was said to have ridden naked through Coventry in protest at her husband's penal taxes, a legend for which there is no shred of contemporary evidence yet which acquired compelling status in the Middle Ages. In 1051 civil war between the supporters of Leofric and Godwin was narrowly averted by the witan expelling Godwin

and his family to France, an early display of power by that body
of royal advisers. Sometime in this period, Edward received an
obscure but significant visit from his mother's great-nephew, the
twenty-three-year-old Duke William of Normandy, at which
William subsequently claimed that Edward had approved his
tenuous claim to the English crown. At this seminal moment in
England's history, no one was taking minutes.

The following year the Godwins returned to London on a
tide of anti-Norman sentiment, expelling Edward's Norman
archbishop, Robert of Canterbury, in favour of an Anglo-Dane,
Stigand. Godwin's son, Harold, became Earl of Wessex and
virtual ruler of England for most of Edward's last decade. It was
now Harold's turn to complicate the succession. On an obscure
journey in the Channel he was shipwrecked on the French coast
and took refuge in William's court, even going with him on a
campaign. During this visit he is said, by the Normans, to have
confirmed the Confessor's acknowledgement of William as
heir to the English throne and paid him due homage. Certainly,
William took this as conclusive evidence of his right to the
crown.

Yet as Edward lay dying at the start of the fateful year 1066,
he turned to Harold and committed 'all the kingdom to your
protection'. The earl was already de facto ruler of England
and was clearly regarded by the witan as most plausible king.
Though he had no blood claim to the throne, he was the next
best thing, a seasoned warrior and in command of the country.
Harold was duly enthroned. When William heard of this he
reacted with fury, sending a message from his capital of Rouen
reminding Harold of Edward's blessing and his, Harold's, oath
of loyalty. The witan, a body now clearly demonstrating quasi-
constitutional authority, rejected the message. It already had a
king.

William the Conqueror

~

1066 – 1087

THE YEAR 1066 is the most celebrated in English history. To every English schoolchild it evokes a Saxon hero, Harold, and a French villain, William, who met and fought at the battle of Hastings. The outcome was decided by an arrow in Harold's eye. But history is seldom as commonly related. Harold, son of Godwin, was at best only half Saxon and had no claim to the throne beyond Edward's deathbed blessing. William was no Frenchman but descended from the Norse warrior Rollo, granted Normandy by the French king Charles the Simple in 911. He too had no claim beyond Edward's apparent, but earlier, blessing. Both were of direct Viking descent.

William was a cunning, ambitious man capable of extreme violence. He ruled a dukedom smaller than Yorkshire for which he paid homage to the French king. His regime was based on feudal ownership of land, which he granted to his barons in return for service in war. In the spring of 1066 William summoned these barons to tell them he meant to claim the English crown and expected their support. Most refused, saying their oath of loyalty did not extend to foreign wars or personal vendettas. William did not control Calais and would have to sail from Normandy across the wider part of the Channel. He would need heavy ships for his horses and a tail wind. On landing, he would face a mature warrior fighting on his own soil. The whole venture was unwise. William was unmoved, but this opposition meant that what began as a bid for a crown and homage mutated into something more embracing. William had to bribe his barons with the promise of land in England, and recruit mercenaries from elsewhere who would need reward. His one tactical advantage was the blessing of Pope Alexander II, angry at Godwin's appointment of Stigand as archbishop of Canterbury. A relic of St Peter was sent for William to carry into battle.

Harold responded by gathering a navy off the Isle of Wight and summoning a fyrd, or Saxon militia, which he deployed along the south coast. This supplemented the king's own corps of 'house ceorls', 2,000 full-time soldiers of his personal guard. Such a defence should have been sufficient, but the first requirement for William's invasion, a south-west wind, failed to materialise. This meant trouble for both leaders. William had to keep a ramshackle army and its transport ships together on the Normandy coast while Harold's forces became desperate to return to their harvest. Harold also now received devastating news. His rebellious brother, Tostig of Northumbria, had travelled to Norway to encourage the Norse warlord Harald Hardrada in his distant claim to the English crown. Hardrada was a blond giant in his fifties who had spent his life fighting and looting his way across the continent, traversing Russia and reaching Constantinople and Sicily. He readily agreed to Tostig's suggestion and in August landed at Scarborough with a fleet of 200 longships. From there he overwhelmed a Northumbrian army at Fulford and accepted the surrender of York.

In the English Channel a storm further imprisoned William's impatient fleet in Normandy, while convincing Harold's commanders that there would be no invasion that year. Harold duly left his home at Bosham near Chichester and headed for London, where he learned of Hardrada's landing in Northumbria. Within twenty-four hours he gathered his army and headed north, reaching York in just four days, one of the greatest forced marches in English history. Here he found that Hardrada had retired from York to Stamford Bridge, seven miles to the east, leaving a third of his army with his ships. Hardrada was surprised by the sudden arrival of the English force. Realising Hardrada was unprepared, Harold's forces immediately charged and, in a fierce encounter, killed both Hardrada and Tostig. The surviving Norwegians were sent home humiliated. The death of Hardrada, 'the last of the Vikings', greatly lessened the threat from that quarter to the English throne.

Harold had spent just a week securing York when he was told the desperate news that William had sailed from France after all, and landed on 28 September at Pevensey. He now had to bring his exhausted army back south to London, where he received a message from William, now camped outside Hastings, restating his claim to the throne. Harold retorted that this was overridden by Edward's bequest to him, by the witan's decision and by his subsequent anointment. The matter was clearly to be settled by arms. Harold left London and reached Hastings on 13 October.

The field of battle, which can be studied today, comprises a ridge and valley and was so confined that probably no more than 8,000 men could fight on either side. William is believed to have had 3,000 cavalry, grouped in platoons, supported by archers and infantry, which he could manoeuvre across the field. Harold's troops fought on foot. They formed into a tight shell of shields on the crest of the ridge, which was defensively strong but hard to discipline or redeploy once it had broken for attack. Such an army lacked any divisional structure, fighting as Saxons (and Vikings) customarily did, with every man for himself and with the king surrounded only by his bodyguards.

On the morning of 14 October the Norman cavalry attacked the Saxon shields, but suffered severe damage to their horses from Saxon axes and spears. The Normans withdrew and regrouped while the Saxons recovered their missiles and cleared their dead. The Norman attack resumed and was again repulsed, but each time the Saxon numbers were reduced, mostly by Norman archers firing from a distance of 100 yards.

A feigned retreat appears to have led the Saxons to break from their shield shell and charge downhill, at which point they became vulnerable to the Norman cavalry. The turning point came, according to most accounts, when an arrow hit Harold in the eye. Seeing their chance, four Norman knights fought their way to him and hacked him to pieces. With the death of their leader, the Saxons fled to the surrounding woods. Harold's body was so mutilated in the melee that his mistress, the charmingly named Edith Swan-Neck, had to be summoned to identify its parts. Harold was buried at Waltham Abbey, north of London.

The narrative of Hastings was recorded in a tapestry, commissioned probably from English needleworkers by Bishop Odo, William's half-brother. Still hanging in Bayeux, it is one of the most vivid depictions of war in medieval history. Although victorious, William had lost a third of his army and many of his battle horses. He had neither reserves nor reinforcements and was alone in a hostile country, whose earls would surely resist when they learned that their land was promised to William's supporters. William ordered an abbey to be founded on the site of the battle and determined to be crowned at the tomb of his claimed patron, Edward the Confessor, in London.

Two decades later, the Domesday Book was to chart a corridor of villages 'wasted' by the Norman army as it progressed from Sussex towards London. It did not test its formidable walls but marched up the Thames and round through Middlesex, waiting until the London bishops and burghers 'submitted from necessity'. William confirmed the liberties granted them by Edward, claiming, 'I will not suffer that any man offer you any wrong.' London was left untouched and William's coronation took place in Westminster Abbey on Christmas Day 1066, by Saxon bishops under the Saxon rite, but with a sullen citizenry outside.

William returned in triumph to Normandy, leaving his new acquisition under the command of Bishop Odo, created Earl of Kent, and William FitzOsbern, Earl of Hereford, with a massive fortress begun at once at Chepstow. He now had to pay his debts, expropriating English land initially on a modest scale. He built castles along the south coast to guard his route home. But rumbles of rebellion required further castles at Exeter, Warwick, York, Lincoln, Huntingdon and Cambridge. Whereas Alfred's burgh fortifications had been built to defend the populace, William's were built to repress them. Initially of mud and wood, they were replaced by stone keeps, where garrisons could seek refuge and imprison rebels.

The inhabitants of England did not submit easily. The most serious revolt was in 1069 in the Northumbrian capital of York. In response William inflicted on the entire region a merciless revenge, torching villages, destroying animals and crops and leaving the starving inhabitants to beg to be allowed to live as slaves. The medieval chroniclers described William as 'yielding to his worst impulses, setting no bounds to his fury'. This so-called 'harrowing of the north' left a legacy of hatred of the Normans that was to last a century. Then in 1071 a Lincolnshire thane, Hereward the Wake, rose in revolt, exploiting his knowledge of the East Anglian fens and evading capture for over a year. He was finally betrayed by the bribed monks of Ely, after which he disappeared and became a Fenland legend.

William now turned his attention to the church, rewarding Norman bishops as he had barons. He replaced the Saxon Stigand as archbishop of Canterbury with Lanfranc, head of the abbey of Caen and a noted lawyer and administrator. Within two decades Norman bishops and abbots had been granted a quarter of England, in return for which they were expected to found monasteries and raise churches. The next seventy years saw church building such as England was not to experience again until the fifteenth century, a sign not just of William's determination to master his new realm but of the wealth that resided in eleventh-century England, comparable even with that of France.

The Norman conquest now took hold. Malcolm of Scotland offered homage to William. In the west, a chain of earldoms from Chepstow through Shrewsbury to Chester commanded the Welsh 'marches'. By the 1070s virtually all of England south of the Tees was subjected to one of the most systematic territorial transfers in European history. Some 4,000 Saxons lost their land to 200 Norman barons, bishops and abbots, with barely 5 per cent of the country left in Saxon hands. An estimated 200,000 Normans, French and Flemings migrated to England. About the same number of English died of slaughter and starvation, perhaps a fifth of the population.

In the process a Saxon ceorl or free farmer became a villein, owing absolute loyalty to his lord, who in turn held land as tenant-in-chief of the king. Though the rigour of this feudal system has been questioned by historians, it supposedly left every villein 'bonded', or obligated to military service and unable to buy or sell land or travel without permission of his lord. The hundred and shire courts, in which free men had administered justice alongside the king's shire reeve, were replaced by manorial courts in which the lord held absolute sway. In the marches of the Welsh and Scottish borders, these lords ruled almost independently of the king, with the right to appoint their own sheriffs, build castles and raise armies. Their names were to echo down the Middle Ages: Mortimer, Montgomery, Osberne, de Broase and de Clare.

In 1085 the ageing William decided to survey the economic geography of his realm, to establish title and value for taxation, and to end disputes among his barons. A cadre of public officials recorded every settlement, a project sealed at a collective oath of fealty from the barons at Old Sarum in Wiltshire. The survey was published in 1086 and dubbed the Domesday Book by the

Saxons, 'because its decisions, like those of the Day of Judgment, are unalterable'. It offered the most complete account of the land of England south of the River Tees until the Victorian censuses. It revealed East Anglia as most populous region, with 165,000 people in Norfolk and Suffolk. After the Norman 'harrowing', Yorkshire had just 30,000. London was omitted because of a fire, but was believed to have 25,000. Only 15 per cent of England was assessed as woodland. No other nation in Europe had anything like Domesday. It did more than record. It marshalled Norman England into an administrative whole. While France remained a confederacy of dukedoms, England was on the road to central statehood.

William's rule was now degenerating. He had lost his powerful but diminutive wife Matilda, whose reputed height of 4ft 2in was recently revised to 5ft on the discovery of a possible skeleton. His eldest son, Robert, had taken up arms and rebelled against him. Another son, Richard, died while riding. William travelled back and forth to Normandy, constantly at war with Philip of France. At the siege of Mantes in 1087 he fell from his horse, rupturing his abdomen. He was conveyed to Rouen where he died. During his burial in the abbey of Caen, where his tomb can still be seen, 'the swollen bowels burst and an intolerable stench assailed the nostrils of bystanders'. William's achievement, the conquest and subjugation of all England, equalled that of Cnut half a century before, but his descendants ensured it was final. Norman politics, language and culture entered the bloodstream of Saxon England. For four centuries it was unhappily and bloodily wedded to continental Europe.

The Conqueror's Children

~

1087 - 1154

THE INSTITUTIONS OF a medieval state were rarely strong enough to survive a monarch's death unchanged. For all the rituals of inheritance and anointment, power defaulted to military strength. The death of the Conqueror left his eldest son, Robert Curthose (or short-stocking), inheriting the senior family domain of Normandy, while the next son, William, took the richer property of England. Known as Rufus from his ruddy complexion, William II (1087–1100) was a competent soldier but lacked his father's self-discipline. He raced from Rouen to be crowned in Westminster before any rival might get there first, and then courted popularity by giving much of his father's treasure to the church, plus £100 to each shire to be given to the poor.

The style of the Anglo-Norman court changed abruptly from the Conqueror's spartan militarism to Rufus's effete extravagance. He was openly infatuated with a Norman clerk, Ranulf Flambard, with whom he ruled and filled the court with French fashion in clothes, entertainment and architecture. Building began on the fortress cathedral of Durham and later on Westminster Hall by the Thames, probably the biggest buildings, ecclesiastical and secular, in northern Europe at the time. Such spending demanded an increasingly severe fiscal policy. Rufus confiscated the revenues of all heirs inheriting under age. When the archbishop of Canterbury, Lanfranc, died in 1089, Rufus left his post vacant to pocket the Canterbury income.

More serious, the new lords of the Welsh marches were allowed to raid deep into Wales, destroying the Conqueror's careful treaties of autonomy with its princes. As a result, for three centuries Wales was to be a thorn in the side of Norman monarchs. Lanfranc's eventual successor, the erudite Bishop Anselm, quarrelled with the king over money, the 'sinfulness' of the court and the 'effeminacy' of its fashions. In return the king openly ridiculed the church and summoned a council of barons to decide whether the king or the pope should rule. They carefully opted for the king.

Rufus was soon besieged by plots. His powerful uncle, Odo, rose against him in favour of his elder brother, Robert, with the support of an increasingly independent Anglo-Norman barony, but he was rescued by an unlikely ally. In 1095 Pope Urban II declared the First Crusade and summoned all Europe to set aside domestic quarrels and free Jerusalem from the infidel. All who died would have their sins remitted. The crusade was portrayed as the ultimate expression of faith, fusing religion with a developing cult of chivalry, of knightly valour and romantic love. Kings, nobles and even humble subjects eager for adventure were to find the call to crusade irresistible. It symbolised the magnetic power of the Roman church over the medieval imagination.

Rufus was a competent soldier but no crusader. He offered Robert £6,600 to go to Jerusalem in return for the entire revenues of the Duchy of Normandy in his absence. Robert agreed, the money being delivered to Rouen in sixty-seven barrels. Five years later, with Robert still absent, Rufus was shot with an arrow while hunting in his father's new hunting ground of the New Forest. What was called an accident was almost certainly murder, in the presence of Rufus's younger brother

Henry. In an extraordinary scene, Henry and his friends left the corpse by the road (the spot, called the Rufus Stone, now lies off the A31) and galloped to the Treasury at Winchester to claim the crown. The body was found by a charcoal-burner and taken for burial at the cathedral. Henry's swift coronation in 1100 pre-empted the arrival of Robert's representatives to assert his claim as the elder son.

Henry I (1100–35) took after his father, the Conqueror. He dismissed Rufus's favourite, Flambard, and in a coronation charter rescinded Rufus's penal taxes and pledged himself to 'end all oppressive practices'. This charter was to be cited as precursor of Magna Carta. Henry enforced priestly celibacy and insisted on short hair at court. His mistress, Princess Nest ferch Rhys of Deheubarth in Wales, widely celebrated for her beauty, was given to the Norman governor of Pembroke castle as a gesture of reconciliation with the Welsh. The king wed a popular Scottish princess, Edith (renamed Matilda), the only British blood to enter the royal line of England until the fifteenth century. When, a year later, Robert returned from the Holy Land to demand the crown, Henry negotiated a deal whereby each acknowledged the other's sovereignty in their respective domains and the right of succession to each other's lands.

Among Normans no such deals were ever secure. In 1106 Robert reneged and had to be defeated at the battle of Tinchebrai in Normandy, regarded by early historians as a 'return match' for Hastings. Robert was captured and imprisoned for life in Devizes and then Cardiff. Henry went on to marry his daughter, Matilda, to Henry V, the Holy Roman Emperor and king of Germany. The pope even agreed a settlement on church homage, with the English clergy owing allegiance to the king in secular matters but to the pope in church ones.

Like his father, Henry saw the need to put in place institutions of statehood. He was fortunate to have an adviser, Roger of

Salisbury, who understood that need. Salisbury was the first in a line of clerical administrators who were to cement the Norman state. He ruled England as 'justiciar' when Henry was campaigning in France, on one occasion blinding and castrating ninety-four minters for debasing the coinage. Salisbury organised the national accounts with a chequer-patterned cloth on which the 'lords of the exchequer' would assess taxes, rents and fines due to the king each Lady Day, at the end of March. This yielded the present 'tax year'. The nomenclature of the law was also established. The king's court of barons was replaced by 'a court of the King's Bench' (hence court of law), with a legal profession residing in 'inns of court' along the Strand. Local courts were subject to appeal to the king's justices travelling on circuit. Henry became 'the lion of justice'.

All this work came to grief when, in 1120, Henry lost his only legitimate son, William, in the wreck of the royal vessel, the *White Ship*, crossing recklessly in bad weather from Normandy after a night of revelry. It was said that half the Anglo-Norman nobility died aboard. Henry was obliged to declare his daughter, Matilda, his heir and next monarch of England, forcing his barons to swear loyalty to her. Such a succession was doubly insecure. There was no Saxon tradition of female monarchy and, following the death of her husband, Henry V of Germany, the twenty-six-year-old Matilda had been married to the fourteen-year-old Geoffrey Plantagenet of Anjou. Anjou was a long-standing enemy of Normandy and what might have seemed a sound diplomatic match for a daughter,was considered unacceptable in a future monarch of England. When Henry died in Normandy in 1135, allegedly of a surfeit of lampreys (small eels), the throne was claimed by a cousin, Stephen of Blois, on the basis of an alleged deathbed change of heart by Henry. Stephen was accepted by the church and the citizens of London. Possession was at least half the throne, but Matilda and her husband strongly contested Stephen's coronation and Anjou declared war on Normandy.

Though Stephen's early years were peaceful, he recklessly expropriated the properties of the bishops of Salisbury, Lincoln and Ely, such that when Matilda landed in England in 1139, she found bishops and barons ready to recall their oath to her father honouring her succession. There ensued fifteen years of civil war, justly to be known as the Anarchy. Royal justice gave way to baronial despotism. Stephen continued to enjoy the loyalty due to an established monarch, while Matilda held that of a declared heiress. In 1141, after her supporters defeated Stephen at the battle of Lincoln, Matilda was briefly declared queen, but she was soon besieged in Oxford castle, escaping disguised in a white cape by walking down the frozen Thames at night to Wallingford. After years of on-going conflict, in 1148 Matilda returned to Anjou, handing her cause to her teenage son by Geoffrey, Henry of Anjou.

This young man was to set Europe ablaze. Thick-set and red-haired, he enjoyed physical endurance and 'a countenance of fire', described as 'a face upon which a man might gaze a thousand times and still feel drawn to gaze again'. Through his father he held the lands of Anjou and Maine and through his grandfather, Henry I, he claimed Normandy. He took the sobriquet Plantagenet, after the sprig of broom (*Planta genista*) worn by the house of Anjou on its war helmets.

In 1151, Henry went to pay formal homage for his domains to Louis VII of France. The French king was a pious, humble man while his wife, Eleanor, was tempestuous. She was a ruler in her own right as Duchess of Aquitaine, and by the age of thirty she had led troops in person on the Second Crusade. When she set eyes on the young Henry she was infatuated. She mocked her husband, Louis, as 'a monk and not a king' and demanded an immediate annulment of her marriage. In May 1152 she wed Henry, ten years her junior, in her capital of Poitiers, thus uniting an empire that ostensibly ran from Scotland to Spain, 'from the Arctic to the Pyrenees'. Europe was scandalised, but history was entranced. Passion and politics gave England's link with France a new lease of life. Despite her age, Eleanor bore Henry eight children and no end of trouble.

With his inheritance contested both in Paris and in London, Henry rose to the occasion. His Angevin knights, many of them hardened crusaders, proved masters of all they encountered. When he landed in England in 1153 with 3,000 soldiers, Stephen did not stand in his way, acknowledging his succession and, in any event, dying within a year. The barons rushed to pay homage to a young soldier who had proved his potency and who offered them what all England now craved, unity and peace.

Henry and Becket

~

1154 - 1189

HENRY II (1154 - 89) was a warrior king as chivalric hero. He was never still, travelling his domains, hardly resting even to feast. When not fighting he was hunting, when not hunting he was legislating, when not legislating he was bedding a mistress, to the fury of his wife, Eleanor. He had a raging temper and a taste for revenge, yet he could be calm and conciliatory, wise and dignified. Henry's attention throughout his reign was divided between the insecurities of his French domain and a desire to re-establish the legal order in England of his grandfather, Henry I.

Monarchs have always had favourites, but few so dominated a reign as Thomas à Becket did that of the young Henry. Son of a Norman merchant in London, Becket was a royal secretary on Henry's accession. The new king recognised in him an able lawyer and diplomat, and the two men became close. Within weeks of the coronation, the twenty-one-year-old Henry made Becket his chancellor. They worked together, ate together, travelled together and played together. 'Never in Christian times were two men more of a mind,' wrote Becket's friend William FitzStephen. Becket lived like a prince in the pageant of Henry's court.

Henry's relationship with Becket was at first fruitful. For two years the king travelled the country, confiscating land from dissidents and razing castles that were symbols of Norman suppression. The feudal duty of military service was replaced

with a tax known as scutage (from *scutum*, the Latin for shield).
Becket, meanwhile, became royal diplomat. Sent in 1158 on
a mission to Paris, he travelled in a splendour that astonished
France. His entourage was 200 strong, all in livery, with hawks
and hounds for hunting and twelve packhorses laden with gifts,
each ridden by an apparelled monkey. To the French, England
was clearly no longer the sodden Anglo-Norse outpost whose
conquest had obsessed Duke William a century before.

Then in 1162, eight years into Henry's reign, disaster
struck. Canterbury became vacant and the king demanded
that a reluctant Becket take the post, combining it with the
chancellorship. Becket claimed that the two loyalties, to church
and king, could not be honoured by one man and at first
refused. When Henry overruled him, Becket is said to have
replied, 'It will be God I serve, before you.' The church was
more powerful in England than anywhere in northern Europe,
largely due to William I's donations and the prosperity of the
Norman monasteries. It employed an estimated one in six of the
population. A frenzy of Norman building was now under way,
with cathedrals and abbeys at Durham, Winchester, Gloucester,
Norwich, Peterborough, Ely and Southwell towering over their
settlements. Only the pyramids of Egypt were of comparable
scale. These churches were the glue of Henry's nation, their
dank naves, flickering candles and consoling chants offering the
people a relief from the daily round that no secular leader could
promise.

Becket now laid aside all trappings of office – including
the perquisites of Canterbury – and became an ascetic. He
wore a hair shirt and in 1163 took his bishops to meet Pope
Alexander III in Tours, returning determined to assert the
independence of church from state. In response, in 1164 Henry
drew up his Constitutions of Clarendon, repeating Henry I's
edict that the monarch be supreme in civil matters. Disputes
over land, taxation and judicial appeals were for the king to

decide. All people in England, whatever their rank and status, were ultimately subjects of the crown, including Becket's clergy. Relations between Henry and Becket collapsed. In 1164 a council held in Northampton heard Becket reassert the liberties of the church, theatrically holding up a crucifix as indication of where his loyalty lay. A furious Henry reminded him of his humble origins. Becket replied, 'We should obey God rather than man,' adding provocatively that St Peter too was a humble man. The clash of arrogant churchman and enraged king saw Becket flee to Paris, where he stayed for six years.

Meanwhile the British lands beyond England rumbled with rebellion. Henry had received the homage of the Scottish king, but had to withdraw from a Wales then in perpetual revolt under the kings of Deheubarth and Gwynedd. In Ireland, Norman-Welsh knights led by the Marcher lord Robert 'Strongbow' de Clare staged a private invasion. By 1170 he had taken the city of Dublin and become king of Leinster. These moves, while formally completing the Norman conquest, showed how far even the most powerful English king was from controlling those parts of the British Isles left unconquered by the Saxons.

On pain of Henry's excommunication, a brief reconciliation took place that year between Henry and Becket in France. Becket returned to England but in heroic style, distributing alms in London and telling his congregation at Canterbury that 'the more potent and fierce the prince is, the stronger stick and harder chain is needed to bind him'. He warned that God would soon increase the number of His martyrs. For good measure he excommunicated those bishops and priests who had collaborated in Henry's measures against him. Becket must have known he was provoking his king beyond tolerance. The unfrocked priests went to plead with Henry in Normandy, finding him sick and in a rage. He cried out (in French but related in Latin), 'What miserable drones and traitors have I nurtured within my household, that they let their lord be treated with such shameful contempt by a low-born cleric?' This was crisply retranslated as, 'Will no one rid me of this turbulent priest?'

Hearing these words, four knights slipped from the king's presence and sailed to England. On 29 December 1170 they found Becket in his palace and demanded he submit to Henry's authority, withdrawing the excommunications. Becket refused, an argument followed and the archbishop retreated to say vespers in his cathedral. The knights followed and tried to arrest him. When he resisted, they cut off the top of his head and fell on him with sword thrusts, leaving him dying in a pool of blood before the high altar. The knights fled the country, first to Rome and then to the Holy Land on a much-needed 'penitent crusade'.

All Europe trembled at Becket's murder. While Henry might protest that he had merely intended Becket's arrest, his notorious words had been heard by too many to question. An archbishop had been slain in the house of God and on the apparent orders of a king. Nothing so demonstrated the power of the medieval church as the reaction. Hell itself was called down on Henry's head. To the archbishop of Sens, it was a crime worse than those of Nero, worse even than that of Judas. Henry fell into three days of mourning, capitulating to papal authority and agreeing that church courts be immune from the royal prerogative. He offered land for new monasteries and shrewdly secured from the pope pilgrimage concessions to St David's and Bardsey Island, much to the benefit of Welsh tourism. He then did penance at Canterbury, walking barefoot to the doors of Becket's shrine, where he stripped and spent the night being whipped by monks.

Though Henry's reign was to continue for another eighteen years, the crisis of 1170 altered the balance of power in his realm. Enemies were less fearful of his wrath. Queen Eleanor, estranged in favour of Henry's mistress, 'fair Rosamund', retreated to the Angevin capital of Poitiers, from where she did everything to undermine her husband's authority. She stirred a revolt by the English earls Robert of Leicester and Bigod of Norfolk, with aid from the ever-obliging Louis of France. By 1175 Henry had stemmed these revolts, mostly at the expense of generous pardons. Fair Rosamund retreated to the nunnery at Godstow outside Oxford, while Henry busied himself furthering the reforms begun by his grandfather, Henry I. Six assize circuits were formalised and trial by grand jury introduced in place of trial by duel and ordeal. County sheriffs were to collect the royal revenues. From this emerged the concept of a 'common law', as opposed to baronial discretion, applicable to every man and woman, high and low. It injected into Norman absolutism the Saxon concept of customary rights based on precedent 'enjoyed since time out of mind', a bedrock of English civil liberty.

Despite this activity, the political and cultural hub of Henry's empire remained France, then enjoying the 'twelfth-century renaissance'. England's court looked across the Channel for its language, culture and fashion. Long pointed shoes, tight bodices and voluminous sleeves were copied from Paris. Education was equally cosmopolitan. The focus of society was the tournament, its legendary role greatly enhanced by the Arthurian romances of Geoffrey of Monmouth, published in 1136, complete with fantastical prophecies by Merlin the wizard. The most extravagant event was staged in 1180 for the coronation of Philip II of France, at which the English champion, William Marshal, broke the lance of every French knight and allegedly the heart of every maiden.

By the 1180s the curse of an insecure succession descended on Henry, as it had on his grandfather, Henry I. In 1183 his eldest son died in Aquitaine, but Henry refused to nominate the next in line, Richard, as his heir, preferring his younger son, John. Richard was goaded by Eleanor in 1188 to defy his father by paying homage to King Philip. Richard was thirty-one and pining to depart on his life's ambition: the Third Crusade to rescue the Holy Land from Saladin. Yet he dared not leave until his father formally named his heir. This Henry resolutely declined to do and a desperate Richard eventually joined the French king in an assault on his father's dukedom of Anjou.

Henry was thus forced to take the field against his own son (and his wife). In the course of one battle, Richard found himself in combat with William Marshal, ever loyal to his king, during which Marshal had Richard at his mercy and pleading for his life. He killed the prince's horse, telling the traitorous Richard that 'the devil may slay you'. But the king was fifty-six and sickening. In 1189 he travelled to Chinon, the place of his youth, where he was told of the fall of Tours to his eldest son. On hearing that his favourite, John, had joined Richard in revolt against him, he wailed, 'I no longer care for anything in this world,' and settled the succession on Richard. He died, said the chronicler, 'a lion savaged by jackals'.

Magna Carta

~

1189 - 1216

THE SONS OF HENRY II returned England to the anarchy of Stephen and Matilda. The reign of Richard the Lionheart (1189–99) was a brief and costly interlude in English monarchy. He was crowned splendidly at Westminster in September 1189, freeing his father's enemies from prison and welcoming his mother, Eleanor of Aquitaine, back to court. Yet his interest in England was limited to its fund-raising potential. He could speak no word of its language and taxed his subjects in every way he could to finance his obsession with the crusade. Such was his greed for revenue that he reportedly said, 'I would sell London if I could find a buyer.' Within a year of his coronation Richard left England for Palestine. He returned only once. England was in the care of his mother, his brother John, and William Longchamp as justiciar, effectively the king's deputy. The result was immediate conflict. High taxation led the citizens of London to form themselves into a 'commune' and elect their first mayor, Henry Fitz-Ailwyn. Since he represented a substantial source of royal revenue, future monarchs could ill afford to disregard this new power.

The battlefields of Palestine proved less glorious for Richard than they had when viewed from the tournaments of Normandy. The crusaders' camp was ridden with disease. Though Saladin could be defeated in the field, Jerusalem defied capture, and in 1192 Richard was forced to negotiate a compromise that merely gave pilgrims access to the holy places. Worse was to follow. Hearing of trouble at home, Richard ordered his trusted aide, Hubert Walter, to return and replace Longchamp as justiciar. John fled to France and formed an alliance with King Philip to usurp his brother.

Before Richard could respond to this threat he was captured and handed over to the Holy Roman Emperor for ransom. In London, Walter now had to repeat Richard's earlier extortion by raising yet more money to free him. The burden was chiefly borne by the City's developing wool trade and Walter was rewarded with the Canterbury archbishopric. Richard was ransomed in 1194 but spent the remaining five years of his life fighting his fellow Frenchmen. He died on the battlefield of blood poisoning when a crossbow wound went septic, chivalrously pardoning his assailant on his deathbed.

His brother and heir, John, was at this point in a state of rebellion against his own country and an ally of its chief enemy, France. A short man of 5ft 5in with his father's red hair, he was nicknamed Lackland for holding no territory as a younger son. He was an avid hunter and collector of jewels, but regarded as a treacherous and unreliable successor. Walter had argued strongly in the royal council for Richard's twelve-year-old nephew, Arthur, to succeed instead. The barons disagreed. They had no affection for John, but an understandable respect for heredity and neither the wish nor the money to fight what would be a certain civil war if they were to reject him. It is widely believed that John had a hand in Arthur's subsequent murder.

Under King John (1199 – 1216) England descended into chaos. The death of Walter in 1206 plunged the king into conflict with Rome over his replacement at Canterbury. The pope was now the powerful Innocent III, his court well stocked with ambitious English clerics. He sent his own man, Stephen Langton, to be the new archbishop. After John rejected him and confiscated church property in 1209, the response was instant excommunication.

With the barons restive and an over-taxed population resentful, John surrendered and in 1213 accepted Langton's appointment. He also capitulated to Innocent's demand that he respect 'the whole of the English church, which by your impious persecutions you are trying to enslave'. In an extraordinary gesture, John turned turtle and presented England as a 'fiefdom' of the papacy.

Enemies continued to crowd John on every side. The Welsh under Llywelyn the Great were capturing one Marcher castle after another. In 1214 John suffered a more crippling blow when the French beat his German allies, supported by an English expeditionary force at the battle of Bouvines. The barons seized on this humiliation to arm against the king who, in a last desperate throw, exploited his recent fealty to the pope by excommunicating them. He even issued tunics to his soldiers carrying the Cross of St George, the saint adopted by the crusaders as their patron.

John and his senior subjects were now in armed contention. He retreated for safety to the Tower of London, while armed citizens roamed outside, precursors of the Ci\ty's 'armed bands'. At this critical point, Archbishop Langton proposed to the barons that they revive Henry I's concept of a coronation charter. They should not demand the king's abdication but set out a demand for specific liberties in the name of 'the community of the whole land'. In June 1215 John travelled upriver to his castle at Windsor where he negotiated, albeit under duress, a sixty-one-clause charter of concessions. He rode out to meet the rebels in a meadow by the Thames at Runnymede. There, sitting on a makeshift throne under canvas, he applied his seal to Magna Carta, and returned angrily to Windsor.

Magna Carta has been subject to centuries of exegesis. It was not the first such charter, as Langton had pointed out, and was to be amended three times under Henry III. Many of the clauses dealt with such matters as fish traps on the Thames, the treatment of Welsh prisoners and the dismissal from court of John's Plantagenet 'aliens'. Yet it was the first charter of rights in Europe specifically to underpin civil liberties in a rule of law.

Clause 12 stated that 'no scutage or aid is to be levied in our realm except by the common counsel of our realm', an early version of no taxation without representation. Clause 39 declared habeas corpus, that 'no free man shall be arrested or imprisoned or deprived or outlawed or exiled or in any way ruined ... except by lawful judgment of his peers or by the law of the land'. Clause 40 embraced a much-abused judicial concept, that 'to no one will we sell, to no one will we deny or delay right or justice'. Clause 52 held that, 'if without lawful judgment of his peers, we have deprived anyone of lands, castles, liberties or rights, we will restore them to him at once. And if any disagreement arises on this, let it be settled by the judgment of the twenty-five barons.'

The charter set a precedent to which constitutionalists returned throughout history, to be granted an importance in retrospect which it perhaps did not merit at the time. It was ignored by Shakespeare in his play, *King John*. But it could not be unwritten. Magna Carta ranks among the foremost documents of the rule of law against raw power, and as such was given great significance by the revolutionaries of the seventeenth century. It also enshrined the powers of the barons in opposition to the authority of the king. As a result of his incompetence and weakness, they had become strong. They were territorial grandees 'in their own right', owning extensive lands and the feudal allegiance of knights, bondsmen and villeins. A shift in the basis of power had occurred, away from monarchical authority and discretion towards the ghost of modern law and a modern parliament.

No sooner had John signed Magna Carta than he wrote to England's new lord, the pope, asking him to annul it. In September the pope obliged, and in extraordinary terms.

Innocent wrote that the charter was 'not only shameful and base, but also illegal and unjust'. He condemned it 'on behalf of Almighty God, the Father, Son and Holy Ghost and by the authority of Saints Peter and Paul and His apostles'. The barons responded as John had responded to his brother Richard, and as Richard had done to their father Henry. They sought aid from France, friend of any foe of England's king, and invited Philip's heir, Louis, to invade England and seize the crown. In 1216 Prince Louis duly landed on the south coast and marched his troops on London, where he installed himself in the Tower and received the fealty of many English barons. Such a thing had not happened since the Conquest.

As always when an English king was in trouble with the French, the Celtic fringe took advantage. In Wales Llywelyn moved his forces as far south into Marcher territory as Carmarthen. The Scots king, Alexander II, took the opportunity to march to the banks of the Tyne to claim the old kingdom of Northumbria. He travelled south, even reaching Dover, intending to pay homage to Louis and thus cement his claim. John meanwhile was a fugitive, roaming his own realm, laying waste to rebel territory and burning towns and villages which refused him aid. October 1216 found him fleeing across East Anglia, contracting dysentery and losing his baggage train in a rushed crossing of the Wash. With it went the crown jewels, which John saw as a symbolic loss of authority.

The king died soon after in Newark, exhausted, sick and friendless, killed some said of poison and others of a 'surfeit of peaches'. His servants stole his possessions before carrying his body to Worcester for burial. Though at times a competent soldier, John ranked among the least popular English monarchs. His lack of piety combined with an ingrained deviousness, was matched only by that of Richard III. The contemporary Matthew Paris wrote that, 'foul as it is, hell itself is defiled by the foulness of King John'. A bard sang that 'no man may ever trust him, for his heart is soft and cowardly'. Yet this evil was catalyst for a greater good, Magna Carta.

Henry III and
Simon de Montfort

~

1216 - 1272

IF A REIGN SUCH AS JOHN'S could advance the rights of English
people through the charter, what might emerge from the
instability normal under a child king? At the moment of John's
death, the nine-year-old Henry III (1216–72) was in the west
country in the guardianship of the Marcher veteran William
Marshal, attended by the papal legate Bishop Guala. Marshal
now acted with speed, rushing the boy to Gloucester Abbey and
crowning him with a ringlet of gold. When John's remaining
courtiers caught up with him, they cried at the sight of the
pathetic child, 'this tiny spark of minute beauty, the sole hope of
the torn kingdom'.

As Marshal realised, an anointed king of whatever age and
one approved by the pope was a powerful symbol of legitimacy.
Barons and court officials who had sided with the French
intruder Louis now rallied to Marshal's authority and Henry's
crown. These included such magnates as Hubert de Burgh,
Peter des Roches and the head of the royal army, Fawkes de
Breaute. Acting as a council they reasserted Magna Carta and
by the summer of 1217 had turned the tide against Louis. His
forces were defeated in a chaotic battle of mounted knights in
the narrow streets of Lincoln, while his navy was beaten by
de Burgh off Dover. The prince retired to France to await his

succession to the French throne as Louis VIII (1223 – 26). In 1219 the great Marshal died, to be buried in the Temple church in London, where he is represented to this day by an unadorned knightly effigy.

The affairs of state passed, for the first decade of Henry's reign, to Hubert de Burgh, soldier, administrator and father figure to the young king. He restored the administration of Henry II, including the assize circuit and the Court of Exchequer, while in foreign affairs he sought an economical peace with France. Thus blessed, England in the 1220s blossomed with the works of imported French architects. They brought with them the lofty choirs and lancet windows of the new Gothic style, replacing the heavy lines of Norman Romanesque with the brightly glazed interiors of Salisbury, Lincoln and Wells, drawing on precursors at Chartres and Beauvais. The new choir at Canterbury was completed by a Frenchman, William of Sens, and work began on what became Henry's greatest obsession, rebuilding the shrine of Edward the Confessor at Westminster. These great structures were in stark contrast to the tumbledown wood-and-rubble buildings of medieval English towns. Archbishop Langton welcomed to England the new mendicant 'preaching' friars, the Dominicans in 1221 and the Franciscans in 1224, their asceticism a welcome contrast to the unpopular laxity of the Benedictines.

Despite attempts across Europe to curb the noble craze for tournaments, there was no waning of the Norman cult of chivalry. As the young Henry passed his teens, de Burgh did all he could to restrain any emerging warrior tendencies, but by 1229 the twenty-two-year-old king was beyond his control. Though lacking a talent for soldiering, he craved glory in battle and duly set sail to recover his grandfather's French possessions lost by John. It was a venture in which he failed and at great cost. In 1236 he married Eleanor, the thirteen-year-old daughter of Raymond of Provence, at an extravagant wedding whose dazzling guest list included King Louis IX of France and 300 attendant knights. Eleanor matured into a bright and assertive queen, avaricious for her relatives. Her retinue came from the royal houses of Poitou and Savoy and her family demanded that they be showered with offices and bishoprics. These were precisely the 'aliens' against which Magna Carta had warned. The Poitevins spoke the southern French language of Occitan, leading the barons to protest at the decline of the 'English tongue', by which they meant French. When Eleanor's barge was rowed down the Thames it was pelted with rotten fruit.

Henry modelled his reign not on the principles of Magna Carta but on the more autocratic French monarchy. He fulsomely honoured the papacy, remarking that 'at a time when we were orphaned and a minor, it was our mother, the Roman Church ... which placed us on our throne'. He devoted a fifth of the revenues of the English church to the pope, displeasing the bishops. Turning to the barons for support he found them reluctant to advance him funds, though this did nothing to relieve his extravagance. He welcomed at court yet more of his wife's Poitevin relatives, and even gave London its first zoo, kept at the Tower. It included a polar bear that swam in the Thames, lions, snakes, a rhinoceros and an elephant. The ostrich died after being fed a diet of silverware. Later visitors had to pay to enter, or bring a cat or dog as food for the lions.

In 1252 the king made a tactical error. He sacked his brother-in-law, Simon de Montfort, from his Gascony governorship, and thus made him a leader of dissident barons on the royal council. De Montfort was son of the headstrong French warrior of the same name and married to Henry's sister, another Eleanor, widow of the late William Marshal. Like any who declare their opposition to a king, he immediately attracted malcontents, from the barons, from the City of London and from a clergy distressed by Henry's 'alien monarchy'. When in 1253 Henry returned to campaign in France, his brother,

Richard of Cornwall, found he could not raise the requisite money, and summoned a 'parlement', a discussion, composed not just of barons and bishops but, for the first time, of shire representatives. This proto-parliament first met at Easter 1254.

The weakened Henry was now floundering on the wilder shores of diplomacy. He had no sooner made peace with Louis of France than he accepted the pope's suggestion that his son, Edmund, become king of Sicily and his brother, Richard, be king of Rome. The catch lay in the cost: an astronomical £135,000 for armies to secure the relevant thrones. Facing years of harvest failure and widespread famine at home, the barons said no, and in 1258 seven magnates led by Simon de Montfort swore oaths of loyalty to each other and demanded further reforms of the king. 'By God's head,' said Henry to de Montfort when out hunting in a storm, 'I fear you more than all the thunder and lightning in the world.' De Montfort was known to demand that the king be 'locked up like Charles the Simple'.

The result was a revision of Magna Carta in the so-called Provisions of Oxford. Under them the barons demanded that 'foreigners' be expelled from all affairs of state, together with papal emissaries and overseas bankers. The provisions went beyond a charter of civil liberties to address the structure of monarchical government. A council of fifteen under Simon de Montfort was put above the king's council of twenty-four, accountable to a parliament that would meet three times a year whether or not summoned by the monarch. Its skirmishes with the king moved to crisis in armed conflict, culminating in a scrappy battle outside Lewes in 1264. Henry was decisively beaten and he and his son, Edward, were taken prisoner by de Montfort's forces.

England now had its first taste of parliamentary rule, and it was not a happy one. A month after Lewes, in June 1264, de Montfort summoned a new parliament including two knights from each shire and two burgesses 'elected' from each city. Its purpose was to discuss not just taxes but any matter of public concern. It was thus regarded as the 'first' English parliament, but it did not meet until January 1265, in a field near Kenilworth castle, and dissolved itself within a month. The attendance is uncertain, though there were only five earls and eighteen barons.

De Montfort overplayed his hand. He found, as often before, that England's barons could unite against the king but soon divided among themselves. At Runnymede England had been ready for a House of Lords, but it was not ready for a House of Commons. Having supposedly rid themselves of Henry's 'foreigners', the barons were equally averse to de Montfort's commoners. The Marcher lord, Gilbert de Clare, defected to the king and began a fortress at Caerphilly in Glamorgan, a phenomenal edifice of keeps, baileys and lake moats. The king's son, Edward, escaped imprisonment and summoned support from barons hostile to the new parliament. The result was that, within a year of Lewes in 1265, de Montfort was confronted by the young Edward at the battle of Evesham. The defection of Llywelyn's Welsh horsemen sealed his fate in 'an episode of noble bloodletting unprecedented since the Conquest'. Henry had been carried into battle in a litter as a symbol of legitimacy by de Montfort, and had to plead for his life after being accidentally wounded. After the battle the peaceable old man professed he dared not look on his rebel son Edward, 'lest I embrace him'.

De Montfort's body was dismembered as a symbol of his lost power and his head put on a spike. His supporters held out for nine months at Kenilworth castle, rendered impregnable with a ring of defensive lakes. Every means – from plague to excommunication – was used to capture it, but the occupants were eventually allowed to walk free. A new parliament summoned by the king revoked many of de Montfort's provisions, though the barons ensured that their property rights were revived in the 1267 Statute of Marlborough. This is the oldest parliamentary statute still in effect, 'ordained in an assembly of discrete men, both high and low … put in writing to be observed by the inhabitants of the realm for ever'. England was at peace.

Henry grew ever more pious in old age, worshipping his hero king, Edward the Confessor, of whom he had murals painted in his sleeping chamber. His gothic rebuilding of Westminster Abbey was completed amid scenes of splendour in 1269. He died in 1272, having ruled after a fashion for fifty-six years. Henry's reign was to prove a high point in the medieval power of barons and parliament. It was followed by three centuries of sometimes tyrannical Plantagenet and Tudor monarchy before parliament was to reassert itself in the seventeenth century. But Magna Carta and de Montfort's parliament had come to pass. To succeeding generations they stood as icons of consent to power, to be cited whenever rulers came to blows with those they ruled.

Hammering the Celts

~

1272 - 1330

HENRY'S HEIR WAS A SWARTHY GIANT of 6ft 2in, as Provencal (through his mother) as he was Plantagenet. Edward I (1272–1307) first heard of his father's death when stopping in Sicily on his way back from a crusade. Such was his lack of urgency that he spent two years in France before arriving in England in 1274. Now aged thirty-five, he had rescued his father from the barons' rebellion, but he had been an early supporter of de Montfort and understood the need for kingly power in a constitutional framework. He also suffered from a Plantagenet temper and habit of violence. He was to treat Celts as he treated Gascons, with a belligerence that sapped his reign of peace and resources. His one apparent gentleness was towards his wife, Eleanor of Castile, who bore him sixteen children.

Edward's coronation in 1274 saw the greatest bout of feasting London could remember. Monasteries were commanded to send swans, peacocks, cranes, pike, eel and salmon. The Westminster hall banquet consumed 60 cattle, 40 pigs and 3,000 chickens. The fountains of Cheapside ran with red and white wine and knights were told to set horses loose in the street, for people to catch and keep. Guided by an able chancellor, Robert Burnell, Edward issued writs summoning juries in every hundred to prepare a census and register of grievances. Commissioners were sent out to gather material for the Hundred Rolls, leading to a series of Westminster statutes which became the first body of English laws founded on the principles of Magna Carta. They regulated land, trade, the church and public order and were passed by a series of parliaments of 'high and low', of barons, knights and burgesses, summoned by Edward over the first fifteen years of his reign. If Henry III can claim parliament's paternity, Edward was its midwife.

The new king's most drastic measure was an inquiry into 'by what warrant' feudal barons held land and administered local law, a Domesday Book of power. They were ordered to appear before circuit justices and prove their inherited entitlements. This was not popular. When Earl Warenne, lord of the Scottish marches, was challenged by inspectors for his warrant, he flourished the rusty sword his ancestors had used at Hastings and declared, 'This is my warrant'. Nor were the barons alone in experiencing Edward's muscle. By the 1270s Wales had experienced its first taste of coherent nationhood. Taking advantage of Henry III's baronial wars, Llywelyn the Great and his grandson, Llywelyn ap Gruffudd, had extended their authority over most of Wales and were recognised by Henry III in the 1267 Treaty of Montgomery. But since ap Gruffudd had been an ally of de Montfort, whose daughter he married, Edward required his homage at his coronation. When the Welshman failed to attend, it was considered rebellion.

Edward's invasion of north Wales in 1277 was the most costly military enterprise ever staged in the British Isles and instilled a hostility that lingers to this day. A large force of 15,000 professional soldiers gathered at Chester, attended by coastal transports, road builders and baggage trains. A Savoy architect, Master James of St George, was commissioned to bring masons from every corner of Edward's domain, and by August the royal army had crossed Gwynedd to Anglesey. The fields were harvested to feed the army and deny food to the Welsh. Llywelyn promptly surrendered without a fight and paid homage to Edward, but the fine imposed on him of £50,000 was unpayable and left the Welsh king at the mercy of English justice. When he failed to pay and his brother, Dafydd, rebelled three years later, the Llywelyns were utterly crushed. Ap Gruffudd died in a skirmish in 1282, while Dafydd was hanged, drawn and quartered, the first victim of what became the standard punishment for treason.

Edward now secured his conquest. Master James's north-Welsh castles, modelled on the crusader castles of the Levant, were designed to 'shock and awe' the Welsh. Caernarfon borrowed motifs from the walls of Constantinople, evoking Edward's dream of a north-European empire. The king adopted the 'crown' of King Arthur and claimed to have found and reburied the remains of Arthur and Guinevere at Glastonbury. Round the castles at Beaumaris, Harlech, Caernarfon and Conwy were built bastides or fortified towns, similar to those in Gascony, their grid plan still evident today. English colonists were introduced and the Welsh banned from holding property or trading within the walls.

After Wales, Edward turned to Scotland. Here the death of Alexander III in 1286 precipitated a conflict over the succession between John Balliol and Robert Bruce. English sovereignty north of the border dated back to the homage intermittently paid by Scottish kings to Saxon ones, which Edward revived by sponsoring Balliol. This so infuriated the Scottish barons that they did something that became habitual when Scotland was in trouble with England, and turned for aid to France.

Edward's military prowess was such that he might have secured a consensual union of the Celtic regions, had he not repressed them so brutally. As it was he found himself in the familiar trap of England's medieval monarchs, encircled by resentful Celts and opportunistic French. In 1290 he supplemented his coffers by the drastic step of expelling England's entire Jewish population and seizing the property of those indebted to them. Some 3,000 Jews made their way to the eastern ports to find refuge in Poland and the Baltic states, not to return until invited back by Cromwell. The same year saw Queen Eleanor die in Lincoln, to Edward's mortification. He had her body carried to London and 'cher reine' crosses erected at each stopping point, the last being at Charing Cross in London.

Edward was now short of money. He converted his private 'wardrobe' into a 'privy' chamber, financed by a privy purse and overseen by a privy council composed of the king's own circle of advisers, circumventing those stipulated under Henry III's charters. But everything had to be paid for somehow. Edward was aware that his subjects were 'fearful that the aid and taxes which they had paid to us out of liberality and goodwill ... may in future become a servile obligation for them and their heirs'. He was the first monarch to articulate so clearly the relation between money and consent. Accordingly, in 1295 he summoned a new parliament, to be dubbed the Model Parliament, to vote money for his continual wars. He gathered earls, barons, bishops and abbots to a baronial chamber, and 292 representatives of the commons, including burgesses from seventy boroughs. It was the first bicameral (two houses) parliament, and it was soon needed. Edward was consuming some £250,000 a year on his wars.

In 1296 Balliol of Scotland was forced by his barons to renounce his homage to Edward, who responded by putting the border town of Berwick to the sword. Balliol was ritually humiliated, stripped of his crown, sceptre and orb, and taken to England as a prisoner. With him came Scotland's 'stone of destiny', the stone of Scone. Apart from a brief theft by students in 1950, it remained in Westminster Abbey under Edward's throne until 1996, when it was returned by John Major's government as an eccentric alternative to devolution.

A Scottish nobleman, William Wallace, next raised the flag of revolt, defeating English soldiers outside Stirling and making a tax-gatherer's skin into his belt. He roamed free for almost a decade until 1305, when he was finally captured, brought to London and hanged, drawn and quartered. Even that was not deterrent enough. A year later, Robert the Bruce took up Wallace's mantle and crowned himself king of Scotland. A furious Edward murdered every one of Bruce's relatives he could find in England, and knighted 300 young noblemen for what he planned as a final campaign against the Scots. On the journey north the sixty-eight-year-old Edward fell ill near Carlisle. He demanded to be raised from his litter and placed on his horse to lead his army onwards, but he died soon after, to be eulogised as 'a great and terrible king ... a conqueror of lands and a flower of chivalry'. On his grimly unadorned tomb in Westminster Abbey is carved *Edwardus primus scottorum malleus hic est* (Edward I, hammer of the Scots, lies here). But the hammering had left no peace, only Celtic lands ground into sullen rebellion.

The new king, the twenty-three-year-old Edward II (1307–27), was so utterly unlike his warrior father that some questioned his paternity. At the time of his accession he was in the process of marrying Isabella, the twelve-year-old daughter of the king of France; she, like many queens of weak English kings, was to be a force in her own right. The new bride was confronted by Edward's frivolous behaviour with his close friend, Piers Gaveston, who had been banished by Edward I as an unsuitable companion for his son, but who was now recalled. Isabella's family were so appalled at the two men's antics during the wedding banquet, which Gaveston attended in imperial purple trimmed with pearls, that they walked out.

Whether or not the king was homosexual, he was clearly infatuated by Gaveston. England now had a free-standing council which the king could not ignore and his early attempt to rescind powers granted to it by his father ensured a reaction. In 1308 the council declared its loyalty 'to the crown' rather than the king's person, and then banished Gaveston. When an obsessed Edward insisted on his return, the man was seized and summarily killed. The grief-stricken king kept the corpse at his side for weeks, until it was dragged stinking away.

Two years later Edward revived his father's campaign to bring the Scots to heel. He proved to be a brave soldier but a hopeless tactician. Leading a large but undisciplined army north to relieve the besieged castle at Stirling, he was enticed into an ambush by a small Scottish force under Robert the Bruce at Bannockburn outside the town. Two battles on succeeding days led to the most humiliating defeat of an English army on British soil since Hastings. Edward lost two-thirds of his men and had to flee by ship from Dunbar.

Gaveston had been replaced in the king's affection by the ruthless and unpopular Hugh Despenser. He was granted the earldom of Gloucester with extensive Marcher lands in Glamorgan and Carmarthen, but he then won the king's approval to seize the de Clare property in Gower and Usk. Such a threat to inheritance in land was too much for the barons to tolerate, and the result was a resumption of baronial wars against the king. The barons were led by the Marcher lord, Roger of Mortimer, who was forced by Despenser to flee to France. There in 1325 Mortimer met Edward's now estranged twenty-nine-year-old wife, Isabella, who shared his hatred of the king's upstart friend. A handsome and intelligent woman, she declared that 'someone has come between my husband and myself. I shall assume the robes of widowhood and mourning until I am avenged.' She did more than that. In Paris Isabella and Mortimer became lovers, to the scandal of the French court, and were banished to Flanders on the orders of Isabella's brother, the king.

Within a year Isabella had amassed enough support from dissident barons in England to risk a return. In September 1326 she and Mortimer landed in East Anglia and, in a swift campaign, forced Edward and Despenser to flee to the west country, where Despenser was captured and tried at Hereford in her presence. He was treated with signal brutality, strung up, castrated, forced to watch his genitals being burned, hanged and, while still (amazingly) conscious, disembowelled and quartered. Not for nothing was Isabella dubbed 'the she-wolf of France'.

The queen had more trouble disposing of her husband. A parliament summoned to Westminster faced the same problem as was later posed by Richard II and Charles I: how to dispose of a legitimate king anointed in the name of God. Even the barons balked at this. Edward had not been tried, nor had he committed any crime. The bishops advised that the head of state could not be deposed but only invited to abdicate. When this was put to Edward in Kenilworth in January 1327, he tearfully agreed, provided his fourteen-year-old child by Isabella, also Edward, was crowned in his stead. That coronation duly took place and the former king was moved to Berkeley castle, where he was murdered later that year, probably on Isabella's orders. Reports of Edward's impalement on a red hot spear, symbol of his rumoured penchant for buggery, are regarded as propaganda. He was probably stifled.

Edward II's twenty-year reign, for all its political and military incompetence, was one of culture and finery. He was a man of taste, expressed above all in his patronage of gothic architecture and illuminated manuscripts. The serene staircase and chapter house at Wells date from his reign. He was the first king to found colleges at Oxford and Cambridge and he commissioned exquisite psalters and gospels. But such qualities counted for nothing in a king who could not hold his crown or secure his legacy. Edward's reign gave way to the dictatorship of Mortimer and Isabella, as notional regents for the young Edward III (1327–77).

The boy was as unlike his father as his father had been unlike Edward I. He lived under what was widely regarded as the tyranny of his mother until, in 1330 at the age of seventeen, he made a bold move. Isabella and Mortimer were staying with the court in Nottingham castle, where Edward and a posse of twenty-three noblemen stole through a secret passage and seized the couple in the keep. Mortimer was taken to London and executed, Edward agreeing only to his pregnant mother's plea that 'gentle Mortimer' be spared the torment of hanging, drawing and quartering. The queen was sent to comfortable banishment at Castle Rising in Norfolk. Edward took the throne in what was to be the apotheosis of chivalric monarchy.

The Hundred Years War

~

1330 - 1377

AT FIRST THE COURT of the teenage Edward III was consumed with play acting. He was a typical Plantagenet male, well built and with long hair and beard, generous and hot-blooded. He was to prove brilliant at arms, considered one of great generals in English history, but less brilliant at statecraft. His early days were consumed with Arthurian feasts, tournaments and dressing-up. Courtiers read literary romances and acted them out in dangerous liaisons. Edward would dress as Sir Lancelot, and when his mother Isabella was eventually allowed back to court, she arrived as Guinevere in a dress of silk and silver, garnished with 600 rubies and 1,800 pearls, 'attended by minstrels, huntsmen and grooms'.

These antics required both money and the stimulus of a regular battle. The Plantagenet aristocracy and their knightly retainers were in constant military array, soldiers in search of employment. Froissart, chronicler of this Anglo-French world, wrote, 'The English will never love and honour their king unless he be victorious and a lover of arms and war against their neighbours.' Edward duly reopened the old question asked since the Norman conquest: of how many nations was the king of England king? He was almost constantly at war with the Scots, and regularly with the Irish, but these wars lacked the glamour of those on the continent. France was the focus of courtly attention. Within its notional borders lived four times the population of England, twenty million against five million. Edward himself was of French stock, a monarch as alien to the people of England as was the French tongue he and the court spoke daily. But of the land of France he had only Aquitaine, thanks to the failings of his ancestor, King John.

When in 1328 Charles of France had died without issue, Edward's mother Isabella had claimed her brother's throne for her son against the rival claim of Charles's cousin, Philip VI of Valois, who ascended it. The succession thus pitted a sister's claim against that of a male cousin. Under French Salic law a female could not inherit the throne. England disagreed and, with Edward's assumption of full power in 1330, the matter went to dispute. Years of tortuous diplomacy led to French support for Scottish raids over the English border and for pirate attacks on England's wool and wine trade with the continent. In 1337 the two monarchs, Edward and Philip, declared themselves at war, and in 1340 hostilities commenced with a naval battle at Sluys. England under Edward's personal command defeated the French for control of the Channel and thus won freedom to transport an army to France. Some 200 French ships were abandoned as their crews dived overboard to escape a hail of English arrows. The sea was so filled with blood it was said the fish spoke French.

Thus began what was later dubbed the Hundred Years War. The episode has been presented as no more than the acting out of a chivalric feud. Yet it was a terrible time in Europe's history. During its course the peoples of northern Europe endured a cooling climate, crop failure, famine and the loss of a third of their population from bubonic plague. Fighting took place largely across the plains of north-west France, which were devastated as a result. Battle was dominated by two weapons, the English longbow and the French cannon, supplemented by an equally deadly enemy, battlefield dysentery. The longbow was up to six feet in length, of yew or elm with ash arrows, wielded most famously by Welsh archers. It had a draw-strength of 200 pounds, and required immense shoulders, altering the skeletal frame of its users. It could outshoot the crossbow, firing ten arrows a minute to the crossbow's two and penetrating conventional armour at 200 yards. So critical was it to English military success that Edward banned all other sports, including football, to make citizens concentrate on archery.

Edward's first major invasion of France in 1346 took some 10,000 English soldiers to the gates of Paris, but its walls proved impervious to arrows and the English were decimated by dysentery. They withdrew to the River Somme, where they were halted by a French army at Crécy. The resulting battle saw the flower of French chivalry, supported only by crossbows, meet the force of the longbow. Froissart wrote that a cloud of arrows fell on the French 'with such force and quickness that it seemed as if it snowed'.

Fifteen times the French cavalry charged, but horses were as vulnerable to arrows as infantry. Knights and nobles were slaughtered in minutes, with Edward complaining at the loss of ransom money by which war was customarily financed. Ten thousand French soldiers are said to have died at Crécy, against just a hundred English. Military historians have suggested that not until the Gatling gun was introduced could an English army deploy such sustained firepower on an open battlefield. The blind king of Bohemia, a French ally, died in the battle, so moving Edward's sixteen-year-old son, the future Black Prince, that he took Bohemia's three feathers as his crest, along with the German motto *Ich dien* (I serve). The Prince of Wales holds them to this day.

Edward advanced to besiege Calais, the base for raids on English wool ships, which held out for a year before falling in August 1347. At the climax of the siege, six burghers of the town came to the English camp offering their lives in return for those of the city's inhabitants. Their offer was accepted but Edward's French wife, Philippa, went on her knees before him to plead mercy for their bravery. The city was spared and the burghers were taken to England as hostages. The incident was commemorated in a monumental statue by Rodin in 1889, one version of which stands in the riverside gardens next to the Palace of Westminster. Calais and its staple (market) were to remain English for two hundred years, until the reign of Queen Mary.

The king returned home to a warrior's triumph, the 'beau chevalier sans peur et sans reproche,' wrote Froissart. He added that 'his like has not been seen since the days of King Arthur', a parallel then bordering on cliché. Edward pondered founding a 'round table' of knights and turned the old Norman castle at Windsor into a facsimile of Camelot, with embattled towers erected by a young court official named Geoffrey Chaucer. Two years after Crécy, in 1348, Edward founded a chivalric order after a garter that slipped, so legend has it, from the leg of a court beauty, the Countess of Salisbury. Her embarrassment was relieved by the king putting it on his own leg and remarking '*Honi soit qui mal y pense*', shame to him who evil thinks. The Order of the Garter took as its patron the crusaders', and England's, St George. The countess, also known as Joan of Kent, later married the Black Prince.

Despite Crécy, Edward could not force the war to a conclusion. He could defeat an army of mounted knights but not conquer an entire nation. To cross north-west France, even today, is to sense the vastness of this land. English troops needed long lines of communication across a war-ravaged country, and had to rely on booty and ransom to pay for each campaign. These soon ran dry. For this reason alone, the Hundred Years War could not ultimately be won by the English. It became more a professional addiction than a realistic strategy.

In 1348 addiction was overtaken by disease. The Black Death was a plague of unprecedented virulence carried by ship-borne rats from the Far East, arriving in a hot June. Seaports were hit first. Bristol lost 40 per cent of its population in a matter of weeks, as did Weymouth. The pestilence spread inland, emptying settlements and villages, some of which remain to this day as no more than a mound in a field. The population of England is estimated to have fallen from five and a half million to four million, proportionally the largest decline in the country's history. The economic impact of the Black Death was swift. Labour shortage saw wages doubling and rents falling. In 1351 a desperate parliament passed the statute of labourers, under which a commission could ban migration, enforce feudal contracts and fix wages at pre-plague levels. The measure was briefly successful, fines being levied on one in eight adults in Essex alone, but it soon fell victim to the market. With land plentiful and fewer mouths to feed, food prices plummeted and many landowners found they had to sell farms to tenants.

Historians debate whether the Black Death altered the balance of political power in England, perhaps expediting the collapse of feudalism and severely denting faith in the church. It certainly aided the emergence of a class of land-owning yeomanry and another of specialist artisans. Workers defied their lords by migrating in pursuit of higher wages. A lack of farmhands accelerated the shift from labour-intensive arable farming to sheep rearing. Wool became to late-medieval England what oil is to modern Arabia, regarded as so critical to national prosperity that the Lord Chancellor sat on a woolsack to remind him where his loyalties lay. In matters of religion, there is little evidence that faith as such weakened at this time. Church building resumed soon after the Black Death, and chantries and colleges were endowed by an increasingly wealthy merchant class. What did emerge from the mid-fourteenth century onwards was individuals critical of the church, such as John Wycliffe and his followers, known as Lollards after the Dutch for 'mutterers'. Wycliffe challenged the authority of Rome and inspired an evangelical priesthood to do likewise. Congregations flocked to hear the new message, filling the airy naves of new, and firmly English, Perpendicular Gothic churches. Their windows were adorned with tales from the Bible and devout depictions of donors and their families. It was said of England in the 1390s that 'every second man is a Lollard'. Wycliffe produced the first translation of the Bible into English and was to be called the 'morning star of the Reformation'. English monarchs were never averse to the message that the Roman church was too rich for its own theological good.

No plague and no religious scepticism could diminish Edward's zeal for combat. He held a tournament at the height of the epidemic, with guests dressed in thick masks. In 1355 he allowed his sons, the Black Prince and John of Gaunt, to resume hostilities in France, marauding across Brittany, Gascony, Armagnac and then deep into the Languedoc, burning even the great city of Carcassonne. Only when the new French king, John II, met the Black Prince at Poitiers in 1356 did a much reduced English force confront a proper French army. Here again a few thousand English troops won a victory even more astonishing than Crécy. Battle was still dominated by longbow-men, but the Black Prince's skill at manoeuvring infantry and cavalry threw the French army off balance. The French king was captured and brought to the Tower of London in lucrative triumph, where he joined David of Scotland, son of Robert the Bruce, as symbols of England's military might.

Edward's reputation was at its zenith, but his reach now exceeded his grasp. An assault on the walls of Paris saw his army exhausted and a French countryside so ravaged by war as to be unable to support him. Disease among his troops forced him to retreat and agree the Treaty of Brétigny in 1360. John of France was ransomed and England recovered a swathe of his country, once owned by Henry II, south from Poitou across Aquitaine. In return Edward renounced Anjou, Brittany and Normandy and his claim to the French throne. In 1362 an act was passed ordering that English, not French, be the language of the law and a year later parliament was opened in English, though paradoxically the act was written in French and French continued to be the language used in speeches.

In 1369 Edward's wife, Philippa, died and the ageing king fell under the influence of his mistress, Dame Alice Perrers. Soon Edward was reasserting his claim to the French throne and sending his sons to resume their campaigns in Aquitaine. Their actions became increasingly desperate. In 1370 the Black Prince massacred the entire population of Limoges, ending any reputation he may have had for chivalry. English fortunes now collapsed. The French used the vastness of the country and the lack of supplies to exhaust the English, whose starving soldiers became little better than bandits. By 1375 Gaunt had lost half his army to disease and famine, and with it most of Aquitaine. He and the Black Prince returned to England to encounter strong baronial and mercantile opposition to a profitless war that had now lasted almost half a century.

Edward had been forced to summon regular parliaments to vote him money, but the one that gathered at Westminster in 1376, the so-called Good Parliament, saw concerted resistance to the fighting in France. It chose the first Speaker of the House, Sir Peter de la Mare, and impeached Gaunt's pro-war associates. It then demanded the removal from court of the increasingly extravagant Alice Perrers, who had reputedly been taking the enormous sum of £2,000 a year from the exchequer. No sooner had it thus asserted its rights than proceedings were undermined by news that the Black Prince was dead. With the ageing Edward incapacitated by a stroke, the succession of the prince's nine-year-old son Richard was imminent, with his uncle, Gaunt, as effective regent.

Gaunt was a giant of the Middle Ages, though a curiously elusive one. He lacked the warrior charisma of his father and elder brother, but through his first wife, Blanche, he headed the mighty house of Lancaster, with thirty castles and 4,000 armed men at his command. Gaunt then married the daughter of the king of Castile, eccentrically demanding that he be addressed as 'My Lord of Spain', though he never made good his entitlement by conquering the country. Meanwhile he had four children by his English mistress, Katherine Swynford, all named Beaufort. After his Spanish wife's death in 1394, he married Swynford and had parliament legitimise her children. All subsequent English monarchs were to be descended from John of Gaunt's wives.

Yet Gaunt was as devoid of political skill as were most Plantagenets. A year after the late Black Prince's Good Parliament had dispersed, he summoned the so-called 'bad' one, which he packed with his supporters to recall Perrers, impeach the Speaker and exile the Lord Chancellor, the powerful and wealthy William of Wykeham. Gaunt also levied a poll tax to pay for a resumption of the French war. The tax was of four pence on every English person over fourteen.

In June 1377, the crippled Edward finally died. He left a nation which he had led to heights of military glory but trapped in an unwinnable war and heavy debt, certain harbingers of domestic dissent. In addition, the achievements of even the greatest medieval king were nothing without a secure succession and a framework for continuing government. The Black Prince's son and Edward's heir, the ten-year-old Richard, offered neither.

The Peasants' Revolt to
the Loss of France

~

1377 - 1453

RICHARD II (1377 – 99) IS OFTEN COMPARED with Edward II,
and not only because both are thought to have been
homosexuals. Neither was well cast for medieval monarchy.
Richard's coronation was presided over by his uncle, John of
Gaunt, and so exhausted the boy that he had to be carried to
his banquet asleep. Gaunt's power incurred such suspicion that
the council denied him the formal regency. Instead, a council of
twelve, excluding Gaunt, was appointed to face the threat of a
nationwide uprising against the poll tax.

This tax had risen to a shilling a head in 1381 and precipitated
the Peasants' Revolt, the first spontaneous rebellion by large
portions of Saxon England against their Norman masters. It was
composed not of peasants but of disparate groups of craftsmen
already protesting against the post-plague statute of labourers,
enforcing loyalty to their masters. There was little coherent
organisation and the rebels marched to London from different
counties in the south-east under leaders whose names were to
become left-wing legends, Wat Tyler, John Ball and Jack Straw.
Ball's ironic couplet echoed down the ages: 'When Adam delved
and Eve span, who was then the gentleman?' For two days in
June 1381 anarchy ruled in the City of London. There was no
competent authority. The archbishop of Canterbury was

murdered at the Tower and Gaunt's Savoy Palace on the Strand was gutted by fire.

Richard, by then just fourteen, displayed remarkable bravery in riding out virtually alone and against the advice of his council to meet the rebels. He promised to grant them their demands, notably relief from the poll tax and an end to the lingering bonds of serfdom. The rebels were appeased and met again the following day at Smithfield, but when Tyler approached the king he became involved in an altercation with the mayor, whom he tried to stab. The mayor cut him to the ground in return. In the ensuing pandemonium, the king again rose to the occasion. He offered himself to the mob as 'your captain and your king'. Though some riots against the tax continued in the provinces, Richard's apparent compromise restored calm. Once that was achieved, penalties were imposed on the rebels and concessions cancelled as made by a minor 'under duress'. Indeed, the king was later recorded as declaring, 'Rustics you were and rustics you are still. You will remain in bondage not as before but incomparably harsher. For as long as we live we will strive to suppress you.' This was not calculated to appease public opinion.

As he matured it was clear that Richard lacked warrior demeanour. He proved delicate and highly aesthetic. His face was described as 'round and feminine, sometimes flushed', and his voice 'abrupt and stammering in his speech'. He displayed a remarkable talent for art and architecture, but also a fatal incompetence at crucial moments in his reign. In 1382 at the age of fifteen, he married Anne of Bohemia, but the king paid more attention to a young courtier, Robert de Vere, Marquis of Oxford. He and Michael de la Pole, a merchant's son elevated to the earldom of Suffolk, became the king's constant companions, dominating what would today be a student fraternity rather than a royal court. With Gaunt absent in Spain, opposition to the king quickly formed, led by another royal uncle, the Duke of Gloucester, and by Gaunt's son by his first marriage, Henry Bolingbroke of Lancaster. Deriding Richard's friends as 'rather knights of Venus' than chivalric warriors, these nobles began a running confrontation with the king, culminating in 1388 in the fall of both Oxford and Suffolk at the hands of a cabal of 'lords appellant' led by Gloucester. The pair fled into exile, the humiliated king being unable to protect them.

As during the Peasants' Revolt, Richard showed sudden resolve, if not tactical sense. Strengthened by Gaunt's return from Spain, he pointed out to his council that he was now twenty-two and old enough 'to take hold of my house and household, not to mention my kingdom'. He declared that government throughout the land was now 'upon his own person', upsetting the long-standing compromise of Plantagenet kingship. The reprise of Edward II's feud with the barons did not augur well.

Richard realised a remarkable taste for flamboyance. He had the first widely celebrated English architect, Henry Yevele, complete the hammer-beam roof of Westminster Hall, probably the largest unsupported span in Europe at the time. Lavish banquets attended its opening in 1396. Richard also commissioned the devotional Wilton diptych, a masterpiece of medieval art, including a delicate and pious depiction of himself. The chancellor, William of Wykeham, restored to power by Richard, founded academies at Winchester and New College, Oxford, and set a new standard of scholastic splendour.

Chaucer's masterpiece, the *Canterbury Tales*, was written at about this time in what was a just recognisable version of early English. In contrast to most European nations at this time, England now possessed the invaluable aid to cohesion, a common tongue. The *Tales* offered a colourful account of late-medieval life in the stories told by pilgrims on their way to Becket's shrine. The poem discussed the Peasants' Revolt and satirised the church, remarking, 'Friars and fiends are seldom far apart.' Like his contemporary Wyclif, Chaucer presented late-medieval England as an open society, prosperous, humorous and questioning of authority. With the Hundred Years War in abeyance, the rich were freed of taxes, and municipal and religious guilds spent copiously on chapels, colleges and ceremonies. England had recovered from the ravages of plague and war, and was emerging as more than a small island off the northern shore of Europe.

In 1397 Richard felt strong enough to take revenge against those nobles who had purged his court of his favourites eight years before. He had his uncle, Gloucester, murdered in France. A committee of eighteen friends replaced the parliamentary council hallowed by Magna Carta and Henry III, and settled a minor dispute between Bolingbroke and Thomas Mowbray, Duke of Norfolk, by personally exiling them both abroad. This act was of reckless stupidity, leaving the previously loyal Bolingbroke as enraged as was his father, the elderly Gaunt. In *Richard II*, Shakespeare has Gaunt reflecting on England at the time as:

> This sceptr'd isle ... now bound in with shame,
> With inky blots and rotten parchment bonds:
> That England, that was wont to conquer others,
> Hath made a shameful conquest of itself.

When Gaunt died in February 1399, Richard confiscated the entire Lancastrian estates that would have passed to Bolingbroke. Such expropriation, usually a sign of royal desperation, always unsettled the nobility. Unwisely, Richard took the opportunity to cross with a small army to Ireland to quell a revolt, leaving the way open for Bolingbroke to return from exile. He landed in Yorkshire and joined forces with the Percys, earls of Northumberland, intent on ending Richard's tyranny. The king was intercepted in north Wales and taken prisoner to London.

The king was forced, like Edward II, to abdicate on pain of his life. Thirty-three charges were read out against him in parliament, including most plausibly that 'the kingdom was almost undone for default of government and undoing of good laws'. Bolingbroke was crowned Henry IV (1399–1413), his usurpation appeased with a vial of holy oil purportedly given to Becket by an apparition of the Virgin Mary. Henry swore to govern not by his own hand, 'nor his voluntary purpose or singular opinion, but by common advice, counsel and consent'. He would be a ruler by general agreement whereas Richard had been a tyrant. But was consent sufficient justification for toppling an anointed monarch?

Henry might be a crowned king but he was a usurper, with his imprisoned predecessor still languishing in Pontefract castle. Irrespective of circumstance, such a situation tore at the continuity and stability of the state. Illegitimacy was to haunt Henry's reign and run as a theme through Shakespeare's history plays of the period. By the following February, Richard was dead, probably through starvation by his gaolers. But Henry was not secure, his crown constantly under threat throughout his reign.

In 1400 this challenge took the form of a charismatic Welsh landowner, Owain Glyndwr, who reacted to a dispute over land by calling on the Welsh to rebel. Glyndwr was a magnet for opposition to Henry and was initially successful. By 1402 he had won support from the Mortimers, earls of March, themselves claimants to Henry's throne, and from the impetuous Henry 'Hotspur' Percy, unwisely rejected by the king as a member of his council, despite the support of his Northumberland clan for his toppling of Richard II. In 1403 Percy marched south to join Glyndwr, but was cut off by the king in person outside Shrewsbury and killed on the battlefield.

By 1404 Glyndwr was holding court across west Wales and even requesting support from Charles VI of France. He was crowned Prince of Wales in Machynlleth. He also proposed to Mortimer and Percy that they divide the kingdom into three, with Glyndwr taking Wales, Mortimer the south and the Percys the north. The Welsh revolt dragged on for seven more years, ending in 1409 when the rebel fortress of Harlech fell to cannons commanded by Henry's son, the future Henry V; Glyndwr vanished into legend.

Though only forty-five, Henry was by 1413 a sick man, obsessed by plots against his throne. Each revolt meant more executions and more potential enemies. Gradually the king's mind began to fail, convinced that his usurpation was the cause of what he diagnosed as incipient leprosy. In March that year he collapsed in Westminster Abbey and died in its Jerusalem chamber, fulfilling a chivalric prophesy that he would die 'in Jerusalem'. The crown passed to the twenty-six-year-old 'Prince Hal' as Henry V (1413 – 22). A warrior king could still excite a medieval parliament, which abruptly voted funds again to invade France and reassert Henry's ancestral claim to its throne. Feuds were set aside in the quest for glory against the old enemy. A Lollard uprising under a Herefordshire knight, Sir John Oldcastle, was savagely suppressed in 1414 and the following summer Henry sailed for France.

The initial siege of Harfleur was a near disaster, with a third of the English army of 10,000 dying from dysentery. A planned march on Paris was abandoned and Henry, desperate not to return home empty-handed, decided to head north for Calais. There he found his way blocked at Arras by a French army four times the size of his own. He hesitated to fight against such odds, but the price demanded by the French was the loss of his French domains. He decided to fight, relying on the tried-and-tested Welsh longbow men against the French cavalry.

The battle of Agincourt, fought on 25 October 1415, 'for England, Harry and St George', ranks with Trafalgar and Waterloo in the annals of English arms. The English knights were dismounted and spread behind a barricade of hidden stakes, flanked by the same array of archers as had triumphed at Crécy and Poitiers. The French, constrained by the lie of the land, advanced against a storm of arrows and fell in such numbers that reinforcements could not advance across what became a rampart of men and beasts caught on the stakes. No quarter was given for fear of counter-attack. The flower of French nobility was slaughtered on the field, at a high cost in ransom forgone.

The psychological impact of Agincourt on both sides was dramatic. The Burgundians firmly allied themselves to the English and recognised Henry V as king of France, as did most of Europe. Henry returned to a hero's welcome, with City aldermen coming to meet him at Blackheath and escorting him for five hours to London Bridge amid shouts of 'King of England and France'. At last England had a victory to celebrate. But it took five years for the French finally to capitulate at the Treaty of Troyes (1420) and Henry to enter Paris in triumph. The mentally disturbed Charles the Mad acknowledged him as his heir, a position secured by Henry marrying Charles's daughter Catherine. Henry had restored the European status of Henry II and Edward III. An English king was at last acknowledged as ruler of France, ironically the first who was believed not to have spoken French.

As so often in the Hundred Years War, supremacy on the battlefield and in diplomacy proved transient. England was unable to hold in peace what it had won in war. To keep an army on the mainland of Europe was expensive and the king's presence as ruler in Paris was impossible. More serious, Henry was mortal. In August 1422, just seven years after Agincourt, he fell victim to the battlefield curse of dysentery and died. The glittering new empire fell on the inadequate shoulders of his baby son by his new French queen, Henry VI (1422–61 and 1470–71).

History now added surrealism to tragedy. Charles the Mad died that same year, leaving a ten-month-old baby king as territorially one of the mightiest monarchs in Europe. Henry V had appointed as regents the royal uncles, the Dukes of Bedford and Gloucester, alongside their Lancastrian cousins, the Beauforts of the Gaunt line, led by Edmund, now Duke of Somerset. They had the awesome task of honouring the legacy of Agincourt and suppressing the rival claim to the French throne of the house of Orléans. While Henry V might have risen to such a task, the regents were in no position to do so. Many in France recognised Charles's son, the Dauphin, as king, leaving their bitter rivals, the Burgundians, as loyal to the infant Henry. War duly recommenced between the English and the French.

After six inconclusive years, a most extraordinary event occurred. In 1429 a seventeen-year-old peasant girl, Joan of Arc, entered the Dauphin's camp during the English siege of Orléans. Exuding serenity, Joan claimed that saints had appeared to her promising the Dauphin the crown of France, but only if his coronation took place in Rheims Cathedral, deep in enemy territory. After much argument she succeeded in so inspiring the French troops that they forced an English retreat and a French advance on Rheims. There the Dauphin was indeed anointed as Charles VII. Joan was later captured by the Burgundians and sold to the English for ransom. When the French refused to pay, the baffled English tried her as a heretic for refusing to renounce her miracles and, in 1431, burned her at the stake.

Though the English were still powerful enough to have the nine-year-old Henry crowned king of France at Notre Dame Cathedral, French forces were now sweeping across land supposedly ceded by the Treaty of Troyes. The exhausted English had no answer. In 1435 the Burgundians further undermined them by switching allegiance to Charles, rendering their position so desperate that Somerset sent ambassadors to sue for peace. This was achieved by Somerset's ally, the Duke of Suffolk, securing the French king's fifteen-year-old niece, Margaret of Anjou, as queen for Henry VI in 1445.

Henry had grown into a young man of twenty-three. He was tall, with a long, sad face and simple manner that ominously recalled the mental instability of his maternal grandfather. Both his piety and 'goodness of heart' were unimpeachable and his response to every argument was meekly to advise his councillors to 'make peace'. He went on to found Eton and King's College, Cambridge, obsessed with making their chapels bigger than a cathedral nave. Later generations even sought his canonisation. His wife, however, was of a different mettle. In her mid-teens, she was already pert and opinionated, unschooled in Plantagenet ways and fixated on making a peace with her French homeland. This put her firmly on the side of Somerset and the Beauforts, Lancastrian relatives of the king.

Peace after defeat in war rarely finds favour with English opinion. The king's house of Lancaster was discredited by military failure and rightly suspected of favouring appeasement with France. Parliament asserted its sovereignty and turned to the opposing faction led by the thirty-nine-year-old Richard Plantagenet, Duke of York, also a descendant of Edward III with a long-standing claim to Henry's throne. In 1450 a leading Lancastrian, the Duke of Suffolk, was murdered and Somerset imprisoned. In 1453, the battle of Castillon signalled England's final defeat in the Hundred Years War. For the first time French cannons were deployed in sufficient numbers to mow down an English army and the age of the longbow appeared over. On hearing of the defeat, Henry had a complete mental collapse. York, as heir apparent, assumed the protectorate with the full support of parliament and took up the reins of government. The Lancastrian cause seemed doomed.

Yet no sooner had York triumphed than, to widespread incredulity, the twenty-one-year-old queen was found to be pregnant and gave birth to a boy. To further astonishment, the king recovered a degree of sanity, sufficient to restore the queen and Somerset to their former ascendancy. York was forced to vacate his new position at court and the stage was set for the most savage civil war in English history.

The Wars of the Roses

~

1453-1483

IF THE HUNDRED YEARS WAR exhausted England in a French dynastic feud, the English dynastic feud that followed was every bit as senseless. The Wars of the Roses were fought over no great issue of principle, such as divided Henry II from Becket or King John from his barons. It was a crude struggle for power between the rival descendants of two sons of Edward III, John of Gaunt and the Duke of Clarence. Gaunt's house of Lancaster (red rose) had by the 1450s held the throne for half a century as the result of his eldest son, Bolingbroke, usurping and killing the Black Prince's son, Richard II. Bolingbroke became Henry IV and the crown then passed to his son, Henry V, and grandson, Henry VI. Though based on usurpation, the Lancastrian claim had the virtue of being acknowledged by parliament and long entrenched.

The Yorkist claim derived from Philippa, daughter of Clarence, who was senior to Gaunt among Edward III's sons. She married into the powerful Marcher family the Mortimers, who became earls of March and dukes of York (white rose). This claim was unsullied by usurpation, but weakened by passing through a female line and being long defunct. The English usually respected Salic law against female inheritance, but tended to waive it for reasons of political expediency, as the Yorkists did now. The truth was that both claims were weak enough to be worth a fight.

The thirty years of ensuing bloodshed engulfed not just the contending parties but the greatest families in the land. These included the Nevilles, earls of Warwick, based in the midlands and the north, into whose family the Mortimers had married and with whom York had formed a close alliance in London. The Nevilles' ancestral foes in the north-east were the Percys, dukes of Northumberland, whose allegiance like that of their neighbours, the Scots, was seldom reliable. In Lancashire and the north-west lay the Stanley interest, while in East Anglia and the south the dukes of Norfolk held sway, traditionally in the king's interest.

Since the coming of the Normans, these families had enjoyed an ambiguous independence under the crown. They owned castles and estates sometimes covering many counties, with incomes to match. They could raise private armies at will, relieving the king of the need for an army of his own when fighting abroad, yet rendering him bereft of one should he need to fight at home. The Wars of the Roses were essentially between these families and their interests. During a battle archers were often told to 'go for the lords, spare the commons'. After the contest was decided, quarter (shelter) was usually but not invariably given by the victors to ordinary soldiers on the opposing side. As the leading protagonists were killed, their sons took the field to avenge them, and the war took on the character of a Montague and Capulet vendetta. By the end battles were often fought between teenage commanders. Executions and confiscations wiped out the nobility on a scale not repeated until the First World War. In Yorkshire's Harewood chapel, frigid effigies of fifteenth-century warriors lie on their tombs like ships at anchor, bearing silent witness to the slaughter.

King Henry's unexpected resumption of sanity on Christmas Day 1454 had driven York from court, but he did not go quietly. While the young queen engineered Somerset's return to power, York and Warwick gathered their prodigious armies in the Midlands and marched on London to regain power. The

Lancastrians under Somerset came out to meet them and battle was joined, in May 1455, in the streets of St Albans. York and Warwick trounced the Lancastrians and Somerset himself was killed. The first blood had been let.

York became constable of England and returned to London as guardian of the enfeebled king. Margaret escaped to take command of the Lancastrian forces in the north. There in 1460 she scored a significant victory over the Yorkists at the battle of Wakefield, where disaster for the Yorkists occurred when the duke himself, the one man who might have asserted authority over England's growing chaos, was killed. Margaret set his head with a paper crown on the gates of York, 'so York may overlook the town of York'.

The civil war now took fire as the sons of Somerset and York sought to avenge their fathers. The eighteen-year-old Edward, the new Duke of York, defeated the Lancastrians at Mortimer's Cross, repaying the cruelties of Wakefield with interest. Margaret won another battle at St Albans, horrifying friend and foe alike by getting her seven-year-old son to pronounce death sentences on enemy noblemen. But with young York advancing on London with a large army, she thought it prudent to flee with the king to Scotland, ally of her homeland of France.

Young York entered London in 1461, accompanied by his powerful cousin and mentor, Warwick, to be greeted with public shows of joy. Though still a teenager, he was a giant for his time, 6ft 4in tall. He declared himself Edward IV (1461 – 70 and 1471 – 83) and a legitimate descendant of Edward III. Once enthroned, he marched north to confront a Lancastrian army regrouped and reinforced from Scotland by Margaret. The two armies met at Towton, between York and Leeds. The battle was one of the most awful conflicts in any English war, and one of the few where the battlefield has been comprehensively excavated. Some 75,000 men are estimated to have been present, approximately 10 per cent of the nation's fighting-age male population. The Lancastrians were again defeated and the exasperated Yorkists declared that no quarter be given. The result was the slaughter of 28,000 men, and Margaret's flight with her husband to the ever-accommodating Scots. The gates of York saw Lancastrian skulls replace the old Yorkist ones.

At this point the war should have ended. Within just a decade, a third of England's 150 noble families are thought to have perished or lost their land. York was king at the age of just twenty, and Henry VI was deposed and in exile. The only wild card was the indomitable Margaret, 'with the blood of Charlemagne in her cheeks'. She now activated 'the auld alliance' of Scotland and her native France, proving herself a ruthless leader and shrewd general. She had Henry, still notionally king, in her retinue and a trump card, their infant son and heir, Prince Edward of Lancaster. With French assistance she skirmished with the Yorkists in the north, holding the Northumbrian castles of Alnwick, Bamburgh and Dunstanburgh. By 1464 Edward had recovered them with massive cannonades, leaving Dunstanburgh the dramatic ruin that sits on the Northumbrian coast today. This time Margaret fled to France.

In London Edward was not yet mature enough to be certain in his authority. Worse, he enraged his closest associate, Warwick, by secretly marrying a commoner, Elizabeth Woodville, when Warwick was carefully negotiating a diplomatic marriage for him in France. Elizabeth was a beauty with, it was said, 'heavy-lidded eyes like those of a dragon'. She was the first English queen since the conquest, and the first commoner. Warwick regarded himself as Edward's protector and friend and felt humiliated. He was even more angry when Edward bestowed eight peerages on his new wife's family, the Woodvilles, who swarmed into prominence at court and threatened the pre-eminence of Warwick's house of Neville.

The result of this crisis was that in 1469 Warwick performed one of the great betrayals of English history, deserting the king to join forces with his erstwhile enemy, Margaret, in France. This cost the Yorkists military strength and political coherence. Warwick married his daughter, Anne Neville, to Margaret's son and royal heir, Prince Edward, and enticed the king's brother, the Duke of Clarence, to join him in France. Warwick's support, in alliance with the French, tilted the balance of power back to the Lancastrians. Hence, when Warwick and Margaret landed in England in 1470, it was Edward's turn to flee into exile, this time to France's enemy, the Duke of Burgundy. Henry VI was reinstalled on the throne in London, under the protection of Warwick, rightly dubbed the 'kingmaker'.

York in Burgundy was no more inclined to accept defeat than had been Margaret in Paris. In April 1471 he returned with a new army and met Warwick at Barnet, north of London. Here he defeated his old mentor in a desperate battle in thick fog, during which Warwick lost his bodyguards and was set upon by soldiers. His visor was raised and his throat slashed before Edward could arrive to save his life. Such was the rage against Warwick's treachery that Edward had to protect his corpse from dismemberment and have it brought to St Paul's in London. Warwick had lived and died the Wars of the Roses. The kingmaker was finally unmade by the king. In the words of his biographer Paul Kendall, 'He left no enduring print upon the English state. He was an adventurer.'

Edward now had to put an end to the Lancastrian cause once and for all. He marched to the west country, where Margaret had gone to summon new troops, and there in May of 1471 he defeated her at the battle of Tewkesbury. Margaret's son and Henry VI's heir, Prince Edward, was slain on the battlefield. No quarter was given and the slaughter reached even the nave of Tewkesbury's Abbey, which was so contaminated it had to be reconsecrated. The bloodthirsty day was immortalised in the opening pun of Shakespeare's *Richard III*: 'Now is the winter of our discontent/ Made glorious summer by this sun of York.'

The supposed speaker of these lines was Edward IV's nineteen-year-old brother, Richard, Duke of Gloucester. He instantly took the dead prince's fifteen-year-old widow, Anne Neville, as his wife, thus uniting the Marcher estates of Gloucester with those of the Nevilles in the Midlands and the north. Overnight Gloucester became the greatest magnate in the land, successor to the Earl of Warwick. On 22 May 1471, Edward IV returned to London to take back the throne for the house of York, with Margaret now his prisoner. That night Henry VI was murdered in the Tower, it is assumed by the only man known to be with him at the time, Richard of Gloucester. Witness to half a century of chaos, the old king died insane, or as one report said, from 'pure displeasure and melancholy'.

Edward IV enjoyed a revival of the chivalric days of his ancestor, Edward III. He restored the Garter ceremony, completing for it the magnificent chapel of St George at Windsor. He formed a library, welcoming Caxton to London in 1476 to produce the first printed editions of the *Canterbury Tales* and Malory's *Morte d'Arthur*. The Wars of the Roses had seen many prosper. Merchants had armies to supply and the conflict did not seriously impede trade, as the wars with France had done. The City of London's cloth merchants were soon powerful enough to pass laws stipulating what fabric different ranks in society should wear, with gold, purple and sable for lords, velvet, satin and silk for knights and no imported cloth for commoners, only English wool.

While peace brought prosperity, some wounds did not heal. In 1478 Edward's turncoat brother, the Duke of Clarence, ally of the disgraced Warwick, was killed in the Tower. He was said to have been 'drowned in a butt of Malmsey wine', possibly a reference to his alcoholism. Then in 1483 Edward himself died of a stroke at the age of just forty, leaving Elizabeth's twelve-year-old son to succeed him as Edward V. Again England had a child monarch, with his uncle, Gloucester, as the only candidate for regent. Under his aegis the Wars of the Roses returned to reach their final bloody climax.

Bosworth and
Henry Tudor

~

1483 – 1509

RICHARD OF GLOUCESTER RANKS with King John and Edward II in medieval demonology. But the truth of his two-year reign (1483 – 5) is hard to disinter from Shakespeare's epic work of defamation, written a century later to justify the Tudor usurpation of his crown. Was he indeed 'rudely stamped, deformed, unfinished', as the Bard claimed? Was he guilty of serial murder, as charged by his biographer, Sir Thomas More? Or was he, as later apologists maintained, much misunderstood?

Gloucester had a grim apprenticeship. He was steeped in the savagery of civil war and helped his brother, Edward IV, preside over the murder of Henry VI and their brother, Clarence. Whether or not he loved Anne Neville, newly widowed wife of Prince Edward, he married her with indecent haste and acquired the greatest fortune in England thereby. Gloucester now found himself guardian of a twelve-year-old king, Edward V, and had good reason to fear the boy's forceful mother Elizabeth Woodville, her brother Earl Rivers and her ally Lord Hastings, all of whom had been Lancastrian loyalists before she married Edward IV. In the desperate aftermath of Tewkesbury, Gloucester might understandably have felt surrounded by conspiracy and menace.

What is clear is that he acted with ruthless decision. When he heard of Edward IV's death, Gloucester enticed Elizabeth to

London from Ludlow with her two sons, the king and the heir to the throne. The party was intercepted at Northampton and their entourage dismissed. Rivers was sent north and summarily executed. When Elizabeth arrived in London she feared the worst and fled to sanctuary at Westminster Abbey. Gloucester took the two boys to be billeted in the Tower 'for their own safety'. Hastings was executed.

Gloucester's Neville power base in the north was summoned to arms and told to march to London. Parliament was summoned and bidden by Gloucester's ally, the Duke of Buckingham, to declare the princes illegitimate on the dubious grounds that Edward IV was already married at the time of his marriage to Woodville. It duly 'called on' Gloucester to become king. On 6 July he was crowned Richard III before a sullen congregation and a sullen citizenry. Rumours were soon rife that the princes, who had been seen playing in the gardens of the Tower, were now dead. They were never seen again. Long after, in the reign of Charles II, the bones of two young boys were found in a walled-up staircase in the Tower.

To combine infanticide and regicide horrified even a nation used to such horrors. By October 1483 Richard's supporter Buckingham could tolerate him no longer and raised the standard of rebellion, only to be pursued to the west country, seized and killed. The king now faced threats from all sides. His son by his new queen, Anne Neville, died in 1484 and Anne herself died a year later. This moved the succession laterally to the twenty-eight-year-old Lancastrian Henry Tudor, Earl of Richmond, descendant of John of Gaunt's Beaufort line. He had been born in Pembroke in 1457 after the death of his father, Edmund Tudor, when his mother, Margaret Beaufort, was just thirteen. The girl almost died giving birth and never had another child. Henry was brought up by relatives in Wales and then moved for safety to the Celtic outpost of Brittany.

By 1485 this tenuous claimant was proving a magnet for Lancastrian exiles from Richard's rule. They brought reports that Richard intended to marry his niece, Elizabeth of York, sister of the princes in the Tower, on whom Henry Tudor had set his sights finally to unite the houses of Lancaster and York. Were a marriage between Richard and Elizabeth to have issue, Henry's claim to the throne would lapse. He dared delay no longer. Landing at Milford Haven in August that year, he marched across Wales, unimpeded by the king's supposed ally, Rhys ap Thomas. Rhys had sworn that the king's enemies would advance only 'over my belly' and stood under a bridge to let Henry pass over him. Like most of Wales he then joined Henry's cause.

There were at the time three English magnates capable of fielding large armies alongside the king and the Nevilles: the Stanleys in the north-west, the Percys in the north-east and the Duke of Norfolk in the south. All were now summoned by Richard, but none was a fully reliable ally. The Percys had long been hesitant in their loyalty to London. Lord Stanley was now married to Margaret Beaufort, Henry's mother. To ensure his loyalty, Richard seized his son, Lord Strange, as a hostage. Richard could trust only Norfolk in the south, along with a cabal of councillors, Ratcliffe, Catesby and Lovell (known as 'the rat, the cat and the dog'). How these forces might align themselves would be determined only on the day.

Battle was joined on 22 August 1485 at Bosworth in Leicestershire. The king had a fresh army supposedly 10,000 strong, while Henry, who had never fought a battle himself, had just 5,000 inexperienced troops. Lord Stanley favoured Henry but dreaded the fate Richard might exact on his hostage son. As the battle began, the king put this to the test by ordering Stanley first into the charge. When he was seen not to move, Richard ordered Strange to be killed. But at this point Percy's forces were also seen to hold back, and the aide told to kill

Strange thought it prudent not to carry out the order. Stanley, claiming 'I have other sons', crucially entered battle on Henry's side.

Seeing these defections, Richard astride a white horse and hurling accusations of treason at his allies, made a desperate personal bid to kill Henry himself. He fought to within striking distance, killing Henry's standard-bearer before falling under a flourish of spears. His performance defied Shakespeare's depiction of his physical inadequacy. The crown was reputed to have fallen into a thorn bush, where it was retrieved by Stanley and placed on Henry's head. The corpse of Richard, last of the Plantagenets, was stripped naked and paraded through the streets of Leicester. The Wars of the Roses ended as they had begun, in scenes of public brutality.

Henry VII, Henry Tudor (1485 – 1509), heralded an emphatic break from the Anglo-Norman past. Yet he was a chip off the old Plantagenet block. His mother was descended from John of Gaunt. His father, Edmund Tudor, whom he never knew, was son of Henry V's widow, Catherine of France, by Owen Tudor. Though only a quarter Welsh, Henry claimed descent from the kings of Wales and rode into battle sporting the cross of St George alongside the red dragon of Cadwallader of Gwynedd. In a final act of unity, he married Richard's intended, Elizabeth of York. The two roses, red and white, were thus conjoined in the Tudor double-rose. The symbol still adorns churches, castles and palaces across England.

Henry is the first king of whom we possess plausible likenesses, with the sharp features and intelligent eyes of a calculating ruler. He enjoyed administration and personally signed thousands of edicts stored in the National Archives. Above all he developed a miserly obsession with revenue, milking the country of money. In this he was abetted by his archbishop, John Morton, whose maxim, 'Morton's fork', held that if a noble was seen to live frugally he could afford the king's taxes, and if lavishly he could also afford them. Today it would be termed Catch-22.

As the reign progressed, Henry became a king 'more feared than loved'. His chief weakness, other than his love for money, was that he never overcame his guilt at the manner by which he attained power. The illegitimacy of his Beaufort ancestors weakened his claim to the throne and, like Henry IV, he was tormented at having usurped an anointed king. Henry did his best to make amends. He named his heir after his notional ancestor, Arthur, and family trees were commissioned with Welsh roots prominently displayed. A Tudor craze for heraldry was initiated. A century later, Shakespeare cleansed Henry's illegitimacy in *Richard III* as he had that of Henry IV.

Barely a year after his coronation, Henry was challenged by champions of a child pretender, Lambert Simnel, as one of the vanished princes in the Tower. He was even crowned as king in Dublin by the ruler of Ireland, the Earl of Kildare. This led in 1487 to a landing in the north and a rebel Percy army reaching Nottingham, where it was beaten by Henry outside Newark. Simnel was acquitted of blame and even became a royal cook. Four years later in 1491 came another pretender, to whom Henry showed no such leniency. A young Fleming, Perkin Warbeck, was one of history's great confidence trickers. He too claimed to be a prince in the Tower and managed to deceive gullible, or perhaps eager, enemies of England in France, Burgundy, Ireland and Scotland. He even married a Scottish princess. Warbeck's intermittent 'invasions' were repulsed and he was captured and later executed in 1499.

For all his parsimony, Henry knew majesty required splendour. After the burning of his palace at Sheen on the Thames, he built a new one on the site, renamed after his old Yorkshire title and seat of Richmond. Built entirely of brick, it was in the Flemish style, with towers, pinnacles and bay-windowed galleries overlooking the river. Churches were still determinedly English gothic. The great Perpendicular wool church at Long Melford in Suffolk, built in the 1490s, was of barn-like proportions, relying on fittings, glass and sculpture for ornament. The chapel at Westminster Abbey prepared for Henry's tomb was vaulted in a celestial starburst of stone fans, a roof device unique to England. There the king's body would lie in a chest of renaissance splendour, designed by an Italian, Pietro Torrigiani.

Henry also dabbled in the Europe-wide passion for discovery following news of Columbus's return from the New World in 1493. In 1496 Henry offered the modest sum of £10 to sponsor a Genoese, John Cabot, to explore America's eastern seaboard. He planted the Tudor flag in Nova Scotia. At the same time Erasmus of Rotterdam brought the humanism of the Renaissance to the universities of Oxford and Cambridge, asserting that a study of the classics was an essential precursor to understanding Christian theology. In London he associated with the church reformer John Colet, dean of St Paul's, and the scholar Thomas More, moving England closer to the mainstream of north-European thought and bringing it into contact with the wellsprings of Protestantism.

In 1501 Henry's cautious foreign policy yielded a great diplomatic triumph in the marriage of his fifteen-year-old son Arthur to the Aragonese heiress Catherine, a deal ten years in negotiating. Two daughters were equally well married, Mary to Louis XII, king of France and Margaret to the king of Scotland, the latter involving an improbably entitled 'treaty of perpetual peace'. Within six months of his marriage, however, Arthur died suddenly in Ludlow castle, to be succeeded as heir to the throne by his brother Henry, Duke of York, then aged ten. The king proposed that Catherine now become wife to this son. But the match was still not concluded in 1509, when the king himself died, leaving England with a minor of seventeen as monarch.

Henry Tudor left England united and at peace with both France and Scotland. Wales was liberated from Plantagenet oppression, and even Ireland was briefly subdued under the ferocious Earl of Kildare. Henry, never popular, was said to have died 'steeped in avarice'. His two unpopular tax gatherers, Edmund Dudley and Richard Empson, were beheaded for corruption and treason after his death, protesting that their actions were only 'as the king would have it so'. But the first of the Tudors had brought to an end a century of civil war and bequeathed his son a full Treasury.

Henry VIII

~

1509 – 1547

HENRY VIII (1509 – 47) WAS the Hercules of English history. Part medieval tyrant, part polymath renaissance prince, he tore up the Plantagenet rule book. He ended the long compromise between Norman ruler and English people, between monarch and church, and between London and the baronial provinces. He took a country salvaged by his father from the splintered wreck of civil war and set over it a single, sovereign king, master alike of its civil and religious being.

When Henry ascended the throne he was just seventeen. A well-proportioned, good-looking but restless youth, until his brother Arthur's death he had been intended by his father for the church. He was educated in the increasingly anti-Roman theology of northern Europe, his marginalia filling the books in his library. He was also skilled at riding, jousting and tennis, as well as at poetry and music. He was once even thought to have composed 'Greensleeves'. Henry cared little for politics. Parliament, regarded by his father as a troublesome tax-factory, continued to take a constitutional back seat, as long as he had his father's full treasury and could ignore it.

Henry's first act, even before his coronation, was to marry his brother's widow, Catherine of Aragon, five years his senior. He respected the Roman church and won ready dispensation from the pope to marry a sister-in-law, on the grounds (strongly asserted by Catherine) that her marriage to the fifteen-year-old Arthur had been unconsummated. There is every sign that Henry and Catherine were happy. She was attractive and intelligent and they remained together for the first twenty years of his reign. The one blight on their relationship was Catherine's failure, after many still-births and a daughter, Mary, to produce a male heir. This was no small matter for an English monarch with a sense of history.

Like his father, Henry chose advisers on merit rather than birth. In place of baronial councillors he turned for advice to younger talents drawn from the church and law, the most prominent initially being a butcher's son from Ipswich, Thomas Wolsey. From a rambling court of some 1,000 favourites and their retinues, he chose a council of personal aides through whom he made proclamations outside the authority of parliament. At this stage in his life, Henry spent most of his time on his leisure, with government delegated to the competent Wolsey, a relationship similar to that of Henry II and Becket. Under Wolsey's influence, the avoidance of foreign wars so scrupulously maintained by Henry VII broke down. His father had fought to rule, but Henry was a Plantagenet throwback, ruling to fight. In 1512 he revived the hoary claim to French territory and, on a trumped-up pretext, sent an army of invasion under the Marquis of Dorset across the Channel, only to see it return defeated. A year later Henry went to France in person, hired German mercenaries, seized the town of Tournai and induced the French to pay him a continuing subsidy to go away. It was Danegeld in reverse.

At home, the Scots took the opportunity to renege on Henry VII's treaty of 'perpetual peace' with a raid into Northumberland. In 1513 it was beaten back and Scottish pikemen were slaughtered by storms of English arrows at Flodden Field. The slaughter shocked contemporaries, with Henry's brother-in-law James IV of Scotland killed, alongside his son and 10,000 soldiers. The Scottish crown devolved on to the head of an infant, the seventeen-month-old James V. The unruly Scots had brought disaster on themselves, and England had brought insecurity in equal measure.

Wolsey was now in the ascendant. Twenty years the king's senior, he became chancellor in 1515 and a cardinal the same year. No friend of baronial power, he tried to ban any further enclosure of common land for sheep. He regulated markets and the professions. He overrode the slow justice of the King's Bench by using the prerogative Star Chamber, delivering summary judgments under his own aegis. Henry meanwhile dabbled in theology. He corresponded with Erasmus and when Martin Luther nailed his anti-Catholic 'theses' to the door of Wittenberg church in 1517, Henry wrote a lengthy denunciation of them. A grateful pope awarded the English crown the title 'defender of the faith', which still graces English coins as FID DEF.

Henry now looked across the Channel at the two great powers of Europe: France and the Holy Roman Empire ruled from Habsburg Vienna. Artists, architects, poets and musicians were summoned from the continent. The king increased the navy from five ships to thirty and personally supervised the design of a seven-tier battleship, *Henry Grâce à Dieu* or 'Great Harry', the biggest in Europe. Then in 1520 came the ultimate folly of a star-struck ruler, a summit conference, the 'Field of Cloth of Gold' at Guînes, near Calais. Pavilions in renaissance designs, courtiers, warriors and entertainers were shipped to France, with a retinue of some 6,000 attendants. Now aged twenty-nine, Henry was in his prime, described by the Venetian envoy as 'much handsomer than any other sovereign in Christendom'. At his own behest, he was the first English monarch to be addressed as 'Your Majesty' rather than 'Your Grace'.

The king and Wolsey were soon out of their diplomatic depths, dabbling in the emerging conflict between the Habsburg Charles V, and the young François I of France. Taking first one side and then the other, England's only reward was to lose the French subsidy won at Tournai and a growing enmity between Henry and Wolsey. The cardinal re-enacted Becket's clerical intransigence, claiming exemption for the clergy from the common law. Henry retorted that 'by the ordinance and sufferance of God, we are king of England, and the kings of England in times past have never had any superior but God alone'. Wolsey's great palace at Hampton Court, outshining Henry's Richmond, was decorated with Italian terracotta and became a source of envy rather than wonder, as did his new Cardinal's College in Oxford.

The king had other worries beyond the pomp of his chancellor. By 1526 Catherine was more than forty years old. Her body was aged by constant miscarriages and the chance of a male heir was slim. Henry was openly infatuated with Anne Boleyn, a lithe, intelligent girl with dark eyes and long, dark hair. Educated in Paris, she dazzled the court with her French clothes, music, dancing and wit. Her sister, Mary, had been Henry's mistress, but Anne rejected his advances, even when reinforced with a shower of jewels and lover's knots. She would have no sexual relations with him while he was still married to Catherine.

England's fate now turned on the conjuncture of Catherine's failure to produce a male heir and Anne's sexual scruple. Henry became a different man. He put on weight. His explosive frustration, exacerbated by a jousting wound in his leg, led him, in Wolsey's words, 'to put one half of his realm in danger ... and set private whim against all Christendom'. While most kings were threatened by external forces, Henry's demons were inside him. He boasted, 'I never spared man in my anger nor woman in my lust.' He was determined to marry Anne.

How far the 'king's great matter' drove forward the clash between church and state is much debated. What is undeniable is that it acquired a furious urgency. Anne is believed to have accepted Henry in 1527, but still only on condition of an annulment from the pope of his marriage to Catherine. The pope was at this moment a prisoner of the Habsburg Charles V, who was Catherine's nephew. Gaining such a licence would be no easy matter. The book of Leviticus ordained: 'Thou shalt not uncover the nakedness of thy brother's wife.' To allow Henry's current marriage to Catherine, the pope had accepted that she had never consummated her marriage to his brother, Arthur. Henry now needed to assert the reverse, that it had been consummated, the pope had erred, his marriage to Catherine was illegal and therefore he could marry Anne. The obstacle was that Catherine stuck to her story, denying the consummation.

Henry was trapped. Wolsey struggled hard to secure an annulment, even warning the pope of 'remedies that are frequently instilled into the king's mind' if it were not secured. He failed. The king turned in desperation to others, seizing on a young Cambridge cleric, Thomas Cranmer, who proposed that the matter circumvent the papacy by being referred to a committee of European scholars. Wolsey's star abruptly fell. He was stripped of his palaces and titles and in 1529 was arrested and summoned to the Tower, dying on his way south from York. Like many who fly so near the sun, he protested, 'If I had served God as diligently as I have done the king, He would not have given me over in my grey hairs.' His Oxford foundation, Christ Church, still stands with its great cloister conspicuously unfinished.

The court was in turmoil. Henry was openly consorting with Anne, though a wealth of inquiry has failed to find evidence of sex between them. Catherine was still queen, resisting with Spanish flair all pressure to say her marriage to Henry was illegal. She had powerful allies at home and abroad, and Henry was sufficiently loyal to his beliefs to be reluctant to defy biblical law even though, as the ever obliging Cranmer pointed out, there was no pope in the Bible.

The king now took his revenge on the church, as Wolsey had predicted. Whether or not goaded by Anne's inclination towards Lutheranism, he recalled parliament in 1529 and had it pass one measure after another against what he saw as clerical abuses. In 1531 he asserted his legal supremacy over the church, qualified only by 'as far as the law of Christ allows'. He denied the church the privilege of sanctuary and the levying of taxes on wills, its most substantial source of revenue. As for the annulment, Wolsey's successor as chancellor, Sir Thomas More, told parliament that 'all men openly perceive that the king hath not attempted this matter of will or pleasure, as some strangers report, but only for the discharge of his conscience and surety of the succession of his realm'.

The king pursued both his will and his pleasure with despatch. He disappeared with Anne for over a month and, on his return, banished Catherine and her daughter from London. He was threatened by Rome with excommunication unless he 'cast off the concubine, Anne', and replied with a bill of annates, potentially removing 95 per cent of subsidies from English churches to Rome. These measures passed the Commons easily but in the House of Lords, where bishops were strong, there was furious resistance. Henry lobbied, cajoled and threatened, demanding ingeniously that the Lords vote for or against 'the king's welfare'. Thomas More balked at a final breach with Rome. In 1532 he resigned rather than concede the king's absolute supremacy of the church, passing his chancellor's office to a brilliant young lawyer, Thomas Cromwell. That same year Henry took Anne on a state visit to France, from which she returned pregnant. He married her privately in January 1533, the bigamy ignored on his continued assertion that the marriage to Catherine was invalid. Cranmer, who probably performed the ceremony, was rewarded with Canterbury, to become the dominant figure of the English Reformation. Anne was crowned queen.

In September 1533 Anne gave birth at Greenwich, but to a daughter, Elizabeth. For Henry this was an apparently unforeseen catastrophe. He had defied his church and fought parliament to beget a son and Anne, like Catherine, had failed him. She instantly lost her charm. Henry was furious to be told that she gossiped about his failing sexual prowess and to hear tales of her infidelity. He was soon comparing her unfavourably with the submissive charm of a twenty-five-year-old court beauty, Jane Seymour, to whom the king shifted his favour. ·

In 1534 Henry enacted the formal Act of Supremacy, under which the king 'recognised no superior in earth but only God, and not subject to the laws of any earthly creature'. The legislation completed the creation of a Church of England, vesting temporal and doctrinal power in the monarch. One of two treason acts imposed the death penalty on any who criticised Henry and his leadership of the church, rendering the king 'a dictator under law'. More, imprisoned for treason under the new act after refusing to support the annulment of Henry's marriage to Catherine, had agreed to remain silent in exchange for his life, but now it was being described as 'a silence that echoed across Europe'. He was beheaded in 1535 and sanctified by the pope.

The following year Cromwell set about replenishing the royal coffers with the suppression and confiscation of some 400 smaller monasteries. The confiscation was not unprecedented. Henry V had dissolved monasteries to pay for Agincourt, as had the king of Sweden in 1527. Many foundations had shrunk to below the supposed minimum of twelve monks. The thirteen Cistercian houses in Wales had just eighty-five monks between them. Most surrendered their wealth in return for state pensions. Within eight years monastic 'privatisation' had brought the crown almost £1 million. The change to the face of England was extraordinary. Monasteries were a presence in the landscape, those such as Rievaulx, Fountains and Wymondham towering over the country as cathedrals did over the cities. Most were stripped and then demolished, often using gunpowder, their contents dispersed at auctions. Many sites became quarries, the stones used to extend private houses and install chimneys in halls. Monastic chapels became parish churches, magnificently so at Sherborne in Dorset and Beverley in Yorkshire. Monastic land was sold to anyone with money to pay, creating a revolution as a new merchant class gained access to a landed status previously confined to the nobility. As after the Black Death, England had a genius for opportunistic social change. No comparable transfer of wealth had occurred since the Norman conquest. The consequence did more than anything to prepare the English nation for the modern age.

In 1536 came an immediate reaction. The so-called Pilgrimage of Grace erupted in the north, in Lincolnshire and in Cornwall. Its leaders protested the king's seizure of church revenue, much of which had been dispersed locally, but many of their followers were simply devout Catholics distressed at the upheaval that the king and parliament had visited on their faith. When a popular army some 30,000 strong moved south from Yorkshire Henry was ruthless in retaliation, promising the rebels that he would 'burn, spoil and destroy their goods, wives, children with all extremity'. He demanded some 250 exemplary executions from the Duke of Norfolk, sent to suppress them.

The methodical Henry now ordered Cranmer to prepare a new prayer book. A version of William Tyndale's English-language Bible, published secretly on the continent in 1526, was distributed to churches across the country. At the same time an elaborate conspiracy was hatched to prove Anne's infidelity. She was condemned and her execution in the Tower in May 1536 was delayed only by her request to be beheaded in the French manner, with a sword rather than an axe. The king married Jane Seymour, who was soon delivered of a son, Edward. Henry's joy turned to deep sorrow when Jane died within weeks of giving birth. She was to be the only queen he asked to be buried with him.

The ever efficient Cromwell now extended his monastic dissolution into a wave of iconoclasm. As Tyndale had written, 'Sacraments, signs, ceremonies and bodily things can be no service to God in his person.' Church roods of Calvary and images of the Virgin were taken down and smashed. Worshippers were ordered 'not to repose their trust and affiance in any other works devised by men's phantasies besides scripture'. The intercession of saints was banned. Henry was particularly keen to eradicate the cult of Thomas à Becket, noted enemy of kingly power. Becket's shrine at Canterbury and the shrine of Our Lady of Walsingham were destroyed and their plate seized for the Treasury in London.

Henry had now to guard his security. His breach with Rome had pitted all of Catholic Europe against him and to declare war on him would be a holy cause. In 1539 he was persuaded by Cromwell to marry a Dutch princess, Anne of Cleves, to forge a precautionary alliance with the Low Countries against France and the Holy Roman Empire. Cromwell told him that Anne's beauty of both face and body 'excels the Duchess of Milan as much as the golden sun excels the silver moon'. The eulogy was enhanced by a commissioned portrait of her as a glamorous young lady by the leading artist of the day, Hans Holbein.

Cromwell's diplomacy foundered on the rock of reality. Anne turned out to be a tall, lanky thirty-four-year-old with a pockmarked face who spoke only German. When she arrived in England, Henry went to Rochester in disguise to meet her, taking with him an extravagant sable wrap as a gift. He was appalled by what he saw, there being 'nothing in this woman as men report of her'. He fled to his barge. Anne was, he declared, no better than 'a mare of Flanders'. In January 1540 he conceded a diplomatic wedding, but carefully did not consummate it on the wedding night, after which he remarked to Cromwell, 'Now I like her much worse.' Parliament annulled the union within months. Henry was once more without a continental ally.

With his Reformation well advanced, Henry was now seized by doubts. He worried that he had gone beyond offending the Roman church and had offended God. Church conservatives round the Duke of Norfolk preyed on this fear, and in 1539 the king passed an act explicitly 'for the abolition of diversity of opinion', the so-called Act of the Six Articles, aimed at extreme Protestant evangelicals. Henry allowed the restoration of Easter sepulchres and the ceremony of 'creeping to the Cross'. Prayers for the dead were also permitted. Protestant Anabaptists were burned at the stake.

Cromwell was damaged by the Cleves fiasco, as Wolsey and More had been likewise damaged by the king's marital woes. An increasingly powerful Norfolk accused Cromwell of corruption and heresy, offering Henry as his new queen his own auburn-haired niece of just twenty, Catherine Howard. Henry was almost fifty, grossly overweight and with constant leg pains. He briefly fell in love and Cromwell's demise was instant. The man who had towered higher even than Wolsey was arrested in June 1540, and shortly afterwards lost his head. Cranmer remarked, 'Whom shall the king trust hereafter?' The answer was no one. Catherine soon suffered the same fate as Anne Boleyn, her flighty disposition and infidelity ill-attuned to the king's tempestuous moods. After being reported in adulterous love with her cousin, she was banished from the king's presence and summarily beheaded in 1542.

The king was left mortified and alone, a despot paranoid and in pain. He could boast fifty-six residences, including Wolsey's Hampton Court, and a catalogue of 100,000 precious objects. Late in life he began a renaissance palace at Nonsuch, south of London, to rival François's Fontainebleau, its shimmering facade crowned with turrets and pennants, evoking the glory days of the Field of Cloth of Gold. He seldom occupied it and it survives only in a few prints. Henry's legislative zeal remained

frenetic. Acts passed in 1536 and 1543 formally merged Wales
and England, ending the privileges of the Marcher lords and
replacing them with MPs in parliament. The law would 'utterly
extirpe alle and singular sinister usages and customs' pertaining
to Wales, including its language. The Welsh Tudors did more to
suppress Welshness than any Plantagenet. In 1541 a parliament
meeting in Dublin also saluted Henry as king of Ireland, while
two years later a treaty with Scotland signed at Greenwich
pledged the infant Mary Queen of Scots as wife to Henry's heir
Edward, an episode later dubbed 'the rough wooing'. For the
first time, the component nations of the British Isles acquired a
sort of unity, as one nation in the case of England and Wales, one
kingdom in the case of Ireland and one kingdom one day in the
case of Scotland.

The king now took a sixth wife, a thirty-one-year-old
north-country widow, Catherine Parr, of Protestant views. She
was studious and calm, nursing Henry, guarding Edward and
reconciling the sickening king with his daughters, Mary and
Elizabeth. The king found little peace. The succession north
of the border of the young Mary as queen of Scotland led to
the repudiation by her French mother of the match with Prince
Edward and her betrothal to the Catholic heir to the French
throne. The implication was that Scotland would become
subject to France, an intolerable provocation to any king of
England. A French invasion was even feared, and in 1544 Henry
led an army to France and seized Boulogne. His armour for the
campaign survives, showing his vast girth. A line of forts was
built along the south coast that still stands today, as at Hurst,
Walmer and Deal. An earlier project of similar ambition, the
warship *Mary Rose*, met with disaster in 1545, when it rolled over
and sank in the Solent during a battle with the French and in full
view of the king.

The king's powers were now waning. As death approached
he appeared to modify his commitment to the Reformation,

founding a monastery at Bisham and even asking for masses to be said for his soul. In his last speech to parliament, on Christmas Eve 1545, Henry pleaded not for the old or the new religion but rather for a reconciliation of the two under a newly 'nationalised' church of England. But it was not a Catholic but his old ally, the Protestant Cranmer, who attended him at his death in 1547.

Henry curbed the two pillars of the medieval state, the church and the barons, bringing both under what amounted to rule by personal prerogative. His declaration of church supremacy was, to many in the seventeenth century, a jump from the frying pan of papacy to the fire of divinely ordained kingship, much exploited by the Stuarts. That battle was to come. But Henry's attack on the Roman church and his dissolution of the monasteries changed the face of the nation. His meritocracy advanced lawyers and clerks such as Wolsey and Cromwell, whom place and corruption enabled to acquire land and thus influence in court and parliament. This shift in the distribution of wealth and thus in the equilibrium of consent posed an obstacle to Henry's first daughter, Mary, in her attempt at Counter-Reformation, but it aided his second daughter, Elizabeth, in reversing it. Henry did what many European monarchs regarded as undoable, he defied Rome and survived. He was one of Europe's great revolutionaries.

Reformation,
Counter-Reformation

~

1547 – 1558

SUCH ARE THE VAGARIES of hereditary monarchy that Henry VIII, symbol of kingly potency, left his crown to a nine-year-old weakling. Archbishop Cranmer had been meticulous in preparing Edward VI (1547 – 53) for Protestant monarchy. He educated him in the reformed religion under a devoted tutor, John Cheke. The boy was precocious, studying history and theology and taking copious notes during sermons. He spoke French and Italian and could translate Cicero into Greek at the time of his coronation. Cranmer referred to him as 'God's vice-regent and Christ's vicar within your own dominions'. The new king might be a loyal Protestant, but the seeds of the Stuart 'divine right of kings' were already sown.

The power of Edward's office was great, but who would wield it? Henry's council of regents collapsed as the king's uncle, the new Duke of Somerset, declared himself Lord Protector. He was openly opposed by another uncle, Thomas Seymour, who curried favour with the boy king by the tried-and-tested method of slipping him extra pocket money. He warned him that Somerset was leaving him 'but a very beggarly king'. One night in 1549 Seymour went too far and tried to kidnap Edward, a crime prevented only by a furiously barking dog at the king's door. Seymour was captured and executed. Princess Elizabeth, whom he had once courted, remarked that he was 'a man of much wit and little judgment'. She would become an expert in the genre.

Somerset proved an incompetent ruler. He built himself a lavish palace on the Thames where Somerset House now stands. He went to war with both France and Scotland and debased the coinage to pay for it, responding to the resulting rise in food prices by fixing the price of corn and reviving Wolsey's ban on further land enclosure for sheep. He declared that the nation must be defended 'with the force of men ... not with flocks of sheep'. Stringent measures were taken to advance church reform and iconoclasm.

Evangelicals now demanded full-blooded reformation. The taking down of roods and abolitions of chantries was extended to the removal of 'all images of stone, timber, alabaster or earth, graven, carved or painted which ... yet stand in a nych or chapel'. Wall paintings were whitewashed and penalties imposed on the hiding of relics. The empty niches on thousands of English church towers bear painful witness to the destruction. Meanwhile Cranmer's new prayer book, revealing in resonant English what had been obscured in Latin, was sent to all churches with orders that it be used exclusively. It was an emphatic gesture of cultural nationalism.

By the summer of 1549 revolts against Somerset's rule emerged, mostly from Catholic sympathisers, in the west country and in Norfolk. Conservatives conspired to topple the king and give the crown to his Catholic elder sister, Mary. The council led by John Dudley, Earl of Warwick, deserted Somerset and summoned the City of London militia to arrest him and take him to the Tower. He was executed in 1552. Warwick, elevated to Duke of Northumberland, now took his place as ruler of England. The change led to no improvement in the quality of government. Only the young king appeared eager to restrain the spreading destruction. He was an uncompromising

Protestant who, at the age of eleven, interrupted a bishop for invoking 'God, the holy saints and all the evangelists' and told him to invoke just 'God through Jesus Christ'. But as orders went out to replace all altars with communion tables, Edward expressed sadness at so much destruction and turned one monastery, Greyfriars in London, into Christ's Hospital school. He even welcomed back to court his sister Mary, who answered his kindness by processing through London with priests, crosses and rosaries. Reformation was by no means secure.

Then in the summer of 1553 the fifteen-year-old king, who seemed set to be both a wise ruler and a safe custodian of the Henrician settlement, died from consumption. On his deathbed Northumberland insisted he name as his successor not Mary, as Henry VIII had ordained, but his impeccably Protestant cousin Lady Jane Grey. This he did, leading Mary to flee to Framlingham castle in Suffolk, where an uprising in her favour won wide support. Northumberland lost his nerve. He faced 10,000 roughly armed men advancing on London and, with just a small force at his disposal, he soon capitulated, accepting the thirty-seven-year-old Mary as queen. It did him no good and within a month he had lost his head. Lady Jane Grey, uncrowned 'queen' for just nine days, was imprisoned in the Tower. Pro-Catholic peers and gentry surged back to power.

Mary I (1553–8) had been brought up under the influence of her much-abused Spanish mother, Catherine of Aragon, and retreated into a retinue of women that was as conservative as a convent. She sought advice on how to rule from her cousin, the Habsburg emperor Charles V, who recommended that she return the English church to Rome and marry his son and heir Philip of Spain. Mary needed no encouragement, claiming to be 'already half in love' with Philip from his portrait. Such a marriage jeopardised the English Reformation and implied an English crown subservient to the most powerful Catholic state in Europe.

The so-called Marian Counter-Reformation saw new instructions going out from court for roods to be recarved and rituals restored, masses sung and holy days celebrated. Edward's bishops, the elderly Cranmer, Latimer and Ridley, were imprisoned in the Tower for heresy, as was Mary's Protestant sister Elizabeth. It was there she is believed to have met and fell in love with the dead Northumberland's young son, Lord Robert Dudley. A revolt in 1554 by Sir Thomas Wyatt against the queen's impending marriage was brutally suppressed, and Lady Jane Grey was executed by royal command as a precaution. Leading Protestants now feared for their lives as, in 1554, Philip of Spain arrived in London to claim his bride. Tiny in stature, he spoke no English – and Mary no Spanish. His only public words heard in English were 'Good night, my lords all' as he led Mary to the bedchamber and did his duty by her on their wedding night. A member of the Spanish party reported that 'the queen is not at all beautiful, small and rather flabby ... and has no eyebrows'.

Henry's Act of Supremacy was repealed and Mary promised to rule in marital obedience. She promised to be 'bonny and buxom in bed and at board'. Their children would fuse the English monarchy with the Habsburg line, though Mary assured a worried parliament that she would be 'unable to permit' Philip's interference in specific decisions of government. Though she was soon declaring her pregnancy, it was widely doubted and Philip realised that it was a figment of a desperate imagination. Within a year he departed for the Netherlands and home, never to return, leaving his wife distraught.

The queen sought to rid her realm of heresy. In November 1555 the elderly Cranmer, who had once declared Mary illegitimate by virtue of her mother, Catherine of Aragon's, 'illegal' marriage to Henry, was toppled as archbishop of Canterbury, and England was effectively ruled by the papal legate, Cardinal Reginald Pole. Protestantism was equated with heresy and heresy with treason, a reprise of the treason acts of Henry VIII. Latimer and Ridley were burned at the stake in Oxford, to be followed by Cranmer. Though he formally recanted his Protestantism, it did not save him. He duly recanted his recantation, dramatically thrusting the hand that signed it first into the flames with the cry, 'This hand hath offended. Oh this unworthy hand.'

Mary became Bloody Mary and gave the Protestant cause some 300 martyrs (as many as the Catholics her father had executed during the Pilgrimage of Grace). They were later celebrated in John Foxe's bestselling *Book of Martyrs*. Religious strife now ran through every parish and every community. Protestantism might seem to some a lacklustre and abstract creed, but over two decades it had begun to take root as England's church. Whatever the affection for the old liturgy, there was little enthusiasm for reverting to the authority of Rome. In addition, though Mary re-established some abbeys, including Westminster, monastic England had passed to a new class of gentry. They might murmur the mass, but even Mary accepted that they would never give their newly acquired estates back to the monks.

Worse news came in 1558 with the eventual marriage of the fifteen-year-old Mary Queen of Scots to the fourteen-year-old French Dauphin amid scenes of great splendour in Notre Dame in Paris. Edinburgh was rocked by Protestant riots and France seized the last English possession on French soil, Calais. Mary in London was devastated, swearing, 'When I am dead and opened, you shall find Calais engraved on my heart.' The Protestant nation established by Henry in the teeth of European opposition now faced an extraordinary fate: England might have a Catholic Spanish king and Scotland a Catholic French one.

Before that prospect could arrive, heredity again played its trump on history. In November 1558 Mary took ill and followed her brother to the grave, reluctantly conceding the succession to her sister, Elizabeth. The Catholic bishop of Winchester, preaching over her grave, warned his congregation that the Counter-Reformation was in jeopardy. 'Soon the wolves will be coming out of Geneva … with their books before them, full of pestilent doctrines, blasphemy and heresy to infect the people.' He was right.

Good Queen Bess

~

1558 - 1603

THE REIGN OF ELIZABETH I (1558 – 1603) is often regarded as England's golden age. She was Good Queen Bess, Gloriana, presiding over an age of toleration, victory, romance and good humour, the cradle of Shakespeare and the English Renaissance. It is a time when English history acquires depth and moves from static tableau to moving picture. We feel we know the Elizabethans as we do not know their predecessors. We know the interiors of their buildings and the style of their clothes. Their speech has moved from Chaucerian obscurity to Shakespearean glory, from a jumble of local dialects to a single national tongue. While previous monarchs are often presented as caricatures, they now become rounded personalities.

Elizabeth was twenty-five when she took the throne. Her appearance was striking, with watchful eyes set in a pale face beneath brilliant red hair. She used copious make-up and dressed with an extravagance that delighted portraitists and impressed visitors to court. Her coronation, on 15 January 1559, was performed with a Protestant ritual that she had herself had edited. It left carefully open what sort of Reformation she intended. Was it to be that of her father's last message, of reconciliation, or of the Protestant extremists and evangelicals who had fled Mary for Calvinist Europe and were returning to resume the puritanism of Edward VI?

The queen's instinct was that English people would rather have no answer to this question than one they disliked. She became a mistress of equivocation, often infuriating parliament and her closest counsellor for almost all her reign, William Cecil. While her father had ruled actively, Elizabeth ruled passively. He led a revolution, she consolidated one. But to do so required intense discipline and personal struggle. Through almost all her reign, Elizabeth was in danger and often at war. Yet she stands with her father supreme among English monarchs. She brought to the office of monarch a quality rare among her predecessors, raw intelligence.

On one matter Elizabeth was clear. There would be no return to Rome's authority, and she reintroduced Henry's acts of supremacy and uniformity. Tolerance was to be permitted over ornament, vestments and ceremonies, but church doctrine was to be Protestant, delegated to a new archbishop, Matthew Parker, culminating in his Thirty-Nine Articles of Anglican faith of 1563. Elizabeth was pious and kept about her such accoutrements of the old religion as the cross, but she was determined to be as tolerant as her security allowed.

The next question to dominate public opinion was, whom should the queen marry? She was bombarded with offers, from the Holy Roman Emperor, from Eric of Sweden, from Mary's widower, Philip of Spain, and from many lesser suitors. While clearly a passionate woman, who loved dancing and the company of young men, she viewed any marriage as dangerous. She was warned by the experiences of her father and her mother. A foreign husband would risk overseas entanglements, while an English one would risk domestic faction and rebellion. Elizabeth knew that England had had enough of both.

There remained the man she had met in the Tower during Mary's reign, Lord Dudley. Such was the gossip about the couple that when in 1560, Dudley's wife, Amy, was found dead at the foot of the stairs in their country house, foul play was suspected. The queen confined herself to creating Dudley Earl of Leicester and a Knight of the Garter, and when pressed by parliament to find a husband, as she frequently was, she asserted that she would 'rule and die a virgin'. England would have 'but one mistress and no master'. She was, however, heard to remark that were she to change her mind, Dudley would be her choice, and he wisely took to wearing a sword-proof jacket. He did not remarry for eighteen years and, when he did, to Lettice Knollys, the queen was furious and banned her from court. He remained close to Elizabeth until his death in 1588.

In 1559 Scotland displayed to the full its capacity for causing trouble. A religious civil war broke out between the Protestant divine, John Knox, newly returned from exile in Geneva, and the Catholic Mary of Guise, mother of the seventeen-year-old Mary Queen of Scots, who was now resident with her husband, the king of France, in Paris. Knox's 'lords of the congregation' drew up a covenant, to 'maintain, set forward and establish the word of God and his congregation'. The Reformation was to arrive north of the border, though Knox displeased Elizabeth with a notorious reference to the dangers of rule by 'a monstrous regiment of women'. The conflict culminated in 1560 in Guise's expulsion, followed by the renunciation of Rome by Scotland's first church assembly. No sooner was this done than Mary Queen of Scots was widowed after just two years of marriage to the king of France, and returned to take up her office in Edinburgh.

Mary was the great-granddaughter of Henry VII and a strong claimant to the English throne, quartering her arms with those of England and France. A beautiful teenager, she devoted herself to romance and wilful conspiracy, to the alarm of her court and the delight of her biographers. She first married a Stuart adventurer, Lord Darnley, by whom she had a son, James, who promptly became the nearest male claimant to the thrones of Scotland and England. A year later, Darnley was murdered and Mary married his assumed murderer, Lord Bothwell. Within three months her exasperated court demanded she abdicate in favour of her one-year-old son and flee into exile. She went south in the hope that her cousin, Elizabeth, would give her sanctuary.

Elizabeth could not bring herself to reject a royal relative, however parliament was appalled. If harm came to the queen, the overtly Roman Catholic Mary would succeed, and was thus a magnet for every sort of trouble and dissent. Under the sway of Cecil, parliament begged the queen to try Mary for suspected treason. She was arrested but remained comfortably imprisoned in Sheffield castle where conspiracy buzzed round her. In 1569 pro-Catholic elements in the north, led by the earls of Northumberland and Westmorland, instigated a plot against Elizabeth in favour of Mary. Their ally, the pro-Catholic Duke of Norfolk, recklessly offered Mary his hand in marriage. The revolt failed and Norfolk went to the Tower where, after much dithering by Elizabeth, he was executed.

In 1570 Elizabeth was excommunicated by the Pope. A blanket of suspicion now descended on English Catholics as their wilder elements played cat and mouse with Elizabeth's spy-master, Sir Francis Walsingham. Catholics were known as recusants. This was a time of codes and secret societies, of the 'five symbols at your door', false walls and Jesuit priests' holes. A recusant house, Harvington in Worcestershire, had as many holes as a Dutch cheese (and still has). They were designed by a carpenter, Nicholas Owen, so cunning that he was eventually caught only by the house in which he was hiding being burned to the ground.

Elizabeth ruled in part like a Saxon monarch, displaying her person and the power of her office by reviving the royal progress. She and her courtiers travelled the counties of England, mostly in the safer south, inducing her rich subjects to lavish hospitality with hope of preferment. At Kenilworth in July 1575 her favourite, Leicester, laid on nineteen days of poems, plays, fireworks, bear-baiting, hunting and sea battles on his lake. The castle's great clock was stopped throughout. When the queen visited the City merchant Sir Thomas Gresham at his house at Osterley in Middlesex, she suggested over dinner that his courtyard would 'look more handsome' with a wall across it. When she awoke in the morning it had been built. Less wealthy grandees would protest bereavement, building delays, plague, anything to avert the financial disaster of a royal visit.

For a decade the queen and the ever-cautious Cecil kept England aloof from the dynastic and religious wars spreading across Europe. Though she was sympathetic to the northern Protestants, she was reluctant to aid them and antagonise Catholic states with whom England had no quarrel. In 1572 such caution was to no avail after the St Bartholomew's Day massacre in France. Some 40,000 Protestant Huguenots were killed at the instigation of Catherine of Medici and thousands sought refuge in a London awash in tales of Catholic atrocities.

Europe's Protestants pleaded to England for help. Elizabeth refused, determined to stay on good terms with both France and Spain. Her one self-interested concession was to turn a blind eye to the antics of English sea captains, such as Francis Drake and John Hawkins, who combined royal authority for exploration with lucrative piracy against Spanish galleons from the New World. This culminated in Drake's epic voyage, begun in 1577, round the east and west coast of the Americas and across the Indian sea in a circumnavigation, during which he seized Spanish gold as he went.

Gradually England found itself drawn into the European conflicts that Elizabeth and Cecil, now ennobled as Lord Burghley, had tried to avoid. With anti-Protestant alliances forming against her, Elizabeth in 1577 agreed to a treaty with the Netherlands and, abandoning all past pledges, agreed to seek the hand in diplomatic marriage of the heir to the French throne, the Duke of Anjou. The bizarre proposal foundered when the duke was told that he would have to abandon the Catholic mass, whereupon he politely suggested that Elizabeth marry his unprepossessing younger brother, the Duke of Alençon. This duke was half Elizabeth's age and reputedly 'the frog who would a-wooing go'. When a pamphlet was published ridiculing the marriage, the queen had its author's hand cut off. Not until two years later did she acknowledge that such an alliance was intolerable to her council and her people. Whether the affair was selfless diplomacy or a forty-six-year-old spinster's fantasy has divided opinion ever since.

Catholic Europe was now consumed with a version of Henry II's question, who would rid it of this heretical monarch? 'She is only a woman, only mistress of half an island,' protested Pope Sixtus V. By 1584 relations with Spain had degenerated into incessant pro-Catholic plots at home and privateer attacks on Spanish ships abroad. Amid invasion hysteria, thousands of Englishmen formed themselves into a Bond of Association, to defend the queen and Protestantism against all Catholics. A year later, Elizabeth abandoned her policy of non-intervention and allowed the ever ambitious Leicester to take an army to the Netherlands to fight the Spanish, though she was furious when on arrival he accepted the governor-generalship of the Dutch states, effectively involving England in their defence against Spain. She publicly demanded he surrender the office.

In 1586, with Spain known to be preparing an Armada, Elizabeth was forced finally to confront the threat posed by Mary. The attentive Walsingham discovered a plot by Anthony Babington to assassinate Elizabeth in Mary's favour, allegedly with Mary's connivance, coincidentally with a Spanish invasion. Both houses of parliament petitioned for Mary's death, as 'to spare her is to spill us'. Even after Mary had been found guilty and a warrant for the execution signed by the queen, Elizabeth could not bring herself to order its implementation. The council decided to act in her name. Mary was convicted of treason in Fotheringhay castle and went to the block in its great hall, theatrically reciting a psalm and dressed in black velvet with the red underskirts of Catholic martyrdom. After her head was severed her dog had to be extricated protesting from under her dress. Elizabeth went into a frenzy of grief and imprisoned the hapless official who had actioned her warrant.

This outrage to Catholic Europe led Philip of Spain to launch his 'enterprise of England', a bid to seize its throne as rightful widower of Mary I. Ireland was poised to rise in revolt and Scotland stood ready to 'let strangers enter England through the postern gate'. In April 1587 Drake sailed boldly into Cadiz harbour and systematically destroyed much of Philip's battle fleet, including thirty galleons, reporting he had 'singed the king of Spain's beard'. Philip waited another year to restore the damage before despatching an Armada under the noble but inexperienced Duke of Medina Sidonia. Setting sail in July 1588, it was the largest assault on England since the Vikings, comprising 151 ships carrying 8,000 sailors and 18,000 soldiers.

The Armada's plan was to sail to the Netherlands to collect the 30,000-strong army of the Prince of Parma and cross to England. As it made its way up the Channel, the waiting English navy, with faster but smaller ships, 'plucked its feathers' but did no more than force it away from shore. At Calais Sidonia found Parma in no position to embark and had to moor in a position that left him vulnerable to English fire ships loaded with gunpowder. These were driven into the Spanish lines, forcing them to break and flee. The pursuing English engaged them at the battle of Gravelines and heavily outgunned them, the galleons being said to carry more priests than gunners. Meanwhile Elizabeth, wearing a silver breastplate, went to Tilbury to address her army gathered there under Leicester's command. She reportedly said, 'I have the body of a weak and feeble woman, but I have the heart and stomach of a king, and of a king of England too … Rather than any dishonour should grow by me, I myself will take up arms – I myself will be your general, judge, and rewarder.' In the event, the army was not needed. Sidonia fled up the North Sea, losing more ships off the coasts of Scotland and Ireland. A meagre sixty arrived back in Spain. England had lost not one. The Armada, for all the glory it brought Elizabeth, showed England vulnerable to attack, its shore defences near useless and its navy almost as ill-equipped as Spain's. It was fortunate that the Armada did not return.

The year 1588 marked a turning point in Elizabeth's reign. Mary Queen of Scots was dead, Spain was repulsed and a Protestant, Henry of Navarre, was heir to the French throne. The queen was eulogised as Gloriana by the poet Edmund Spenser in his saga *The Faerie Queene*, 'O goddess heavenly bright!/ Mirror of grace and Majesty divine,/ Great Lady of the greatest isle.' The court now saw a reprise of the chivalric antics of Edward III, typified in the glorification of the soldier/poet Sir Philip Sidney, killed fighting the Spaniards. A landed aristocracy and merchant class had begun to settle into its post-monastic wealth. Palaces were no longer built at the monarch's expense, but at the expense of the rich to please the monarch. Houses fit for purpose became houses fit for show. Longleat, Hardwick, Burghley and Wollaton displayed the glory of the Tudor Renaissance, symmetrical in plan and adorned with towers, pierced parapets, pilasters and strapwork. One courtier, Christopher Hatton, built both Kirby and Holdenby in the Midlands, to greet a queen who never came. Another, Edmund Harman, adorned his memorial in Burford church with American Indians to boast the reach of the Cotswold cloth trade.

In 1588 Elizabeth lost her beloved Leicester, whom she called 'my eyes'. She locked herself away for days on hearing of his death, until Burghley broke down her door. His last letter she kept to her death. Leicester shared with Burghley pre-eminence in Elizabeth's court, but while the latter is regarded as a wise and selfless counsellor, Leicester is seen as more equivocal. Variously vain, scheming and reckless, he both survived and contrived to absorb the queen's passionate nature without destabilising her reign. With his going something of Elizabeth's brilliance dimmed. The 'Armada portrait' shows her in imperial mode, resting her hand on a globe as if possessing it and wearing the necklace of 600 pearls bequeathed her by Leicester. She was approaching sixty and losing her political caution. Drake was sent in 1589 to destroy the remains of the Armada, and returned with failure. He also failed in his sideline of piracy, in which the queen had invested her own money. Similar failures by Hawkins and Sir Walter Raleigh increased Elizabeth's anger at the reckless young gallants who crowded her court.

Still she indulged them. A new favourite was Leicester's hot-headed stepson, the Earl of Essex, who in 1591 persuaded her to send him to aid the Protestant Henry of France against the Catholic League. The venture, potentially vital for the defence of the realm after the Armada, ended in fiasco and the queen swore she would never send Essex abroad again. In 1598 Burghley died, removing the hand of caution that had counter-balanced the hawkish influence of Walsingham and Leicester in her council. A year later Elizabeth's diminishing sagacity saw her capitulate to Essex's petulance and let him take the largest army ever sent to Ireland, 16,000 men, to confront Hugh O'Neill, Earl of Tyrone and uncrowned monarch of Ireland.

Essex was a poor commander. He used his licence from the queen to lavish honours on favourites. It was said he 'never drew a sword but to make knights', and when outmanoeuvred by Tyrone he sued for peace. Parlaying alone with the Irish leader, Essex promised him all of Ireland, while he would return and seize control of England 'in the queen's name'. Leaving his army without a leader, he returned to England to plead his cause with the queen, daring to disturb her when still in her nightclothes at Nonsuch. She could not save him. He was arrested for desertion and dismissed, eventually plotting a coup in league with Catholic and other dissidents in 1601. His enemy Robert Cecil, son of Burghley and now chief minister, went for the kill. At Essex's trial for treason, Cecil derided the elderly queen's courtiers for their 'pre-eminence for wit, nobility and swordsmanship' and damned them for their dishonesty and treachery. Essex lost his head.

As these events were taking place, the darkening of Elizabeth's reign was illuminated by the rising star of Shakespeare. As Bede had opened a window on the Dark Ages and Chaucer on late-medieval England, so 'the bard of Avon' displayed Elizabethan England as a pageant of humanist sensibility. While his poetry was for private clients, his plays were staged mostly in London theatres for a paying public. A dramatic genius which, in most of Europe, would have been shared with an elite, in England was shared with all who could get to a theatre. Shakespeare wrote of the politics of medieval England as a metaphor for Elizabeth's reign, using the past to glorify or expiate the present, notably the characters of Henry IV, Henry V and Richard III. Fictional creations such as Hamlet, Shylock, Malvolio and Falstaff seem so immediate that they can be re-enacted with ease in modern dress. Through them, the world to this day has become familiar with the voices, the emotions, the imagination and the turmoil of the human condition in Elizabethan England.

By the turn of the seventeenth century Elizabeth cut a lonely figure. Her favourites had gone to death, treason or both. Her foreign ventures had emptied the Treasury and her captains, for all their piratical bravado, had made little impact on the growing empires of Spain and Portugal. To most of Europe England was a great nuisance rather than a great power. When parliament complained in 1601 that she was selling trade monopolies to her courtiers, the sixty-seven-year-old monarch retorted in her 'golden speech' that she was not a 'greedy scraping grasper' but rather the upholder of a burdensome crown. She ended the last oration of her reign, 'Though you have had, and may have, many mightier and wiser princes in this seat, yet ye never had, nor ever shall have, any that will love you better.' Love was Elizabeth's code word for mutual consent.

On 24 March 1603 Elizabeth died in her grandfather's palace at Richmond, saying that 'none but' the Protestant James, thirty-six-year-old son of Mary Queen of Scots, should succeed her. Tired though her reign had become, she passed away loved and mourned. Her private prayer was an apt epitaph: 'When wars and seditions with grievous persecutions have vexed almost all kings and countries round about me, my reign hath been peaceable, and my realm a receptacle to Thy afflicted Church.' She had established the supremacy of the crown in her father's image and bonded the English nation under it. She had brought her nation glory and peace. Elizabeth was surely the greatest of England's rulers.

Early Stuarts

~

1603 – 1642

MOST PEOPLE WHO MET James I (1603 – 25) as he rode south in the summer of 1603 had known only Elizabeth as monarch. Loyalty to her person had soothed the conflicts of Henry's Reformation. Beyond the familiar confines of village and town, the queen had come to embody a united England, a nation at peace, at least with itself. She enjoyed what Macaulay called 'English king-worship', a consent which she deftly identified as a bond of love between herself and her country.

How would James compare? He was short, garrulous, self-consciously a scholar and lacking in self-discipline. His upbringing was dreadful. His father had been killed, probably by his mother, Mary Queen of Scots, who in turn had been killed by the English over whom he now ruled. As boy king of Scotland he had survived four regents dying violent deaths round him, not to mention an attempt on his life, a sadist for a tutor and a witches' conspiracy against him. To the English, he was an outsider from an enemy state. Cecil, fearful of Spanish plots, urged him to hasten south.

As he travelled, James billeted his retinue of 'coarse and beggarly Scotsmen' on English grandees, dispensing his new prerogative at will. He hanged a man without trial in Newark and knighted any host who cared to ask. In London the new king indicated a break with the past. After the dowdy last years of Elizabeth's reign, he put London en fête. Shakespeare's now celebrated troupe was taken under royal patronage and became the King's Players. James patronised John Donne, Ben Jonson and the composer Orlando Gibbons. Masques on classical themes were ordered from Inigo Jones, as was the exquisite Italianate Queen's House at Greenwich, a gift to James's Danish wife Anne. What came to be called Jacobean architecture spread to every mansion and manor in the land, with long glazed galleries overlooking formal parterres.

The new reign began with the best of intentions. At a Somerset House conference a year after his coronation James achieved what had eluded Elizabeth, peace with Spain. It silenced Spanish demands for a Catholic restoration in England in return for an end to English attacks on Spanish interests in Europe and the Americas. That same year, James declared a united monarchy of England and Scotland to be known as 'Great Britain', with a distinctive flag named after an abbreviation of his Latin name, the Union Jack, though he was unable to merge the two nations in one parliament, any more than he was able to bring Ireland to heel.

Finally in 1604 the king summoned representatives of the bishops and the Puritans to Hampton Court in the hope of ending conflict between them. He was not a wholly impartial chairman. Despite a Calvinist upbringing he was an 'episcopalian', acknowledging the authority of bishops. He garrulously warned all who cared to listen that, if bishops were replaced by assemblies, 'Jack, Tom, Will and Dick shall meet and, at their pleasure, censure me and my council.' It would be tantamount to a parliamentary republic. Yet the Hampton Court conference reconstituted a Church of England that has survived ever since. Bishops were entrenched. Matters such as baptism, ordination and the civil role of the church were agreed. James also ordered a new translation of the Bible, published in 1611, involving no fewer than fifty-four scholars, overseen by a commission of twelve. Though based on its precursors, the bibles of Tyndale and Coverdale, it remains one of the masterpieces of

English literature and a tribute to the art of the committee. 'It lives on the ear,' said the Victorian theologian, Frederick Faber, 'like music that can never be forgotten, like the sound of church bells, which the convert hardly knows how he can forgo.'

As ecclesiastical diplomacy Hampton Court was less successful. Where Elizabeth convinced both sides she favoured them, James left both dissatisfied. His hectoring manner extended beyond theology to all aspects of the nation's welfare, with a treatise opposing tobacco smoking, a habit 'loathsome to the eye, hateful to the nose, harmful to the brain'. Nor did James's tolerance extend to the Catholics, excluded from Hampton Court. In 1605 a group of them reacted to his failure to hear their pleas by taking the drastic step of plotting to blow up parliament. Only when a conspirator warned a friend to stay away on the night of 5 November was parliament thoroughly searched and Guy Fawkes, with forty barrels of gunpowder, found in the basement. There is little question that, had they exploded, the king and ruling class of England would have been wiped out. An appalling atrocity was averted.

The retribution was ferocious. The plotters' trial concluded that 'from the admirable Clemency and Moderation of the King ... he is graciously pleased to afford them, as well as an ordinary Course of Trial, an ordinary Punishment much inferior to their Offence.' This ordinariness meant each being drawn from prison backwards by a horse-tail, then hanged, cut down when still alive, 'have his Privy Parts cut off and burnt before his face, as being unworthily begotten and unfit to leave any generation after him. His Bowels and inlaid Parts taken out and burnt ... after to have his Head cut off.' Then his body was to be quartered. If this was ordinary, we could only wonder what 'extra-ordinary' punishment might involve.

Fawkes's bomb did not explode, but a different fuse was lit, that of anti-Catholic frenzy. To show even-handedness, James persecuted Catholics and radical Puritans alike. The Church of England identified 'uniformity' with state security and treated dissent as treason. One consequence was a wave of emigration to the New World. It began in 1607 with John Smith's doomed colony of Jamestown, Virginia, named after the king, and culminating thirteen years later in the Pilgrim Fathers and the *Mayflower*. By the end of James's reign 80,000 Britons had crossed the Atlantic in one of history's most significant migrations.

James regarded parliament as a compulsive spender might a tiresome bank manager, to be ignored except in time of need, and then resented. Yet times were always of need. The king suffered from the curse of the house of Stuart, extravagance, coupled with antagonism towards parliament when it refused him money. He told parliament that its privileges were at his disposal as a 'matter of grace'. His divine right to rule was not a matter of negotiation. Had he not written a book on the subject in which he stated explicitly, 'Kings are called gods, and are appointed by God and answerable only to God'? Those who obstructed him were 'spitting in the face of God'. Parliament begged to differ, with an 'apology' that the aforementioned privileges 'are at an everlasting stand ... being once lost are not recovered but with much disquiet'.

After 1614 an exasperated James did not even summon parliament for seven years, turning to sources of revenue not dependent on the Commons. He sold honours much as Henry VIII had sold monasteries. He invented minor hereditary titles called baronetcies for £1,095, cloaked as subsidies for troops in Ireland. By the end of his reign he was selling knighthoods for as little as £220. But he could not escape his judges. The lord chief justice, Sir Edward Coke, one of the first great exponents of common law against royal absolutism, ruled that even the king was subject to the law: 'The King cannot take any cause out of any of his Courts and give Judgement upon it himself ... the King ought not to be under any man, but under God and the law.' In 1616 James sacked him, but he could not sack his argument.

Robert Cecil, royal counsellor since 1590, had died in 1612, as had the much-acclaimed heir to the throne Henry Stuart, who fell to typhoid at the age of eighteen. Henry was succeeded by his diminutive younger brother Charles. The court was dominated instead by the dashing George Villiers, Duke of Buckingham, who mesmerised the king and was called by him 'my dear, sweet Steenie'. Courtly behaviour took on a bizarre glamour, depicted by the artist William Larkin, in costumes of unprecedented brilliance. Never had the English male been so ravishingly adorned, with lace collars like wings, voluminous pantaloons, embroidered stockings and shoes with giant pompoms. Forced to recall parliament for funds in 1621, the king found it still intransigent, urging him to join a European Protestant alliance against Spain. James recklessly sought help from the latter, cavorting openly with the Spanish ambassador. He had already, at Spain's bidding, executed Walter Raleigh, held in the Tower of London since Elizabeth's reign, putatively for treason.

In 1623 James approved a wild venture by his son and Buckingham to visit Madrid with a view to Charles marrying the Spanish infanta. The two young men offered to convert England to Catholicism, or at least to raise future English kings as Catholics, an extraordinary suggestion within living memory of the Armada. The infanta took an instant dislike to Charles, who was told by her father he would have to receive mass and stay a year on probation in Madrid if he wanted her hand. The two Englishmen fled.

The king was now ailing and Buckingham, with Charles firmly under his influence, played with fire. He switched to supporting war with Spain, turned his attention to France and found Charles a wife in the daughter of the French king, the fifteen-year-old Henrietta Maria, a pert girl no more than 5ft tall whose front teeth were said to be 'coming out of her mouth like tusks'. Before any marriage could be arranged, in 1625 James died, carrying with him the comment of a French courtier that he was 'the wisest fool in Christendom'. He was at first scholarly and sincere in seeking to resolve the conflicts inherent in the state bequeathed him by Elizabeth, but a nation rife with religious pluralism required a more subtle statecraft than James possessed. Nor could it tolerate his creed of divine kingship, which would soon bring the monarchy into collision with parliament and people.

James's son Charles I (1625–49) was an indecisive but cultured man, compensating for his small stature and stammer with a zealous love of art and an adherence to his father's belief in his divine appointment. He patronised Rubens and Van Dyck, and amassed one of Europe's great art collections. Rubens called him 'the greatest amateur of painting among the princes of the world'. He married Henrietta Maria by proxy and it was not until shortly before his coronation in 1626 that Londoners witnessed with dismay their new queen's arrival with a 200-strong retinue of French priests and papists. She infuriated the public by stopping to pray for the souls of Catholic martyrs at Tyburn. As a practising Catholic she and her party could not join the coronation ceremony, and Charles ordered his guards to limit her retainers to seven at state functions.

When the new king addressed parliament, it found his brevity a relief after his father, but was shocked by his demand for a larger subsidy. The Commons were strongly Protestant and dominated by independents such as John Pym and John Eliot. They now denied the king revenue from trade duties for more than a year at a time, and debated the impeachment of Buckingham, who retained his hold over the king. The confrontation led to the most explicit charter of political liberty since Magna Carta, the 1628 Petition of Right. It was sponsored by the indomitable Coke, who declared that 'Magna Carta is such a fellow he will have no sovereign'. It told the king he could not imprison without trial, or tax without the will of the Commons. Nor could he impose his prerogative on parliament or support a standing army. The petition served as the foundation stone of all later declarations of civil rights, including that of American independence. Charles dismissed it on the grounds that 'kings are not bound to give account of their actions but to God alone'.

That same year Buckingham was stabbed to death in Portsmouth, an event that apparently jolted the king, after four years of marriage, to attend to his queen. She bore him an heir, also Charles. In 1629 he dissolved parliament, not calling another for eleven years of what some called personal rule and others 'the tyranny'. Charles relied instead for advice on his conservative archbishop of Canterbury, William Laud, and a former parliamentarian, Thomas Wentworth, Earl of Strafford. The latter was sent to pacify Ireland and returned, like many put to that task, with a reputation for ruthlessness (and a nickname: 'Black Tom').

The tyranny was the last sustained test of English monarchical sovereignty. Charles could dispense with parliament but not with his need for money. In 1635 he used his prerogative to extend one of the few duties outside parliamentary control, 'ship money' levied on coastal towns for their defence. The king now declared it a national tax. A former MP for Buckinghamshire, John Hampden, refused to pay. 'Grant [the king] this,' wrote the radical John Milton at the time, 'and the parliament hath no more freedom than if it sat in his noose.' When at a subsequent trial the court found for the king, Henrietta Maria reacted with delight, creating an elaborate ballet in which she danced as Luminalia, or light defeating darkness. The gesture did little to increase her popularity or that of the tax. Ship money proved near uncollectable, only 20 per cent being gathered by 1639.

When, in 1637, Charles had sought to impose Laud's new high-church prayer book on his Scottish subjects it led to riots in Edinburgh and a Presbyterian 'covenant' against bishops. Despite the pleadings of Strafford, Charles declared a 'bishops' war' on Scotland. He saw his under-resourced army beaten back to the gates of Newcastle, which had to be ceded to the Scots. Charles was desperate for funds and finally summoned the so-called Short Parliament to give him money. This it refused to do. A new parliament was elected, at which 399 out of 493 MPs, led by Pym and Hampden, declared themselves firmly opposed to 'the king's advisers'. This so-called Long Parliament of 1640 became one of the great institutions of English history. It lasted in one form or another through the English Civil War, displaying radical, republican and conservative phases until it oversaw the Restoration twenty years later. Its composition reflected the crucial shift in wealth that had taken place in provincial England and Wales under the Tudors, from the medieval church and territorial magnates to an emerging middle class of smaller landowners, city burgesses, merchants and the professions. As it argued with itself and grew in confidence, the Long Parliament was the key that unlocked the door to modern England.

This institution moved swiftly to assert its control over the king, impeach Laud and execute Strafford. When the king was forced to sign the latter's death warrant, Strafford remarked, 'Put not your trust in princes,' a pathetic echo of Wolsey's cry a century before. In 1641 the House of Commons recast the Petition of Right as a Grand Remonstrance with 200 clauses. It demanded that the prerogative court of Star Chamber be abolished, ship money ended and taxes regularised. A freely elected parliament should meet every three years and be dissolved only by its own decision. It should control the church, the appointment of ministers and judges, and the conduct of the army and navy. There should be no bishops in the House of Lords and the king should rule in name only. Such an assertion of parliamentary sovereignty was the most radical in any European state at the time, and was only narrowly voted through. Even in the twenty-first century its programme has not been fully realised.

Charles now had to fight to save his crown. He responded hesitantly to the Grand Remonstrance, but was goaded by Henrietta Maria 'to pull these rogues out by the ears or never see my face again'. He did what no monarch had done before. On 4 January 1642 he tried personally to arrest the five most extreme MPs, including Pym, for treason, entering the Commons with armed men in attendance. Members stood amazed as the Speaker, William Lenthall, vacated the chair for the king, but refused to hand over the five, remarking famously, 'May it please your Majesty, I have neither eyes to see nor tongue to speak in this place, but as the House is pleased to direct me, whose servant I am here.' Realising the MPs had by now escaped, Charles abjectly declared 'all my birds have flown', and beat an ignominious retreat. No monarch was ever to set foot in the chamber again.

Within weeks, armed bands from the City invaded Westminster, rumoured to be seeking the queen's arrest. The royal family fled to Hampton Court and then to Greenwich, where Charles and Henrietta Maria spent a poignant night together at the Queen's House. Even today it seems a place of sadness, its curved steps like teardrops running down its facade. The queen gathered her children, seized the crown jewels and headed for Dover and the pawnshops of France. The king went north to Nottingham where, that August, he summoned his subjects to defend his rights on the field of battle. Consent had called the bluff of divine kingship and, after a century and a half, the horror of civil war returned to England.

Civil War

~

1642 – 1660

THE MONARCHY THAT EMERGED from the Middle Ages ruled
with the consent of barons, bishops and burgesses, rooted in a
secular contract with parliament, that the latter would vote
for taxes in return for regular redress of grievances. When
the contract broke down, as under Edward II, Richard II and
Richard III, the monarch was toppled but monarchy survived.
In the seventeenth century, monarchy too was toppled. A Tudor
king had declared himself head of the church and a Stuart king
had interpreted that as making him sovereign over parliament.
Even Henry VIII had secured parliamentary approval for his
tyranny. The true English revolution was by the king against
parliament not, as popularly supposed, the other way round.

During the summer of 1642, the argument divided not just
the king from parliament but Protestant from Catholic, north
from south, even father from son. The St John tombs in Lydiard
Tregoze in Wiltshire record a family torn apart, with three sons
dying for the king and two surviving for parliament. Still today
people challenge each other by asking, 'Which side were you
on at Marston Moor?' contrasting parliamentarian Roundheads
(so-called for wearing their hair short) with royalist Cavaliers
as a metaphor for rationalist democracy against a romantic
attachment to authority.

From the outset, parliament had logistics on its side. It had
access to taxes, sea ports and the City of London as well as the

support of enlightened opinion, John Milton and the rights of man. That, however, did not assure it of victory. Englishmen were attached to their monarch and, whatever the issue, were disinclined to see him defeated. They had a long-standing horror of usurpation.

The first battle at Edgehill in Warwickshire, in October 1642, was a nervous affair. The royalist standard-bearer, Sir Edmund Verney, had been a member of parliament but remained loyal to his king. His corpse was found after the battle, with the royal banner gripped in his rigid hand. The royalist cavalry, commanded by the king's dashing twenty-two-year-old nephew Prince Rupert, drove back the parliamentary horse and chased them from the field, but it failed to regroup and continued an undisciplined chase. The royalist infantry, unwisely commanded by a king who had no battlefield experience, was left floundering until Rupert returned. The outcome was considered a draw. The parliamentary general, the Earl of Essex, marched back to London and the king failed to pursue him, preferring to set up court at Christ Church in Oxford. It was to be his capital for the remainder of the war.

In the north at York, Prince Rupert's Cavaliers checked the Roundheads under Sir Thomas Fairfax, and by the middle of 1643 the king could confidently prepare a three-pronged assault on London from north, west and south-west in the new year. The capital was nervous of any drawn-out war, especially against a king whose person they professed to respect. The Commons were careful always to treat him as captive of his advisers, though they were less tolerant towards the queen. Most people assumed that the sporadic battles of 1643 had been trials of strength, to force the king to a new political settlement. Some counties and cities would have nothing to do with the conflict. Coventry refused the king entry unless he came without his soldiers, though it was later strongly parliamentarian and was used to house royalist prisoners (the probable derivation of 'being sent to Coventry').

The chief parliamentary leader, Pym, now played the Scottish card. In August 1643, after lengthy negotiations, the Edinburgh assembly sent as many as 18,000 infantry and 3,000 cavalry south in return for parliament's agreement to bring 'the covenant' to England and abolish the hated bishops. There would be a subsidy of £31,000 for each month a Scottish army was in the field. Pym died shortly afterwards, but in the summer of 1644 this essentially mercenary army marched south and linked up with the Roundheads outside York. Here they were reinforced by East Anglian cavalry under a Cambridgeshire MP of the lesser gentry, Oliver Cromwell. On 2 July 1644 they closed on Rupert's army at Marston Moor outside York, when the day was already drawing in. Cromwell's disciplined 'Ironsides' attacked Rupert's cavalry immediately. In what turned out to be the greatest battle of the war, Cromwell and the Scots outnumbered Prince Rupert and gave no quarter. Three thousand royalists were slaughtered on the field. Cromwell declared that 'God made them as stubble to our swords'. The war was now in earnest.

Marston Moor lost the king the north of England and the ports of the east coast. Rupert retreated south to Shrewsbury and Charles, hard pressed by the Earl of Essex, headed for Worcester. A series of manoeuvres and counter-punches in the south-west saw the royalists gain some ground, even forcing a parliamentary surrender in Cornwall. Another parliamentary general, the Earl of Manchester, with Cromwell in support confronted the king in October 1644 at Newbury. Largely through the incompetence of Manchester, the battle was inconclusive and the king was able to withdraw to Oxford. A furious Cromwell rode to London to rail in parliament against the incompetence of its aristocratic generals, Essex and Manchester. He declared that he 'hoped to live to see never a nobleman in England'. The Commons sacked the two commanders, replacing them with the modest but professional Fairfax. It conceded Cromwell's proposal for a New Model

Army, a properly recruited and paid force of cavalry, infantry and artillery, with Cromwell heading the cavalry. So far, English armies had been over-eager to return home. The New Model Army proved all too eager to stay in the field.

Cromwell was now an overwhelming presence, one of those English leaders who briefly bestrode the stage and carried all before them. A strongly built man, a religious Independent, humourless and honest, he told his portraitist to portray him 'warts and all'. He was foe of Catholics, bishops and Puritan extremists alike. He led men, so he said, who did not seek fortune but regarded 'that which they took for public felicity to be their end'. Dubbed 'God's Englishman', he regarded himself as sent by his maker to save his country from superstition. His supporters included Milton and Andrew Marvell, who called him 'angry heaven's flame'. It was sometimes hard to distinguish Cromwell's concept of divine mission from the kingly divinity of the Stuarts he so opposed.

Parliament's newly recruited army spent the winter of 1644 training and preparing for a decisive campaign in the new year. The showdown came in June 1645, at Naseby in Northamptonshire. Again the royalist cavalry under Rupert was effective but not the royalist infantry, which was cut down by the Ironsides. The battle was so intense that Charles had to be restrained from rushing personally into the throng. He was able to escape the carnage, but Naseby was the end. The king escaped but three months later Bristol fell and Charles found himself besieged in Oxford. The following year he turned up in disguise in the Scottish camp outside Newark, begging sanctuary from what he still regarded as his compatriots. His cause was not helped by the disclosure of letters to the queen in which he begged for an Irish or French army in return for bringing England back to Rome. The Scots spent almost a year bargaining with parliament over money before handing the king to Fairfax and heading home.

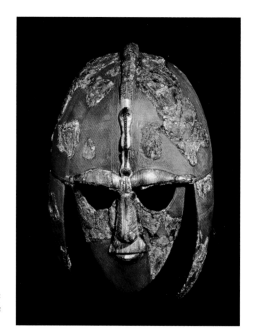

England was born of the aggressive settlement of the eastern coast of the British Isles by Germanic Anglo-Saxons: warrior's helmet from Sutton Hoo in Suffolk, now in the British Museum.

The reign of Offa in the ninth century marked a shift of power in Saxon England, from Northumbria south to the Midlands kingdom of Mercia: medieval depiction of the king with his abbey of St Alban's.

Ethelred the Unready presided over the disintegration of Alfred the Great's kingdom and its eventual conquest by the Danes under Cnut.

A medieval depiction of William of Normandy, whose ruthless conquest and Norman settlement of England supplied the framework of the future nation state.

Norman fraternisation with the natives was encouraged: William's son, Prince Henry, in bed with his mistress, Princess Nest of Wales. He went on to wed a Scottish princess. Such concord did not last and future monarchs married overseas

The murder of Becket in December 1170, within Canterbury cathedral was a deed that shocked Europe. It ended Henry's bid to establish secular authority over the Roman church in England.

The execution of Hugh Despenser in the presence of Queen Isabella was peculiarly sadistic, involving castration, disembowelling, hanging and quartering. It was so popular as a ritual punishment for treason as to be imitated into the seventeenth century.

The Peasants' Revolt (1381) was a rare popular uprising against the English crown. One of its leaders, John Ball, is shown assembling the rebels outside London, all careful to display patriotic standards, including the crusader cross of St George.

The battle of Agincourt, fought on 25 October 1415, was the climactic of English success in the French wars. Yet victory could not be turned to political advantage and it was soon reversed.

The succession of the infant Henry VI dissolved the Anglo-French empire won by Henry V at Agincourt, despite his later coronation as king of France in Paris.

Richard III was the last of the Plantagenet kings. He was ruthless and cruel even by the standards of his age and his death signalled the end of the Wars of the Roses.

Henry VIII (1509–47) in his youth: a revolutionary tyrant, who 'never spared man in my anger nor woman in my lust'. He created the Church of England and a new class of landowner by dissolving the monasteries.

Allegorical depiction of the marriage of the Lancastrian Henry VII and Elizabeth of York, under a combined red and white Tudor rose.

Henry chose as his councillors talented men, often from humble backgrounds, who had risen through the church and the law: Cardinal Wolsey (top left) and Thomas More (middle), Thomas Cromwell (top right) and Archbishop Cranmer (left).

Elizabeth revived the Saxon tradition of an itinerant monarch visiting her subjects across the land, with ostentatious displays of queenly wealth and power.

James I was a talented intellectual who patronised the arts and the new Bible, but his extravagance and advocacy of kingly divinity sowed the seeds of eventual civil war.

Charles I and Henrietta Maria of France. Their marriage was close but politcally disastrous and ended on the scaffold.

Oliver Cromwell, 'Angry heaven's flame', who told his portraitist to depict him 'warts and all'.

Painted ceiling in the Royal Hospital in Greenwich: though firm Protestants, William and Mary revelled in Stuart grandeur and understood the potency of monarchical symbols.

Tapestry showing the Duke of Marlborough at the battle of Blenheim. His mastery of battlefield tactics made him one of England's, and Europe's, premier commanders.

Walpole, left, was the master of party politics and the first minister to make the House of Commons pre-eminent in government.

William Pitt the elder, later Earl of Chatham. His global strategy in Europe, India and America laid the foundations of the British empire.

The death of Wolfe at Quebec. The victory marked England's final triumph over France in north America.

John Wesley's oratory to large congregations often in spartan churches spurred the cause of anti-slavery and galvanised Anglican church reform.

The Peterloo Massacre (1819) panicked Lord Liverpool's government into repression yet it proved a powerful impetus to parliament to advance the reform of the franchise.

The growth of new industrial cities such as Leeds, seen here in c.1840, threatened the unreformed parliament with irrelevance. The 1832 Reform Act brought them within the political pale and made further reform inevitable.

After the tawdry Hanoverians, Victoria and Albert restored the reputation of monarchy and embodied marital bliss as a central 'Victorian value'.

Keir Hardie, first leader of the Independent Labour Party, speaking at Trafalgar Square.

The two most dynamic personalities of the 1906 Liberal government, Lloyd George and Churchill. They laid the foundations of the welfare state, though soon went separate political ways.

The suffragette, Emmeline Pankhurst, under arrest. Until the social upheavals of the Great War, even Liberal reformers found votes for women a step too far.

The Jarrow 'hunger march' of 1936, though at a time of economic recovery, illustrated the growing gulf between north and south of England.

Chamberlain's return from Munich after his agreement with Hitler was wildly popular in London. It appeased a dictator but it also bought time that was to prove vital in confronting him.

Victory in Europe produced scenes of relief and euphoria in the streets of London: Churchill mobbed on his way down Whitehall to parliament.

The coronation of the young Queen Elizabeth in 1953 boosted morale. Her reign was predicted to rival in longevity and prosperity that of Queen Victoria.

The marriage of Prince Charles to Lady Diana Spencer attracted global attention and displayed England's continued talent for ceremonial.

Margaret Thatcher, Britain's first woman prime minister, took office declaring, 'We have had no end of a lesson; it will do us no end of good.' She was the first political leader to confront the welfare consensus head-on.

The death of Princess Diana in 1997 produced an outpouring of grief and briefly unsettled the monarchy: flowers outside Kensington Palace.

Blair and Brown turned Labour from a mass movement into a modern political machine under a strong leader. They brought the party thirteen years of uninterrupted rule.

The 2010 coalition of Cameron and Clegg was forced to introduce drastic measures to confront the consequences of the 2008 financial crisis.

A nation tired of war greeted the king with a strange warmth as he travelled south in February 1647. The expectation was of a new settlement. The Long Parliament ordered the New Model Army to disband and fined the royalist gentry to pay for it. It unwisely proscribed Independents and Baptists, strong in the army, and denied its soldiers their backlog of pay and pension. A majority of MPs took the view that they had defeated the king's argument, but wanted no standing army, let alone one of strongly 'leveller', or egalitarian, tendencies.

Cromwell was again angry and his soldiers refused to disband, protesting that they were not a mercenary force but infused by a desire to protect the people's 'just rights and liberties'. Led by Cromwell's able lieutenant Henry Ireton, the army seized the king on his way south and carried him as hostage to Hampton Court. London was in turmoil, with moderate Presbyterians in parliament ranged against Cromwell and his army council, who in turn were contending with Levellers within their ranks. This culminated in a series of impromptu debates, held at Putney church from 28 October to 9 November 1647, on the fate of the king and the future course of the revolution. Every rudiment of political philosophy was aired, including the rights of individuals against the state, property against community and votes for all, including women. On one thing every speaker agreed, 'That a man is not bound to a system of government which he hath not had any hand in setting over him.' Consent was not a bargain but an absolute. Though of little influence at the time, the Putney debates became an icon of English socialism.

In November the king escaped from Hampton Court and secured refuge in Carisbrooke castle on the Isle of Wight. There, comfortably entertained by the local gentry, he received reports of a revival in his popularity and recklessly courted support in Scotland for a resumed civil war. In 1648 an invasion from the wayward Scots was allied to risings in the north and west. Cromwell and Fairfax fanned out across England, where they everywhere prevailed. Rebels were mostly executed though some, as at Burford, were offered the grim alternative of being preached at for hours by their Puritan chaplains.

Cromwell had been inclined to leniency towards Charles, but now the king was too great a menace. He was brought to London where in December 1648 a 'rump' of the Long Parliament was purged by a soldier, Colonel Pride, of some 370 Presbyterian and royalist sympathisers, leaving just 154, mostly radicals, approved by the army. A commission was set up to try the king for treason. Fearing the worst, Charles now found a constancy of purpose he had lacked throughout his reign. He viewed the proceedings in Westminster Hall with scorn, refusing even to remove his hat. The trial was full of drama. The charge was that the king, 'trusted with a limited power to govern by and according to the laws of the land ... hath traitorously and maliciously levied war against the present Parliament'. Charles's plea was simple and unanswerable in its own terms, that the king could not be tried by any superior jurisdiction on earth: 'England was never an elective kingdom but a hereditary kingdom for near these thousand years ... The king can do no wrong.' Topple him and the result was tyranny or anarchy.

Argument was unproductive. The commission condemned Charles for treason and required that 'his head be severed from his body'. On 30 January 1649 his execution took place on a platform outside the Banqueting House in Whitehall, the king wearing two shirts so he would not be seen to shiver. For Charles it was said that 'nothing in his life became him like the leaving it'. At the moment of execution, according to the young Samuel Pepys, the crowd did not cheer but groan, sensing a terrible deed had been done. Even Cromwell was rumoured to have visited the corpse the next day and bewailed its 'cruel necessity'.

The Rump Parliament now declared a republic with the words, 'The people under God are the original of all just power ... The commons in parliament assembled, being chosen by and representing the people, have the supreme power in this nation.' The monarch's image was struck from the seal used to approve acts of parliament. The House of Lords was abolished. Censorship was introduced. England would be ruled by a forty-one-strong council of state with Cromwell unchallenged as its most prominent citizen. Cromwell paid off the army, taking part of it to Ireland for a campaign of repression. This culminated in the slaughter of the citizens of Drogheda in retribution for an anti-Protestant massacre (not involving the town) in 1649. Some 80,000 Irish were branded traitors and thousands were dispossessed or sent into slavery in America, to free land for English soldiers. Drogheda was an act of extraordinary brutality, even for the times. Cromwell joined Strafford in Irish demonology.

Meanwhile the Scots, who had helped destroy Charles I, entertained his eighteen-year-old son Charles Stuart, and even crowned him Charles II. In the summer of 1651 they set out to invade England, both in his cause and in the ostensibly contradictory one of imposing Presbyterianism on England. This force was finally defeated by Cromwell at Worcester. Charles fled the field and hid for a night in an oak in the grounds of Boscobel house in Staffordshire, before escaping to France disguised as a servant. Thousands of pubs were later to be named the Royal Oak.

Cromwell had had his fill of Celts. He imposed his will on Scotland and Ireland by enforcing political union with England. What Henry VIII and James I had attempted Cromwell achieved. He ruled a united state with MPs in parliament to be elected from throughout the British Isles. It was to prove a short-lived union. Relations between Cromwell and the four-year-old Rump worsened until, on 20 April 1653, he marched his troops to the Commons, listened awhile to the meandering speeches and did what many have wished to do before and since. In one of the most intemperate parliamentary speeches ever heard he shouted, 'Ye sordid prostitutes ... Ye are grown intolerably odious to the whole nation. The Lord hath done with you ... Go, get out, make haste, ye venal slaves, be gone. I will put an end to your prating.' He ordered the mace seized as a mere 'bauble' and sent the MPs home.

Cromwell had now to confront the reality of his own power. His 'commonwealth' had beheaded one king and defeated another in battle. He had disposed of the Lords, the bishops and the Commons, and had Marvell's admonitory lines ringing in his ears: 'The same arts that did gain / A power, must it maintain.' First Cromwell summoned a religious assembly of 'godly' members chosen from local Independent congregations. This became known as the Barebones Parliament (after a preacher member, Praise-God Barbon). He told them, 'Truly ye are called by God to rule with him and for him.' When it proposed the abolition of virtually every institution of state, he quickly dismissed it.

Cromwell was now outdoing the Stuarts. He agreed to be named as Lord Protector and was installed as such in December 1653, musing that 'somewhat of monarchical power would be very effective'. A united kingdom now came, albeit briefly, into life under a written constitution or 'instrument of government'. Newly elected parliaments were summoned by Cromwell and dissolved for varying degrees of radicalism as the Protector struggled to balance his own tolerance with the need to discipline a burgeoning pluralism. The Levellers, who believed in social egalitarianism split with the Diggers, who sought an agrarian communism. Baptists split with Anabaptists, Quakers and even Ranters, who believed in no religious or moral discipline at all. Cromwell also welcomed the Jews back from the continent. It was no wonder that the House of Commons was a nervous, fractious place.

In 1655 Cromwell imposed what amounted to a military regime on the provinces, dividing them into eleven military regions under major generals. They were ordered to introduce puritanical rules, including execution for adultery, the suppression of theatrical performances and games, the closure of taverns and brothels, the outlawing of swearing and the banning of church ritual. Censorship was intense. The Revolution was brought home to every community throughout the country, but by conveying a sense not of personal freedom but of oppression. The smashing of church ornaments, begun by William Dowsing in East Anglia in 1643, was intermittently revived. Extreme sects were gradually suppressed. Nothing did more for the eventual cause of Restoration than the imposition across the country of Cromwell's revolutionary regime.

Constitutions were now being rewritten by the day. In 1657 a group of lawyers and MPs took it upon themselves to propose to Cromwell a 'humble petition and advice' for a new constitution, restoring a monarch as answerable to a new bicameral parliament. Cromwell refused the title of king, though sensing a public desire for some symbolism – 'but dross and dung in comparison of Christ' – he agreed to sit on Edward the Confessor's throne, wear a purple gown and be addressed as 'Your Highness, the Lord Protector'. This did not last long. On 3 September 1658 Cromwell died aged fifty-nine, naming his son Richard as his successor.

Richard Cromwell, a well-meaning but ineffectual man, held office for eight months before the army reassembled the Rump to vote in May 1659 to end the protectorate. England was at the mercy of feuding army officers in a 'committee of safety'. A commonwealth devoid of authority had come to anarchy and craved a leader. The only one to hand with a coherent army was Cromwell's governor in Scotland, a Devonian general named George Monck. He had served both his king and parliament and had stabilised authority in Ireland and Scotland. He demanded the Rump resume control and marched south with his troops. All England was in suspense. Monck kept his counsel and bided his time. Not until February of 1660 did he reach London, where dictatorship was within his grasp. Had Monck shared Cromwell's ambition, England's history might have been very different. But he took the mood of the country and of parliament and reached the conclusion that the 1657 humble petition for the restoration of monarchy, ironically addressed to Cromwell, was the only basis for constitutional progress. There was just one king available, Charles II, and he was in the Netherlands. Would he agree to what were certain to be stringent parliamentary terms?

Monck was punctilious. He ordered that the full 1640 Long Parliament be reassembled and asked it to dissolve itself by deputing a new convention to negotiate the king's return. This body would create a king, not be summoned by one. This news alone set London church bells ringing and citizens drinking toasts round street bonfires. Monck's emissaries to Charles found they were negotiating with Edward Hyde, an aide as wise and temperate as was Monck himself. Hyde was a former parliamentary lawyer whose daughter Anne had recently married the exiled king's brother James. A plain, sensible girl, she gave birth to two daughters brought up as Protestants. Both of them, Mary and Anne, would one day ascend the throne.

Hyde well understood the state of play in London. The 1660 Declaration of Breda, signed by an eager king and an exhausted parliament, offered a general pardon for those who had participated in the war. It agreed to tolerate those 'of tender consciences', pay off the army and accept the supremacy of parliament. The veteran general Fairfax was sent to accompany Charles from The Hague. He landed at Dover on 25 May 1660 and progressed to London amid much rejoicing. Ironside troops even paraded as a guard of honour on Blackheath. In the language of the age, the English people felt they had passed through the valley of the shadow of death and now saw a great light. It was a moment of national reconciliation.

Restoration

~

1660 - 1688

WHAT WAS RESTORED? The events of 1660 had been England's
first act of collective intelligence. The country had done
something terrible. It had gone to war with itself and
decapitated its king. Two decades had seen theocratic tyranny,
parliamentary government, republican commonwealth and
military dictatorship, as if England were trying constitutions on
for size. Now, after this monumental exercise in trial and error,
it decided it wanted the monarch back, and not any monarch
but the son of the one it had just killed. But if it was a similar
monarch, it was not a similar monarchy.

The reign of Charles II (1660–85) could not have been more
different from that of Cromwell's grim commissioners. A six-
foot, debonair extrovert, the newly restored king radiated the
confident promiscuity, in every sense of the word, of the court
of Louis XIV, where he had spent his early exile. Theatres, race
courses, brothels and taverns reopened. Orchestras returned to
church galleries and the festivals of the seasons were celebrated
with their old gaiety. Drury Lane saw the foundation of a
Theatre Royal. The 'merrie monarch' perambulated London's
parks with his eponymous spaniels, chatting with members of
the public.

Charles's sexual behaviour was equally expansive. The
barrenness of his wife, Catherine of Braganza, was his lame

excuse for some seventeen mistresses, by whom he fathered at least fifteen children, most of whom he ennobled. The chief of these ladies were Lucy Walters, Barbara Villiers and the actress Nell Gwynne, all much depicted by portraitist Sir Peter Lely, with characteristic bulging eyes and long noses. When visiting Winchester, Charles was forbidden by the dean to lodge with Nell in the close, so he gallantly stayed with her in a neighbouring house. His last words on his deathbed were, 'Let not poor Nelly starve.'

The king patronised the new Royal Society, an association of scientists founded in November 1660, with a paper on astronomy by Christopher Wren and an early membership that included Wren, Isaac Newton, Robert Hooke and Robert Boyle. Charles built a laboratory in Whitehall and wrote to the society asking for advice on such matters of national concern as the male erection. He also brought with him from the continent a mania for building palaces, with lavish projects at Whitehall, Greenwich, Hampton Court and Winchester, mostly begun under Wren's aegis. His rooms at Windsor are still among the most splendid in England.

The so-called Cavalier Parliament, as packed with monarchists as its predecessor, the Long Parliament, met in 1661. It was packed with monarchy's critics. To Charles's dismay it promptly overrode the Breda pardons and ordered the bodies of the regicides, including Cromwell, to be disinterred and gruesomely hanged. Under a code drawn up by James's chancellor, Edward Hyde, now Earl of Clarendon, the Anglicans reinstalled Laud's bishops and the Book of Common Prayer. They also renounced Breda's commitment to 'liberty of tender consciences'. It was thus parliament not the king that purged the church of Puritans and proscribed the Nonconformist sects. After 1664 a fifth of Anglican clergy were evicted from their livings and Nonconformists were imprisoned. Among them was the Baptist John Bunyan, who wrote the most powerful work of

Protestant morality, *The Pilgrim's Progress*, when in Bedford gaol. If the Catholic bishops once defended their closed shop, so now did their Anglican successors. For the next two hundred years they were to be a vigorous force for parliamentary reaction.

On one matter there was no return to the past, parliament's hard-won sovereignty. MPs were soon at loggerheads with Charles as they had been with his father, over extravagance, not least in the matter of mistresses. For a while, concord was maintained by the time-honoured means of a foreign war. London merchants, with Cromwell's aggressive support, had been eager to break Dutch trading monopolies in the Americas and the Indies and there had been sporadic battles in that cause. Charles was happy to fight the Dutch, but for a different reason, his continued good relations with his former host, Louis XIV. Parliament duly voted the enormous sum of £2.5 million for a fleet of 150 ships. A series of naval encounters starting in 1664 caused heavy losses to both sides, a lasting outcome of one being the transfer to England of the Dutch colony of New Amsterdam on Manhattan island, renamed after the king's brother, the Duke of York.

The war was interrupted by a devastating outbreak of plague in 1665. London briefly reprised the horrors of the Middle Ages as diseased rats proliferated in the open gutters and sewers of the close-packed city. Crosses appeared on doors. Vestries had the ghastly task of organising biers and plague pits. Streets echoed to the cry of 'Bring out your dead'. An estimated 100,000 Londoners died, one in five of the population. The diarist Samuel Pepys wrote, 'Lord, how empty the streets are, and melancholy.' No sooner had this horror passed than, in September 1666, a fire broke out in a baker's shop in Pudding Lane near London Bridge. Seized by a strong wind it took hold and within five days nine-tenths of the buildings within London's medieval walls were destroyed. Inhabitants fled to the suburbs or took to boats on the river. The Duke of York won plaudits for leading the rescue attempt, largely by blowing up buildings in the path of the flames.

The result was a tussle between court and City fathers over rebuilding. Wren offered the government a plan for a new city of straight, wide streets and piazzas in a classical style. The City vestries had no time for such grandiosity and no money for land acquisition. Businesses needed to get back to work. New regulations confined themselves to dictating wider streets and less combustible brick facades. The rich now moved out of the old City. With London free of the need for defensive walls, its citizens colonised the spacious developments of Covent Garden and St James's Square to the west, profiting families owning land there, such as the Jermyns, Berkeleys, Audleys and Grosvenors. Everywhere in the capital rose new churches in a sedate English baroque style, while over them floated Wren's new St Paul's Cathedral. The sense of England 'restored' in every sense must have been palpable, but it was not to last.

Within a year of the London fire, the Dutch took the opportunity of brazenly sailing up the Thames to Chatham, where they burned thirteen ships and towed away the navy's flagship, the *Royal Charles*. The nation was humiliated. To the navy secretary, Samuel Pepys, 'the whole kingdom is undone'. Charles's licentious lifestyle was openly blamed for the defeat. Clarendon was impeached and sent into exile, while power shifted to a new group of the king's supporters, their names Clifford, Arlington, Buckingham, Ashley and Lauderdale donating the word cabal to the English language. Charles's feckless foreign policy descended into chaos. A popular treaty reached with Holland against France, within a year of the Medway debacle, was undermined in 1670 by a contradictory one with France against Holland, struck by Charles in secret at Dover with emissaries of Louis XIV. This stipulated that England would fight the Dutch in return for a French subsidy to Charles, relieving him of the need to summon parliament. In addition, and for yet more aid, Charles would return the English church to Catholicism 'as soon as the welfare of his kingdom will permit'. It was a flagrant revival of his father's secret offer to Spain in 1623, and an equally flagrant defiance of the Breda agreement and of parliament's sovereignty in such matters.

The country was now ringing with talk of a twenty-two-year-old Dutch Protestant hero, William of Orange, who in 1672 resisted a French assault on the Netherlands by flooding the dykes and promising 'to die in the last ditch'. As details of the secret Dover treaty began to leak out, an angry parliament denounced it and, in 1673, passed the Test Act, excluding all Catholics from public office. Matters were exacerbated when the king's brother and heir, James Duke of York, resigned his post as lord high admiral rather than abjure Catholicism under the Test Act. His wife, Anne Hyde, having died, James now married the Catholic Mary of Modena. The leading figure in the Cavalier Parliament, the Earl of Danby, had been handling the degenerating relations between Charles and parliament, and had negotiated a popular marriage of James's Protestant daughter, Mary, to the heroic William of Orange. This supposedly secured a Protestant succession to James. But what if Mary of Modena now had a son?

Anti-Catholic ferment recalled the popish plots of Guy Fawkes' time. In 1678 a deranged clergyman, Titus Oates, reported to the privy council a Catholic conspiracy to kill the king, burn London, raise a Catholic army and take England under the wing of France. Oates was found to be an imposter, but hysteria ran wild and parliament demanded an extension of the Test Act that would specifically exclude James and any Catholic heir from the throne. This was too much for Charles. In 1679 he dissolved parliament, summoning and dismissing three more in two years. Each was increasingly hostile, demanding he sign the bill disinheriting his brother. He refused and the bill eventually died. It was at this hectic time that so-called 'parties' began to emerge in parliament. Danby's royalists, broadly sympathetic to the king, were branded 'Tories' after a group of Irish papist bandits. The king's pro-Dutch opponents were dubbed 'Whigs' after wild Scots fundamentalists. The new parliaments were so strongly Whig that, from 1681, an exasperated king decided to rule personally, as had Henry VIII, James I and Charles I, through a privy council of allies. He met his expenses with subsidies from the king of France. His mistresses were so alarmed as to form an incipient trade union, to demand post-office revenues for their pensions.

Through all these machinations, Charles struggled to remain jovial and tolerant. He disliked fanaticism of any sort and, though suspected of Catholic sympathies, kept his beliefs to himself. In 1681 he even blessed the Pennsylvania colony of the outlawed Quaker William Penn. When Penn was invited to meet the king, he refused to remove his hat, upon which Charles good-humouredly removed his own, pleading that the custom was 'for one of us to be bare-headed' on such occasions. In 1683 the king and James escaped assassination by so-called 'Rye House' plotters on their way back from racing at Newmarket. The rumoured involvement of Whigs in the plot gave the royal pair some political respite, but two years later Charles died suddenly of a stroke. Though only fifty-four, he had passed an extraordinary life of recklessness and debauchery, but his reign was a struggle to maintain religious tolerance. His failing, like that of all Stuarts, lay in his extravagance and in the means by which he sought to pay for it, from Catholic Europe. The iron parliamentary grip of no taxation without redress of grievances, reasserted at the Restoration, was his undoing. Charles converted to Catholicism on his deathbed and passed the crown to James, but he had no illusions of his brother's political skill. He predicted that James would not last long on the throne. He was right.

James II (1685–8) came to power after a distinguished military career, but he was a humourless and brittle personality.

Nell Gwynne called him 'dismal Jimmy'. Parliament voted him new expenses, but these were soon spent on suppressing a revolt by a pretender, the Protestant Duke of Monmouth, Charles's oldest illegitimate son. The rebellion was initially popular and took brief flight in the west country in 1685, backed by an ill-equipped force of former Roundheads. It ended in mass slaughter at Sedgemoor in Somerset. Second in command of the king's forces was the young John Churchill, a handsome and ambitious officer who had shared the attentions of Charles's mistress Barbara Villiers. He was married to an equally ambitious maid of honour to the queen, Sarah Jennings.

Monmouth was executed and his followers treated with peculiar ferocity. The 'bloody assize' under Judge Jeffreys executed 300 people and flogged or transported hundreds more, revolting even James's Tory sympathisers. After Sedgemoor, James refused to disband his army, staffing it with Irish troops and 100 Catholic officers. When the king demanded pay for this army and the repeal of the Test Act, parliament refused and was promptly dissolved. James packed the judiciary and the privy council with Catholic sympathisers and even removed the fellows of Magdalen College, Oxford, for refusing his appointment of a Catholic president. He knew neither tact nor tactics.

In 1685 Louis XIV made things no easier for his English friend by revoking the Edict of Nantes, previously assuring French Protestants of tolerance. London was flooded with refugees from what was reported as an imminent Catholic pogrom. Despite James's censorship, every pulpit resounded to denunciations of Catholic atrocities, further bonding Anglicans and Nonconformists against the king. James offered a 'declaration of indulgence' towards all Protestants, to be read from every pulpit, but by also indulging Catholics it further antagonised the Anglicans. When seven bishops refused to read out the indulgence from the pulpit, James had them arrested and tried for sedition, but they were acquitted. James was suspected of wishing to put the Catholic church on an equal footing with the Church of England, if not ahead of it. One of James's closest advisers was Father Petre, a Jesuit.

Whig leaders began openly negotiating with William of Orange, whose Protestant wife Mary was still heir to the throne. In this they were abetted by William's assiduous London agent, Hans William Bentinck. This path to a possible transfer of power to the next in line was sabotaged in June 1688 when the king's wife, Mary of Modena, gave birth to a son, James Stuart. Whether or not the boy was produced from a Jesuit warming pan, as implausibly rumoured, he took precedence over Mary as James's successor. For Protestant England this was a disaster. As in 1660, all sides, Whig, Tory, Anglican and Nonconformist, combined to prevent a Catholic succession and what seemed the certainty of resumed civil war. The Restoration compromise had fallen apart and needed somehow to be re-established.

Emissaries from William's court in The Hague invited six peers plus a bishop and including the Tory Danby, later to be known as 'the Immortal Seven', to send a letter, possibly drafted by Bentinck, requesting military intervention. It claimed that 'nineteen parts of twenty people are desirous of a change [of monarch]'. William needed no encouragement. He was concerned urgently to avert an alliance between James and Louis XIV against the Netherlands, while eager also to secure his wife's succession to the English throne. In that sense, the events of 1688 were a dynastic conquest similar to that of William's namesake in 1066. The Dutch assembly refused to sanction the expedition as being conducted in its name. Nor did William dare risk an invasion of England, which might well be contested, unless he knew that France would stand aloof and not take the opportunity to attack his country. Soundings during the autumn of 1688 indicated that Louis was, for the moment, happy to see England plunged back into civil war.

After frantic preparations, William's huge fleet of 463 ships, including 53 warships, and some 40,000 men, finally set sail on 1 November. This was a force three times the size of the Armada. As it passed through the Straits of Dover it spread across the entire Channel, guns blazing a salute to Dover castle as it went. A 'Protestant wind' landed it four days later at Torbay in Devon. Parliament had not requested such an invasion and the king had certainly not done so. William's invitation from six peers was constitutionally irrelevant. England was attacked by a foreign ruler to usurp a legitimate monarch. The invitation was clearly treasonable but, as the saying goes, 'if treason prosper, none dare call it treason'.

Glorious Revolution

~

1688 - 1714

AS WILLIAM OF ORANGE marched in full array across southern
England in the autumn of 1688, James II's army evaporated. Chief
among those turning their coat was the king's commander, the
opportunistic victor of Sedgemoor, John Churchill. William's
arrival in London on 18 December was carefully stage-managed.
Crowds were issued with orange ribbons and Dutch soldiers lined
the king's path through Knightsbridge. For two years Dutch
troops garrisoned the capital. London's streets, inns and courtly
chambers rang with the alien sound of the Dutch language. There
was no question: England had been occupied by a foreign power.

James fled to France with William's connivance. He even
tossed the Great Seal of England into the Thames as he went,
giving parliament the excuse of assuming a symbolic abdication
in favour of his daughter. However, in usurping him William
had no intention of acting merely as Mary Stuart's consort. The
couple would reign jointly and, were Mary to predecease him
before producing an heir, a member of the house of Orange
would be next in line. The two were jointly enthroned as
William III (1689 – 1702) and Mary II (1689 – 94) at Westminster
the following April. The Calvinist William mocked 'the comedy
of coronation', but none the less swore to govern according to
the 'statutes of parliament'.

Much was made by later Whig historians of the 'Glorious
Revolution'. To them it asserted pragmatic, bloodless reform,

in contrast to the current and future convulsions elsewhere in Europe. Yet it was bloodless only because James capitulated. The truth was that the Civil War and Restoration had failed to cure England of religious autocracy, and had failed to entrench parliamentary consent in anything stronger than vague precedent. James had preferred flight to fight, but a sizeable body of opinion still regarded him as England's legitimate monarch. William's Dutchmen had invaded illegally and with main force, from a land with which England had only recently been at war.

This time parliament took no chances. It wanted no more Catholics in charge. The Toleration Act of 1689, the 'Magna Carta' of religious liberty, restated Breda's freedom of worship, but only to Protestant dissenters such as Baptists, Independents and Quakers if they affirmed the Trinity. It excluded Catholics and Unitarians, though it undoubtedly led to a wider tolerance than the act formally stated. It was followed the same year by the Bill of Rights, re-enacting freedoms previously asserted by Magna Carta and the Petition of Right. Parliament alone now claimed the right to levy taxes, raise an army and wage wars. Judges were to be independent. Above all the bill declared, 'It hath been found by experience that it is inconsistent with the safety and welfare of this Protestant kingdom to be governed by a popish prince, or by any king or queen marrying a papist.' Never had the word 'experience' carried such force. A later addition was a Triennial Act stipulating that parliament should last for three years, irrespective of the wish of the monarch. Parliament had again declared itself sovereign, on this occasion in a body of legislation that lies at the heart of the British constitution. This time it held.

William faced a rebellion from the displaced James. The former king landed in Ireland in March, with French men and money at his disposal, to instigate the civil war for which his friend Louis XIV had hoped. Churchill, now the Earl of Marlborough and a recognised master of the battlefield, was sent to defend William's Dutch borders while William concentrated on Ireland. It took a full year to defeat James, culminating in the battle of the Boyne in 1690. As at Bosworth two centuries before, two kings claiming the throne of England faced each other across a field. Though William was wounded by a cannonball, it was James who was beaten and forced to return to France. For Ireland's Protestants, William became the heroic King Billy, and the toast of 'Orangemen' ever after.

While a seasoned military commander, the new king no longer seemed the youthful hero of Dutch resistance. He was very much a foreigner who preferred the company of his Dutch courtiers. He was asthmatic and ill tempered, departing urban Westminster for the clearer air of Kensington and bickering with all round him. He disagreed with Marlborough on the conduct of the army and quarrelled with his sister-in-law, Anne, a close friend of Sarah Marlborough. The two court ladies nicknamed him King Caliban after Shakespeare's monstrous creation in *The Tempest*. However, Queen Mary was popular and the royal couple were soon displaying typical Stuart extravagance. They commissioned Wren to design duplicate apartments of 'equal precedence' at Kensington and Hampton Court. A later mural by Sir James Thornhill in the Painted Hall of Greenwich Royal Hospital depicted William as Alexander the Great, crushing the tyrant Louis underfoot. The chief objective of the house of Orange is clear: there is no sign of James II.

William's reign was bedevilled by the emerging conflict between parliament's Whigs and Tories, to him reminiscent of the tiresome political feuding of the states-general of the Netherlands. The Whigs, led by the so-called Junto of leaders, had championed his usurpation but were wary of any sign of the king reviving Stuart autocracy. The Tories, still led by Danby, were relaxed about kingly power, but fiercely opposed to financing William's French war, which led to his returning home to the Netherlands every summer, when Mary would rule alone. In 1694 a partial compromise was reached in a new Bank of England, through which the king could raise loans to finance the army. But the same year William was mortified when Mary contracted smallpox – he had to be removed from her room for his loud crying. When she died soon afterwards he was so bereft he contemplated returning to the Netherlands.

In 1701, with Mary six years dead and her Protestant sister Anne showing no sign of producing a male heir, parliament confronted the probable demise of Stuart Protestantism. It passed an Act of Settlement, formally conferring the succession away from the Stuarts to the house of Hanover, by descent through James I's daughter Anne of Bohemia. The act insisted that monarchs swear allegiance to the Anglican church, abjure overseas wars without parliament's consent, live in England and not travel abroad without permission, a pointed reference to William's absences. Parliament was growing meticulous about its rights.

At which point yet another monarchical incident convulsed Europe. Charles II of Spain had died without issue in 1700, soon turning William's running conflict with France into a wider war over the Spanish succession. The ageing Louis XIV claimed the crown of Spain for his grandson, Philip of Anjou, combining in one vast state the empires of France and Spain, with much of Flanders and Italy. This merged Catholic Europe and unbalanced power across the continent. As Louis said, 'the Pyrenees are no more'. William was suspicious of any French king on the warpath. His concern was widely shared when, also in 1701, James II died at St Germain outside Paris and Louis provocatively recognised his son James, the 'Old Pretender', as king of England. Parliament was united in fury and voted William money for war. Despite William's dislike of Marlborough, he recognised his supremacy as a commander and allowed his appointment to lead a grand coalition of Dutch, Prussian and Austrian forces against the French. The war with

France, initially over the Spanish crown, was to last in various forms for more than a hundred years. It reversed the dismal outcome of its medieval predecessor. Previously France had resisted English expansionism while this time England resisted that of France. The conflict relegated France while awarding England the grandest of global empires.

Hardly had hostilities commenced than William's horse tripped on a mole-hill in Richmond park and he fell and broke his collar bone. The injury led to pneumonia, from which he died in March 1702. Jacobites, or supporters of James II's cause, for years afterwards would raise a toast to 'the little gentleman in a black velvet waistcoat' and smash their glasses. Mary's plain, diminutive, gout-ridden sister ascended the throne as Queen Anne (1702 – 14). Afflicted by eighteen miscarriages and infant deaths, Anne settled down with her favourite, Sarah Marlborough, at her side and the agreeable Lord Godolphin leading the government. Alexander Pope wrote of her palace at Hampton Court, 'here thou, great Anna, whom three realms obey / Dost sometimes counsel take – and sometimes tea.' Tea, and the 'china' named after the country from which it came, was now widely fashionable.

On the continent Marlborough cleared the French from the valley of the Meuse, and in 1704, staged one of the most remarkable forced marches in military history. He advanced at speed up the Rhine to join his ally, Prince Eugene of Savoy, at Blenheim on the Danube. Here they met and defeated a large French force, victory being due largely to Marlborough's skill at positioning cavalry and infantry on the battlefield and manoeuvring them with speed. Blenheim kept the French from the gates of Vienna, and public opinion in normally war-shy England was delirious. Anne gave Marlborough a dukedom and land at Woodstock outside Oxford, where Vanbrugh began the great mansion named after the victory, the only private house in England to be called a palace. Two years later Marlborough again beat the French at Ramillies, when over 40,000 cavalry took to the field. Still Louis refused to admit defeat.

Back in England, Anne's longing to conjoin the two Stuart crowns of England and Scotland was taken to formal union. This was driven in part by England's continued need for security against the long-standing French threat 'through England's back door', reinforced by a counter-threat to exclude Scottish merchants from English markets in the new American colonies. Furious debates over union took place in London and Edinburgh, where most Scots were plainly against it. Sent north to scout for the government, Daniel Defoe reported that 'for every Scot in favour there is ninety-nine against'. The houses of pro-union Scots were even sacked by rioters. But bribery and cajolery eventually delivered enough votes to push union through the Scottish parliament.

The 1707 Act of Union awarded Scotland forty-five MPs in what was to be called the parliament of the Kingdom of Great Britain. Anne was separately queen of Ireland and, for good measure, France. On 1 May Anne rode to St Paul's to give thanks for the union, wearing the Order of the Garter alongside the Scottish Order of the Thistle. She declared her wish for the two nations, 'that so it may appear to all the world they have hearts disposed to become one people'. The word 'appear' was appropriate. The Scots, like the Welsh and the Irish, were to play a significant role in the British army, the British empire and the Industrial Revolution, quite apart from Scotland's own intellectual renaissance in the eighteenth century. Over the coming century something called 'Great Britain' was forged from the component peoples of the British Isles and it became sensible to use such terms as the British government and the British people except in explicit reference to England. But the forging relied heavily on the perception of Britain on the world stage, usually in the heat of war and imperial expansion. Even in the twentieth century England still tended to be used for Britain: soldiers fought 'for England' and poet Rupert Brooke's foreign field was 'forever England'. Anne might speak of 'hearts disposed to become one people,' but there were not many of them north or west of the border. The English might refer to Britain as 'England', but the Scots, Welsh and Irish most certainly did not. The Scottish parliament closed in 1707 but was reopened three centuries later.

In 1708 the first Anglo-Scottish election put the Whigs emphatically in power. This rendered the fervently Tory Anne inconsolable. She remained a Stuart and deeply distrustful of the Whigs who had toppled her father. Her misery was deepened when the same year she lost her beloved husband, George. She was the last monarch to chair ministerial meetings in her private 'cabinet' and disliked having to admit to it politicians she detested. But on one matter she was in full agreement with the Whigs, the continuation of what was now seen as Marlborough's 'great war'. Campaigning had taken on a medieval character, with summer battles giving way to winter rest and recuperation. By 1709 it was clear, even to Louis XIV, that peace should be sought, but the Whigs demurred, recklessly demanding that Louis withdraw his grandson, Philip, from the Spanish throne. This he would not do, and hostilities resumed.

In 1709 the two sides, replenished with fresh troops, returned to the battlefield at Malplaquet near Mons. Here Marlborough and Eugene of Savoy deployed a vast force of 30,000 cavalry. The outcome was another triumph for Marlborough, but the deaths of 20,000 allied troops sickened public opinion. The carnage of Malplaquet infuriated the Tories and finished the Whigs. Peace was preached from every pulpit and Anne dissolved parliament. At the resulting 1710 election, the anti-war Tories secured a majority and took power under Robert Harley, a dissenter, bibliophile and astute political operator.

Harley became leader and chancellor of the exchequer, while his headstrong and overtly Jacobite colleague Henry St John, later Lord Bolingbroke, took charge of foreign affairs. The new government coincided with a furious breach between the queen and Sarah Marlborough, who was now replaced in the queen's affections by a Harley protégée, Abigail Hill, leading to bitter accusations by Sarah of lesbianism. Marlborough, long the champion of war, now lost both political and court influence. His corrupt abuse of army commissions was savaged by the satirist, Jonathan Swift, as that of a British Midas who 'now neglected stands / with asses' ears and dirty hands'. The Tories began secret negotiations with Louis that led to Marlborough's dismissal and the appointment as allied commander of the openly Jacobite Duke of Ormonde. His orders from Bolingbroke, kept secret from the allies, were to avoid battle and seek peace. The French were delighted. A gleeful Louis remarked that the turn of events 'does for us all we desire'.

The outcome was the diplomatic edifice of the 1713 Treaty of Utrecht. While curbing Louis's ambition, it awarded the allies less than they might have won after Marlborough's victories four years earlier. Austrian control of what is now Belgium was agreed and British interests extended in the Mediterranean and north America. As part of the deal, Gibraltar was ceded to Britain by the Spanish. Utrecht was a triumph of negotiation rather than conquest. Though the Tory Commons supported the treaty, the Whig-dominated Lords did not and Anne had to create a dozen Tory peers to secure its passage. This was the first use of this method to enforce the will of the unelected chamber on the elected one. Marlborough went into self-imposed exile in Hanover with Blenheim Palace as yet unfinished.

The queen was now sickening. She felt she had usurped her half-brother, the 'Old Pretender' James, and encouraged Jacobite and Tory emissaries to France to get him to renounce his Catholicism in order to succeed her. This he firmly refused to do. Bolingbroke continued to build a Jacobite faction in parliament in opposition to his partner, Harley. Alarm bells now rang. The Whigs warned the legal successor to Anne's throne, Prince George of Hanover, that, like William of Orange before him, he might have to threaten force to secure his throne. The veteran Marlborough was already in self-imposed exile at George's court, reportedly ready to lead a new invasion force.

On 27 July 1714, in the ailing queen's bedroom in Kensington, a bitter personal argument broke out between her two leading ministers, Harley, now Earl of Oxford, and Bolingbroke. As they denounced each other, the queen sided with Bolingbroke and demanded Harley resign in his favour. Confusion surrounds what happened next. Bolingbroke, in regular communication with James in Paris, left the palace to rally parliamentary support for a Jacobite succession. However, the following day a group of privy councillors induced the dying queen to name a senior statesman, the Duke of Shrewsbury, as head of a ministry to honour the Act of Settlement and the Hanoverian succession.

Had the queen survived another week, Bolingbroke might have won parliamentary support to offer the crown to James, though this would have defied the act. The likelihood would have been renewed civil war. As it was, the royalist Jonathan Swift wrote that 'fortune turned rotten at the very moment it grew ripe' and the death of Anne marked the end of the Stuart era. Though there were said to be fifty-five people with a stronger lineal claim to the Stuart throne than George of Hanover, he was generally acknowledged as king. With his accession, England's monarchy lost its prominence in England's history. Kings moved from centre stage, and gave way to party politicians.

Walpole and
Pitt the Elder

~

1714 - 1774

THE HANOVERIANS WERE BORN not as monarchs but as princelings. They came to power not by the sword or politics but by descent from a distant Protestant princess. They were mostly bewigged, powdered nonentities, who could neither handle their children nor say boo to a parliamentary goose. As such they collectively advanced the cause of parliamentary government more than any monarch since Henry III. The Georges cared chiefly for their mistresses and their cards, and let the body politic breathe and mature. As a result, statesmen no longer danced attendance on kings but lived as separate political personalities in their own right, tossed back and forth by parties, opinions, voters and economic forces, all of which acquired a new significance.

The arrival in London in 1714 of the fifty-four-year-old George I (1714–27) was greeted with relief rather than enthusiasm. He spoke little English and had visited his new domain only once, when he declared he 'did not like it'. He regarded himself as having done England a favour by saving it from the Stuarts. A Hanoverian autocrat, he had imprisoned his wife in a castle for thirty years for having an affair with a courtier, who had been murdered and dismembered. In her place George brought with him two mistresses, one fat and one thin, known as the Elephant and the Maypole, who played cards with him on alternate nights. New courtiers were said to 'have names like a bad cough'. They built themselves houses in the new Hanover Square with facades borrowed from patterns back home. The king's son, George Augustus, hated him and formed a separate court with his lively wife, Caroline, at Leicester House in London. She referred to Hanover as 'a dunghill'. If the majesty, let alone the divinity, of kings had any lingering appeal to the English, it died with the electors of Hanover.

The king's lack of English and his frequent absences from London conferred independence and status on the cabinet. Meetings were chaired by senior ministers, of whom Lord Stanhope emerged as the 'first', alongside a rough-hewn Norfolk landowner, Robert Walpole, as chancellor of the exchequer. They faced an immediate challenge in the form of a revolt sparked by the Old Pretender, James Stuart, in Scotland in 1715. The Duke of Argyll, on behalf of the government, halted the insurgents before they moved south of Stirling and James no sooner landed on Scottish soil than he had to flee back to France. The so-called '15 rebellion' was over before it had begun.

Like William of Orange, George of Hanover saw the crown in part as an invitation to engage England's support for his conflicts back home. The post-coronation election of 1715 saw the Tories trounced for their supposed Jacobite sympathies and the Whigs returned to power. Though traditionally the war party, they split over the question of how to pay for past wars and whether to support George's current ones. Walpole resigned from the government as the national debt rose to £50 million. In 1720 a scheme to redeem it was devised by exploiting a trading monopoly granted to the South Sea Company after the Utrecht treaty. This led to frantic speculation in the company's shares, with government ministers flagrantly talking up their value to line their own pockets. Within weeks a £100 share was worth £1,000 and subsidiary companies were enjoying equally swift inflation. It was said to be impossible to buy a carriage anywhere in London, such was the credit boom.

The so-called South Sea Bubble burst in September that year and stunned the nation. Thousands, mostly in London, were ruined and the Riot Act had to be read in the lobby of parliament. Stanhope had a stroke in the House of Lords and died. The postmaster general took poison and the chancellor of the exchequer (no longer Walpole) was thrown into prison. It was proposed that bankers who had loaned against the shares 'be tied up in sacks filled with snakes and tipped into the murky Thames'.

By 1722 Walpole was back as leader of the Whigs and head of an anti-war government which was to be the longest in English history. He was a man weighing twenty stone, hard drinking and high living, who shared the Tories' opposition to expensive military adventures. This enabled him to reduce land taxes and reassure all sides that a semi-detached Hanoverian king in harness with a Whig government was no threat to the established order. As first lord of the Treasury, Walpole was the first minister to be dubbed 'prime minister' and to be awarded a modest town house in a speculative housing development just off Whitehall named Downing Street. He wisely insisted this perk go with the job hereafter.

Walpole's political motto was 'Let sleeping dogs lie'. Government debt was moved into a sinking fund and policy was dictated by the avoidance of war and the promotion of trade. 'Walpole's peace' came to be regarded as a golden age. Politics was subject to the wit and satire of Pope, Swift, Defoe and Johnson. Liberal opinion gave currency to the philosophy of Locke and Berkeley. The political conversation began to widen from the confines of the court and parliament to a broad intellectual elite. In religion a lethargic Anglicanism, protected by the Test Acts, stimulated the 'Methodist' preaching of John Wesley, describing himself as 'a brand plucked from the burning' to galvanise the Church of England. The new middle classes delighted in the upward social mobility practised by Beau Nash in public assemblies in the elegant surroundings of Georgian Bath. Meanwhile the poor could drown their sorrows in cheap gin. By the 1730s there was one gin shop to every eleven dwellings in London and a person 'could get drunk for a penny and dead drunk for tuppence'. The 1720s and 1730s were the only time that London's population boom stagnated, at about 700,000, until the 1736 Gin Act taxed and licensed gin shops and curbed consumption.

Aristocrats returning from the Grand Tour laden with works of art stimulated a battle of styles. On one side stood the English baroque of Vanbrugh, Hawksmoor and Gibbs, displayed from Blenheim and Castle Howard to the 'Queen Anne' churches of east London. On the other stood the Italian Palladianism of Lord Burlington and his protégés, Colen Campbell and William Kent, represented by Burlington House in Piccadilly and Chiswick House on the Thames. The latter style was lampooned as foreign and effete by the 'British Bulldog', William Hogarth, but it came to dominate British architecture throughout the eighteenth century. The world of music was equally enlivened by a German immigrant, Frederick Handel, a great Hanoverian favourite.

On the king's death in 1727 Walpole's association with the old regime might have led to his dismissal by the apostate George II (1727–60). But his friendship with the new queen, Caroline, and his abuse of the Civil List to reward political allies rendered him near immovable. George was more popular than his father, but he became indolent and irritable, detesting his own son, Frederick, as his father had detested him. When the queen saw Frederick in the street, she remarked: 'I wish the ground would open this moment and sink the monster to the lowest hole in hell.' The Hanoverians found it hard to be nice, even to their own.

George II, devoid of historical personality, was none the less a prudent monarch. On matters constitutional he 'defied any man to produce a single instance wherein I have exceeded the proper limits'. He made peace with Walpole, who continued to govern for a further fifteen years. Walpole had Kent build him the magnificent Houghton Hall in Norfolk, where he amassed a fine art collection, partly on the proceeds of office and partly on credit. He was lampooned in the hugely popular *Beggar's Opera*, opening in 1728, and was the model for the treasurer Flimnap in Swift's *Lilliput*. His proudest boast was made to the queen in 1734, 'Madam, there are fifty thousand men slain this year in Europe, and not one Englishman.'

Walpole was eventually felled by precisely the foreign adventurism he had made it his mission to oppose. Spanish piracy was harming London's ocean trade and merchants put pressure on Walpole to take action. A young parliamentary orator, William Pitt, demanded war with Spain, so delighting the elderly Duchess of Marlborough that she left him a large legacy. Walpole negotiated a settlement with Spain in 1738, but disagreement over implementation led to the outbreak of war in 1739. It was popularly known as the War of Jenkins' Ear. Sea captain, Robert Jenkins, claimed to have had his ear cut off by a Spaniard, the wrinkled organ being waved in parliament. Walpole found the national mood of belligerence distasteful, remarking, 'They now ring the bells, but they will soon wring their hands.' The war achieved little beyond the renewed hostility of Spain and France. The general election of 1741 saw the prime minister's long ascendancy weaken. In 1742 Walpole lost a motion of confidence and retired to the House of Lords, his fall reputedly the basis of the nursery rhyme 'Who Killed Cock Robin?', first published at the time.

The new government was still dominated by the Whig patronage machine, which was now run by the Pelham brothers, dukes of Newcastle. They were described as having every talent for 'obtaining ministry, none for governing the kingdom'. The king, who enjoyed absolute power in Hanover, bemoaned his lack of authority in London: 'Ministers are the kings in this country,' he said. 'I am nothing there.' There were some who still wished him not even king. In 1745 the Old Pretender's son, Bonnie Prince Charlie, raised again the flag of rebellion in Scotland. The highlanders responded to the call and a Scottish army marched south against England's king, supposedly also theirs. The government sent the Duke of Cumberland to meet the prince, who had advanced as far south as Derby where the lack of an uprising in his favour broke his nerve. Cumberland drove him back to Scotland, as far north as Inverness. In April 1746 battle was joined at Culloden outside the town, but Charles fled the field, to be called 'a damned Italian coward' by his bodyguard.

The rebel highlanders were outnumbered. They fought 'like wildcats' but were overwhelmed and no quarter was shown. The Scots were massacred, their clan rights ended, their tartans banned, their leaders either executed or imprisoned. Charles fled 'over the sea to Skye', thereafter to live out a dissolute exile's life in France and Italy. Cumberland was nicknamed the Butcher for his ruthlessness, but most English and Scottish opinion was relieved at this emphatic end to the long Stuart feud.

Commons opposition to Newcastle's Whig government now cohered round Pitt. He was brilliant, eloquent and aloof. Despite the popularity of his anti-French rhetoric in the London streets, his association with Frederick, Prince of Wales, and the Leicester House set, made the king desperate not to appoint him to office. Pitt had also secured George's hatred for opposing subsidies to the continued Hanoverian wars against France. During one of these encounters at Dettingen in 1743, George even became the last English monarch to command troops in battle, winning renown at the age of fifty-nine for being unhorsed and then charging at the enemy, sword in hand.

By 1746 Pitt's status could be ignored no longer. He was appointed pay-master of the forces, electrifying his colleagues by declining to accept bribes. While Lord Newcastle remained head of the government, Pitt became its moving spirit and master of the Commons. His policy was clear. While he had opposed Walpole's passivity, he was equally averse to European wars. He disliked standing armies for their expense and for the belligerence they instilled in the political community. 'We ought to support our allies upon the continent with our money and our ships,' he declared, but it was 'dangerous to our liberties and destructive to our trade to encourage great numbers of our people to depend for their livelihood upon the profession of arms'.

The world beyond Europe was a different matter and here Pitt was wholly aggressive. The loss of Minorca to France in 1756 saw mobs in the streets demand that England fight for their return. Pitt was carried to prominence on a tide of pro-war sentiment. He was dubbed the Great Commoner, the first truly popular politician. Dr Johnson remarked that 'Walpole was a minister given by the king to the people, Pitt a minister given by the people to the king'.

The Seven Years War of 1756–63 encircled the globe and is regarded as the first truly 'world war'. The conflict was rooted on the continent of Europe, essentially between England allied to an emergent Prussia under Frederick the Great, and an alliance of France, Spain and Russia. It soon spread to the fast-growing trading posts of these powers in the Americas and Asia. British opinion, supported by the king, was strongly pro-Prussian, shown in the number of pubs named the King of Prussia and the Marquis of Granby, an allied general. Pitt struggled to stand aloof from this theatre, giving money and a few battalions to the Prussian cause but with his attention concentrated on the navy and overseas.

In India, the collapse of the Mogul empire enabled a French general, Joseph Dupleix, to capture Madras from the British East

India Company and thus control most of south India. Dupleix carried all before him until halted by Robert Clive, a talented twenty-three-year-old company officer turned soldier. In 1756 an Indian nawab, acting with French compliance, captured the company's trading post in Calcutta, where he imprisoned and suffocated 123 Europeans in a basement that became known as 'the black hole of Calcutta'. Arriving to seek retribution with 3,200 troops, Clive defeated an Indian army of 40,000 at the battle of Plassey, largely by terrifying them with cannon shot. By the time a French attack on Madras was defeated in 1759 Calcutta, Madras and Bombay were in company hands. This embryo British empire was acquired, so the Victorians remarked, 'in a fit of absence of mind'. It was through Clive's personal enterprise rather than any strategy on London's part and when Clive was later accused in parliament of widespread corruption, his reply was that, in view of his achievements, 'By God, Mr Chairman, at this moment I stand astonished at my own moderation.'

Skirmishes on the American continent with the French began in 1754 with an abortive attack by a young British officer named George Washington on a fort of 'New France'. This territory expanded from Canada down the Ohio and Mississippi rivers towards Louisiana and threatened to encircle the thirteen 'New England' colonies on the east coast. Pitt resumed hostilities on this frontier in 1758 when British units moved in strength into the Ohio valley, where French lines were cut and the principal fort, Duquesne, renamed Pittsburgh. To the north General James Wolfe advanced up the St Lawrence and in 1759 seized the French colony of Quebec. This was achieved with a nocturnal scaling of the adjacent cliffs, known as the Heights of Abraham, with Wolfe reputedly reciting Gray's 'Elegy Written in a Country Churchyard'. He died during the ensuing battle, honouring Gray's line 'The paths of glory lead but to the grave'. By now the French had been driven from most of Canada and virtually all of what is now the United States of America.

Horace Walpole remarked after the so-called annus mirabilis of 1759 that 'our bells are worn threadbare ringing for victories'. By 1760 Pitt's strategy had ended France's dreams of an empire stretching from Bengal to Montreal. His policy of fighting abroad and subsidising others, notably Frederick of Prussia, to fight France in Europe had succeeded. He had, he said, 'won Canada on the banks of the Rhine' and humiliated a nation that had always been bigger, richer and more magnificent than England. Pitt's achievement was a brilliant exposition of pro-active foreign policy, an epic chapter in English history and one never to be repeated.

George II died in 1760 and was replaced not by his son, Frederick, who had predeceased him, but by his grandson, the twenty-two-year-old George III (1760–1820). The new king disliked Pitt as had his grandfather, regarding him as having 'the blackest of hearts', and Pitt retired unthanked by the nation to become a cantankerous backbencher and popular champion. The 1763 Treaty of Paris confirmed Pitt's achievements, acknowledging Britain as master of India, Canada and most of the West Indies. But empire had not come cheap, doubling the national debt and absorbing half the annual revenue in interest.

The young George III tried, unwisely and briefly, to revive the Stuart monarchical prerogative. He boasted he was not a German immigrant but 'a true-born Englishman' and formed a governing clique with his old tutor, the Earl of Bute, and the Marquis of Rockingham. He assumed he could handle the Commons, as had Walpole, by manipulating patronage. His government struggled to repair Pitt's financial legacy by introducing levies and stamp duties that caused fierce opposition in the American colonies, followed by further duties on corn, paper and tea. These imposts, designed to relieve public debt, were clearly damaging to a central purpose of the new colonies: the promotion of trade.

By the middle of the eighteenth century industry and commerce had become crucial to England's story. The population of England, Wales and Scotland had almost doubled from five million at the start of the century. Manufacturing productivity was rising under the Industrial Revolution, with factories driven by fast-running rivers and produce moved by a new network of canals. Initial patents on spinning machines, steam engines and bar iron all expired in the 1780s. As a result spinning jennies and steam engines were soon proliferating driven by England's abundant supply of the new gold, coal. This output needed markets immune to the politics of Europe, in other words an empire.

With Pitt on the backbenches, the king could not find a coherent party or body of opinion in parliament from which to fashion a government. Thrust into a position of having to choose ministries for himself, rather than have them delivered to him by the Commons, he was changing cabinets by the year, while Pitt in caustic opposition was daily cheered in the London streets. This could not last, and in 1766 the king finally pleaded with Pitt to return to power. The statesman was now sick and gout-ridden, often speaking in the House of Commons wrapped in flannels and supported by sticks. He agreed to office only if he could move to the House of Lords as Earl of Chatham. This decision by the Great Commoner horrified the poet Thomas Gray, who called it 'the weakest thing ever done by so great a man'. Chatham soon became depressed and a virtual recluse, at one point hiding for days in his room and being fed through a hatch. He resigned on grounds of ill-health two years later in 1768.

By the time of Chatham's fall, new forms of popular politics, divorced from royal or aristocratic patronage, were coming into play. A rabble-rousing MP for Middlesex, John Wilkes, contrived in 1763 to be imprisoned in the Tower for attacking the ministry, on the grounds that he had attacked 'the king's speech'. He was later re-elected by his voters, rejected by parliament, elected lord mayor of London and defended by the lord chief justice among others. Chatham made a celebrated speech in his defence, declaring that irrespective of his character Wilkes was 'an English subject, possessed of certain rights, which the laws have given him and which the laws alone can take from him'. Unlimited power, said Chatham 'is apt to corrupt the minds of those who possess it, and this I know, my Lords, that where law ends, tyranny begins'. Wilkes was subsequently restored to his seat. The saga enraged the king and delighted the London mob. Wilkes had a fine, derisive turn of phrase. When Lord Sandwich told him he would 'die on the gallows or of the pox', Wilkes replied, 'That, sir, depends on whether I embrace your principles or your mistress.'

In 1774 a young MP of Irish origins, Edmund Burke, was acquiring a seat in Bristol. In addressing his new constituents, he asserted the role of the MP to be that of a representative not a delegate. An MP, he said, 'is not a member of Bristol but he is a member of parliament … he owes you his judgment; and he betrays, instead of serving you, if he sacrifices it to your opinion.' The radicalism of Wilkes and Burke established the rights of MPs against the executive, setting the stage for the nineteenth century's age of reform. But before then, their radicalism was tested in the fire, as a significant corner of Chatham's new empire abruptly and spectacularly disintegrated.

From Boston to Waterloo

~

1774 – 1815

THE ENGLISH PARLIAMENT responded to American protests against new taxes by repealing at least some of them. George III was appalled by such repeal. 'It is with the utmost astonishment,' he said, 'that I find any of my subjects capable of encouraging the rebellious disposition which unhappily exists in some of my colonies in north America.' His lack of understanding was shared by his prime minister, the plump, genial, ineffectual Lord North, who he had described ungraciously as 'very much my last choice'. North was the worst statesman to preside over the American War of Independence.

The war began as nothing of the sort. It was essentially an argument between loyalist and radical British subjects over trade and taxes, only gradually acquiring the rhetoric of civil rights and liberties. Even today that argument is mired in chauvinism. London protested that a derisory £1,400 a year in revenue was being gathered from the thirteen colonies, to pay for having been rescued by Britain from French autocracy in the Seven Years War. To call this rescue, as the Americans did, 'absolute despotism' was absurd. The protested Stamp Acts were imposed throughout the empire, as were other trade restrictions, while the colonists enjoyed their own assemblies and were for the most part autonomous. America was far better treated than Ireland.

Though most of the taxes were repealed, one remained on imported tea. When, in 1773, the hard-pressed East India

Company was relieved of the duty and allowed to ship tea tax free to America, rival tea merchants, mostly smugglers, dressed up as Indians and tossed the offending merchandise into Boston harbour. The government in London, lacking intelligence on the ground and with messages taking weeks to cross the Atlantic, over-reacted by passing five so-called coercive acts, closing Boston harbour and reasserting direct rule by the Massachusetts governor. The acts stimulated a 1774 congress in Philadelphia, which wrote a declaration of rights, boycotted British imports and requested the repeal of laws 'penalising' American trade.

When London rejected these requests, local militias called 'minutemen', as they were supposed to be 'ready at a minute's notice', took up arms. They were backed by a wide coalition of colonists, many with mixed motives. Some genuinely desired freedom but others were fearful of London calling in land debts, requiring respect for Indian treaties or regulating slavery. In April 1775 an attempt by the British governor of Massachusetts to capture militia bases at Lexington and Concord saw his force beaten back to Boston with a thousand casualties. The following year, 1776, the same exasperated delegates who had earlier sought accommodation with London gathered again in Philadelphia. Tom Paine published a republican tract entitled 'Common Sense', accusing loyalists to the British crown of having 'the heart of a coward and the spirit of a sycophant'. A Declaration of Independence, largely written by Thomas Jefferson, was published on 4 July, declaring George III to be 'unfit to be the ruler of a free people'. Its most celebrated passage asserted that, 'We hold these truths to be self-evident, that all men are created equal, that they are endowed by their Creator with certain unalienable Rights, that among these are Life, Liberty and the Pursuit of Happiness.' This ringing phraseology was a classic product of the European enlightenment. It did not, of course, apply to slaves or Native Americans. England's most successful creation, the United States of America, was born.

A cat-and-mouse war between rebels and loyalists was waged up and down America's eastern seaboard for five years. Opinion back in Britain was divided. The elderly Chatham fumed against the folly of fighting an America 'which cannot be conquered'. When the king recruited mercenaries in Hanover, Burke attacked him for using 'the hireling swords of German boors and vassals' to repress 'our English brethren in the colonies'. The war destabilised domestic politics, with anti-Catholic Gordon riots breaking out at the height of the war in 1780, instigated by a mild government measure to relieve Irish hardship. Some 60,000 people rampaged through London for almost a week, leaving more than 200 dead.

The American rebels found allies in France and Spain, eager for any chance to avenge their humiliation at the hands of Chatham. The French entered the conflict after the American victory at Saratoga in 1777 and their support was critical. A French fleet soon commanded the American coast and prevented the easy movement of British forces. By 1781 the British general, Cornwallis, was forced to surrender at Yorktown in Chesapeake Bay to the French and to the rebel commander and first American president, George Washington. When news of the defeat reached London, a despairing North cried, 'Oh God, it's all over!' George III was shattered. To the delight of radicals, the Yorktown surrender was accepted as final. Under a treaty signed in Paris in 1783, Britain held Canada and India but lost its jewel, the American colonies.

North lost a motion of confidence after Yorktown. The old Whig and Tory cohesion dissolved and in desperation George III in 1783 asked Chatham's son, also William Pitt, to become prime minister at the tender age of twenty-four. At an election the following year, Pitt won a majority that he was to retain for seventeen years. Though he called himself an independent Whig, Pitt was a new Tory, attuned to scientific innovation and the mercantilism of the Industrial Revolution. He was an enthusiast for the ideas of Adam Smith, whose *Wealth of Nations* appeared in 1776, with its stress on the division of labour and the significance of trade. Pitt had his father's ability, energy and guile, but was of a more outgoing personality. Like his father, he understood the damage that ill-judged wars could wreak on the nation's finances. Like him too, he dreaded European entanglements and saw his duty as to promote sound finance at home and profitable trade abroad.

Britain had lost America not to a rival European power but to something less humiliating and more radical: self-government. The response at home was not so much humiliation as a sense of intrigued resignation. When the new American ambassador, John Adams, arrived in London in 1785, George III amiably remarked that he wanted to be 'the first to meet the friendship of the United States as an independent power'. It was the war's victors who faced the tougher future. For the first time America had to tax itself for its own protection, and its income per head fell 46 per cent in the next fifteen years. Britain's rose, partly through trade with its former colonies. In France the legacy of the American wars was desperate, the unleashing of a revolutionary populism which the Bourbon establishment could not contain. In 1789 the citizens of Paris rose in rebellion and seized the Bastille. The French revolution was at first welcomed by the young Pitt and by reform-minded Britons. France appeared merely to be moving belatedly down the same road as had Britain a century earlier. Wordsworth declared, 'Bliss was it in that dawn to be alive,' and 'corresponding societies' were formed to liaise with allies in France.

For the time being events in America and France fostered a new radicalism in Whig ranks. A radical aristocrat, Charles James Fox, formed a close friendship with the Prince of Wales, a dissolute but clever and cultured young man, following in the Hanoverian tradition of opposing his father. They were joined by Burke, champion of the American rebels and now a noted debater and commentator. Fox called George III 'a blockhead' and Burke attacked crown patronage and so-called 'rotten boroughs', small constituencies with few electors usually in the patronage of landed grandees. Only on the French revolution was Burke trenchant in hostility. He said it had 'subverted monarchy but not recovered freedom', which should go forward not by revolution but in step with wider social and economic change. France, he shrewdly predicted, was on the road not to reform but to dictatorship. Burke's attack was to be a classic text of British conservatism.

Pitt remained an optimist. In his 1792 budget speech, three years after the Bastille fell, he foresaw fifteen years of peace in Europe. He was proved wrong within a year. Louis XVI went to the guillotine in January 1793 and the Terror began. The revolutionaries, led by a firebrand orator, Georges Danton, determined to topple all Europe's monarchies, and hurl 'at their feet as gage of battle the head of a king'. French peasant armies marched across France's borders, annexing Belgium and declaring war on the Netherlands. Within two weeks of the king's execution, France declared itself at war with Britain in the republican cause.

This was a European conflict from which not Walpole or either of the Pitts could have stood aloof. French soldiers were now roaming the continent carrying all before them. The revolutionary Directory in Paris kept them abroad for fear of what they might do if they returned home. By 1797 a young Corsican officer, Napoleon Bonaparte, campaigning in Italy, was delivering his masters so many triumphs that the French minister, Talleyrand, feared a military coup if he returned. He duly sent Napoleon to Egypt, to attack British interests in the Mediterranean.

Pitt galvanised himself for a resumed conflict with France much as his father had done for the Seven Years War. 'We must anew commence the salvation of Europe,' he said. He took the opportunity, like many governments under guise of national security, to impose a raft of curbs on habeas corpus, 'seditious meetings' and 'treasonable practices', evincing complaints from Fox of 'Pitt's Terror'. The charismatic Captain Horatio Nelson was sent to the Mediterranean where, in August 1798, he found Napoleon's fleet moored off the delta of the Nile. Nelson daringly steered his ships to its landward side and almost wiped it out with his guns. Only four French ships survived out of seventeen. Nelson's Nile victory was the talk of Europe. He had by now lost an arm and an eye, and his celebrity was as widespread as his affair with Emma Hamilton was scandalous. Napoleon fled back to France where, in 1799, he staged the coup that Burke had predicted and Talleyrand feared. Pitt's response was to introduce Britain's first income tax, two pence in the pound, rising to two shillings for incomes over £200.

Meanwhile America's rebellion did not pass unnoticed on England's Celtic fringe. The spread of the nutritional potato had combined with the teachings of the Catholic church to increase Ireland's population to six million, approaching a third of the British Isles total of twenty million. The continued treatment of Ireland as an English colony was seen as increasingly indefensible. In 1800, after an argument similar to that which preceded Scottish union a century earlier, an Act of Union was passed in London and Dublin, merging the English and Irish parliaments. But the king refused to countenance any concession of votes to Irish Catholics, rendering the reform near meaningless. Since Pitt had committed himself to such enfranchisement he felt obliged to resign. As with the American rebellion, empire was to be the last refuge of English monarchical prerogative, with disastrous consequences. The resulting Irish curse on British political leaders was to last more than a century.

The government in 1802 made peace with Napoleon, now chief consul of France, leading to a rush of British tourists to Paris to see the ruins of the Bastille and admire Napoleon's plunder of Europe in the Louvre. This included the horses of San Marco from Venice and the Apollo Belvedere from the Vatican. But within a year Napoleon reneged on the peace and shocked Europe by resuming his warpath. Britain realised this was war to a sort of death. Talk of political reform was condemned as revolutionary. Paine's *Rights of Man*, which had sold 200,000 copies, was proscribed. Habeas corpus was suspended and judges made liberal use of deportation to the new colony of Botany Bay in Australia. Income tax, having been abolished, returned at a shilling in the pound on incomes above £150 a year.

In 1804 Pitt was recalled to government and plunged into a frenzy of preparation. As Napoleon massed an invasion army at Boulogne, Martello towers were built along the south and east coasts of England, named after defences first built at Mortella in Corsica. Nelson was ordered back to sea, to find and destroy the French fleet that would be needed to escort a French invasion. Not until October 1805 did he corner his French and Spanish prey off Cape Trafalgar outside Cadiz. There he drove his ships at right angles to the extended opposition line, reducing the target for their guns while slicing the line and destroying twenty-two out of thirty-three enemy ships. He lost not one of his own. Nelson died in his moment of victory, shot by a sniper on his quarterdeck. When his body arrived back in London, posthumous praise knew no bounds. He was commemorated by a funeral at St Paul's and by a new square and column at Charing Cross. England was saved from invasion. As for Napoleon, thwarted by his loss of sea power, he led his grand army eastwards against the Austrians and Russians, crushing them both at the battle of Austerlitz. On hearing the news, Pitt remarked of a map of Europe, 'Roll up that map. It will not be wanted these ten years.' For Pitt Trafalgar was the end. He died exhausted in January 1806.

In May of that year a Whig government pushed through parliament an act banning British subjects from conducting trade in slaves, following a campaign by Fox and an independent Hull MP, William Wilberforce, with Methodist help from John Wesley. Fox declared the trade 'contrary to the principles of justice, humanity and sound policy' and its passage the finest thing he had done in forty years. It took another quarter-century for slavery, as opposed to the trade, to be outlawed across the empire, and then not in America, whose new independence saved it from abolitionists. Fox died shortly after the act passed. He was a defining personality of the late-Georgian era, a compulsive and monstrous gambler, drinker and womaniser, ridiculed alongside the Prince of Wales by the cartoonist James Gillray and one origin of the phrase 'a right Charlie'. Yet he was intellectually alert and witty, a sincere defender of civil rights, Catholic emancipation, franchise reform and anti-slavery. With Burke and others he had pushed the mainstream of Whiggery firmly towards liberalism. At this critical phase in England's political history, reform never lost touch with parliament, or parliament with reform. However unrepresentative it was of the nation, the floor of the House of Commons offered a bridge between conservatism and radicalism which each felt it could traverse.

Pitt's death in 1806 left a vacuum in the conduct of the war that was difficult to fill. The two leading Tories were a brilliant upstart, George Canning, and an Irish aristocrat, Lord Castlereagh, whose dislike of each other culminated in a farcical duel on Putney Heath in 1809. Not knowing that protocol required him to shoot high to miss, Canning aimed and missed, whereupon a furious Castlereagh demanded a second shot and tried to kill Canning, hitting him in the thigh. The two men had to resign public office, with the nation still at war. At the same moment, George III subsided into mental illness and two years later the Prince of Wales was declared Prince Regent. This was no time for the nation to lack a helmsman.

By 1808 Napoleon had invaded Spain and Canning had sent Arthur Wellesley, an army commander from India, to harry his forces across the Iberian peninsula from Portugal. This led to a costly and probably unnecessary four-year campaign that became an epic of military history. Not until 1812 did Napoleon begin to withdraw from Spain, turning his attention to a resurgent Russian nationalism. The result was his march on Moscow and eventual retreat after the battle of Borodino. The French emperor made his way back to Paris, disgrace and exile on Elba. In 1814 the allied powers summoned a peace congress in Vienna finally to dispose of revolutionary France.

Within months the congress was interrupted by news of Napoleon's escape from Elba. In February 1815 he landed at Antibes and marched on Paris. Reforming his imperial army, he marched into Belgium where he was confronted by an allied force hurriedly assembled under Wellesley, now Duke of Wellington. On 15 June a ball was given in Brussels by the Duchess of Richmond at which it was dramatically announced that the French army had arrived outside the city. The two great generals, both in their forty-sixth year, first skirmished at Quatre Bras and then, two days later, met at Waterloo. All Europe hoped it would be the battle to end all battles. Both armies were composed of roughly 70,000 men, but the allies had summoned an additional 48,000 Prussians. The battle saw horrendous losses on both sides as French cavalry swept against the volleys of British infantry 'squares'. Only the belated arrival of the Prussians turned the tide of battle, with Wellington admitting it was 'the nearest run thing you ever saw in your life'. When Napoleon's imperial guard was finally committed and seen to falter, the French army turned and fled. With darkness falling, the emperor's carriage was captured by the Prussians and his diamonds later incorporated in the Prussian crown jewels.

Napoleon's defeat was final. He wrote to George III, 'I have terminated my political career ... I claim from your Royal Highness the protections of the laws, and throw myself upon the most powerful, the most constant, and the most generous of my enemies.' He hoped to escape to America, the nation that had inspired the revolution of which he was the beneficiary. But he was captured and sent for the remaining six years of his life to the isolated south Atlantic island of St Helena, where he died in 1821. Britain's second hundred years war with France was over.

The Road to Reform

~

1815 - 1832

IN THE WAKE OF WATERLOO, the Vienna settlement was regarded as a triumph of European diplomacy, but it was deeply conservative. While it punished France for its revolution and shored up autocracies in Austria, Spain and Russia, it could not suppress the spirit of revolution. The American genie was out of the bottle and had already spoken French. It hovered over every capital in Europe and seemed certain to find an English voice. The British government from 1812 to 1827 was under the leadership of the Earl of Liverpool, a man of instincts so conservative it was said he would have opposed Creation to preserve Chaos. He was now to preside over a critical period in English history. How would the constitution, largely unchanged since the Glorious Revolution of 1688, stand amid the revolutionary storms still raging across Europe?

The end of the French war saw 200,000 disbanded soldiers and sailors flooding the labour market. Government spending fell and recession set in, causing widespread disorder. The 1815 parliament, still representing the landed interest, introduced an Importation Act which imposed a tariff on overseas wheat as a means of sustaining farm incomes. This 'Corn Law' increased the price of bread and led to riots in the cities, while in the factories so-called Luddites smashed labour-saving machinery. This unrest, which was widespread across the provinces, terrified the authorities, with their recent memories of the 'sans culottes' of Paris.

In 1819 a peaceful demonstration in St Peter's field in Manchester was dispersed by panicking troops at the cost of fifteen deaths and six hundred injuries. The incident was dubbed the Peterloo Massacre in ironic reference to Waterloo. Liverpool was shocked into passing the 'six acts' as draconian as those of Pitt, restricting freedom of speech, publication and assembly. Shelley's anti-government poem – 'I met murder on the way / He had a mask like Castlereagh' – could not be published for fear of his imprisonment. Meeting to promote reform was considered 'an overt act of treasonable conspiracy'. The following year a plot to assassinate the cabinet by five republicans meeting in Cato Street, London, was foiled only at the last minute.

Britain's political establishment creaked under the strain. Even the monarchy seemed insecure. The insane George III, blind, deaf and long incarcerated in Kew, finally died in 1820. His successor, George IV (1820–30), was a glutton and a spendthrift, obsessed with outdoing Napoleon in splendour. His coronation saw him decked in a costume copied from the French emperor's robes and he was horrified when his estranged wife, Caroline of Brunswick, returned from France to attend the event. Though her appearance and behaviour were unprepossessing, the king was so unpopular that the London mob gleefully took her side. George could not rely on his guards and had to hire thugs to exclude Caroline from Westminster Abbey. She banged on the doors to be let in, dying shortly afterwards, possibly of a drug overdose.

Industrial progress was now transforming the demography of Britain. The population of the British Isles, excluding Ireland, had been five million in 1700, barely double its medieval level and with only five provincial towns of more than 10,000 people: York, Bristol, Norwich, Exeter and Newcastle. By 1800 the population had risen to nine million and in the next quarter century to twenty million. It was driven by urbanisation, which appears to have increased longevity and fertility, and by improved nutrition. The old cathedral cities were swamped by the new industrial ones, Manchester, Birmingham, Leeds and Sheffield. They poured smoke into the atmosphere and attracted awe and horror in equal measure.

These changes turned Britain into the world's first industrial nation, but they put parliament at risk of political irrelevance. Its constituencies in no way reflected the new Britain, while its leadership was that of a rural oligarchy. Local government was based on borough aldermen, parochial vestries and justices of the peace. The Anglican church was moribund, its clergymen pluralist and taking large incomes from parishes they left in the care of curates. Church buildings unrepaired since the fifteenth century lay derelict, their roofs open to the skies. Nonconformity soon had as many adherents as Anglicanism. While trade unions were still banned by Pitt's Combination Acts, friendly societies blossomed, delivering alternative leadership to that of the aristocracy and the church. The government could imprison such cantankerous journalists as the anti-monarchist Leigh Hunt and William Cobbett, a conservative radical who assailed 'borough-mongers, sinecurists and tax-eaters'. But news and opinion were bursting from every political seam. The *Manchester Guardian*, the *Leeds Mercury* and the *Scotsman* newspapers appeared on the streets in the 1820s, read by unenfranchised citizens and financed by unenfranchised merchants.

The natural home of reaction was the Tory party and some Tories, such as the Duke of Wellington, responded by suppressing dissent. Others were aware that some change in political life to reflect the new Britain was inevitable. For all his conservatism, Liverpool was a pragmatist of genius, fashioning a coalition of these two elements. At the Home Office, Robert Peel was influenced by the philosopher Jeremy Bentham and the prison-reform campaigner Elizabeth Fry, to end the worst of the prison system's barbarities. He drastically cut the number of crimes meriting capital punishment and went on to found an unarmed metropolitan police force for London. Its constables were dubbed 'bobbies' and 'peelers' after him. William Huskisson, president of the Board of Trade, reduced food prices by lowering import duties. He was to be the first passenger killed by a railway engine, at the opening of the Liverpool to Manchester railway in 1830.

The star of Liverpool's ministry was Canning, returned from his post-duelling exile to the Foreign Office, where he championed a liberal view of empire. In 1823 he supported the Monroe doctrine of non-interference in South America, calling 'the New World into existence to redress the balance of the old'. This enraged George IV, who detested 'the new liberalism'. Canning later promoted Byron's cause of Greek autonomy from the Ottomans.

In 1827 this progressive Toryism met an abrupt crisis when Liverpool suffered a stroke and Canning, who took over as prime minister, died almost immediately afterwards. The ailing king turned in desperation to the Duke of Wellington, hero of the old guard, to take charge. Even Wellington, while he opposed an altered franchise, continued down the path of piecemeal reform. He needed the support of the Canningites in parliament, and repealed Charles II's Test and Corporation acts, confining public office to Anglicans, a move opening up local government across Britain to new and radical blood. In 1829 Wellington shocked conservatives by promoting Catholic emancipation in Ireland, a measure that had defeated the younger Pitt. The impact on Westminster was drastic, eventually creating a solid block of Irish Catholic MPs increasingly committed to self-rule. The reform led to a bizarre duel between the old soldier and the Earl of Winchilsea, who accused him of betraying the Protestant cause. Unlike Canning versus Castlereagh, both parties shot to miss.

The king died at Windsor in 1830, bloated, unloved and derided. When he came to power he had demanded the cabinet find £550,000 to pay his debts. Having commissioned Henry

Holland to rebuild Carlton House and Brighton Pavilion, he then demanded that John Nash rebuild Buckingham House as his London residence, to emerge as Buckingham Palace. The king also commissioned from Nash a plan of quadrants and terraces linking St James's to Regent's Park, London's only town plan to rival those of Rome, Vienna and Paris. By then the king, grotesquely fat, had retreated to Windsor castle. On his death even *The Times* remarked that, 'never was an individual less regretted by his fellow creatures than this deceased king'. The throne passed to the king's sixty-four-year-old brother, William IV (1830 – 37), an unsuccessful naval officer who never expected the office and showed little interest in it. He had ten children by his long-standing mistress, an actress named Dorothea Jordan, yet no legitimate male heir.

At the 1830 election the only talk was of franchise reform. Though the Tories retained a majority, Wellington fatally remarked that the current franchise was ideal and, 'as long as I hold any station ... I shall always feel it my duty to resist' any steps to reform. This public intransigence sent radical mobs prowling the streets. Cabinet ministers could go nowhere without armed guards. Wellington lost a vote of confidence and was forced to resign.

Into office came the sixty-six-year-old aristocrat and Whig leader Earl Grey, attended by the liberal-minded Lord Melbourne, Viscount Palmerston and a talented and radical lawyer, Henry Brougham. With these men committed to reform and the Tories split between the conservative 'ultras' and the reformist Canningites, battle was joined. In March 1831 the Whig Lord John Russell introduced a reform bill in the Commons abolishing sixty rotten boroughs such as Old Sarum, and reducing the plural representation of forty-seven more, thus removing the seats of 168 MPs out of 658 surviving from the Act of Union with Ireland of 1800. The franchise would be modestly extended from 400,000 citizens to 650,000, but for the first time, the great manufacturing cities of Manchester, Birmingham and Leeds would be represented in parliament.

The bill passed the Commons by one vote on the highest ever turnout of 608 members, but was defeated by the Tories in committee. Grey resigned in April and called a single-issue election, for or against the bill. Political unions were formed across the country and the second election returned an overwhelmingly pro-reform Commons. In September 1831 Russell's bill was reintroduced and passed the Commons, but was rejected by the Lords, with the bishops voting 21 out of 22 against. Riots broke out in Bristol, Nottingham and Derby. In Birmingham muffled bells were tolled. Wellington was nicknamed the Iron Duke not for Waterloo but for the shutters he had to put over his windows. There were rumours of armed groups forming, taxes being refused and money being withdrawn from banks. Britain's 1789 moment, so long feared, was at hand. How would parliament, and perhaps the monarch, react?

In December 1831 Russell's bill was presented for a third time in diluted form, but again it was rejected by the Lords. Grey now demanded that the king create enough peers to pass the bill, a tactic last employed by Queen Anne to pass the Treaty of Utrecht in 1713. When, in May 1832, the king refused, Grey again resigned, warning him that 'the spirit of the age is triumphing and to resist it is certain destruction'. The ensuing weeks, known as 'the days of May', saw constitutional politics hanging by a thread. Wellington was summoned by King William to form a government, which he could not do. The duke knew the game was over and advised the monarch to concede Grey's demands forthwith. A radical peer, Lord Stanley, even demanded the entire brigade of guards be ennobled.

Faced with the prospect of such a dilution, the Lords capitulated. The great Reform Act became law on 7 June 1832. Most rotten boroughs vanished and 125 new seats came in their place. The franchise rose by an estimated 60 per cent. Though it was still based on property, was not secret and was confined to men, the dam had burst. For the first time since the English Civil War a new distribution of power was established in Britain. Grey promised that further reform would move only 'according to the increased intelligence of the people and the necessities of the times'. But the implication was that move it would. The year 1832 ranks as one of the great turning points of England's history. Violent uprising had been forestalled because Britain's parliament and political community were, albeit belatedly, supple to the mood of the time and responded to it. Eighteen thirty-two, not 1688, was the true 'glorious revolution'.

Victorian Dawn

~

1832 - 1868

WELLINGTON'S SARDONIC REACTION to the first reformed parliament in 1833 was, 'I never saw so many shocking bad hats in my life.' Yet it was to be as radical as the Long Parliament of 1640, and its reforms more lasting. Grey's reassembled ministry honoured the mandate of the new electorate with a burst of liberal legislation that set all Europe on its ear. It abolished slavery in the West Indies, as opposed to the already illegal trade in slaves. It limited factory employment of children under thirteen. A poor law offered 'indoor relief' for the destitute, albeit with a regime so harsh as to move Charles Dickens to write *Oliver Twist*. Elected borough councils took over from corrupt municipal corporations. When the Tolpuddle 'martyrs' were deported to Australia in 1834 for union activity, public opinion demanded their reprieve and return. It was granted. The old order departed symbolically when the Palace of Westminster burned to the ground in 1834, a scene vividly recorded by J. M. W. Turner. The building was replaced in the Perpendicular gothic of Charles Barry and Augustus Pugin, a majestic evocation of the old camouflaging the new.

That same year Grey retired as prime minister and it was the amiable Melbourne who three years later welcomed William IV's eighteen-year-old niece, Victoria (1837–1901), to the throne. She was told of her uncle's death by the archbishop of Canterbury and the lord chamberlain, waking her at five in the morning in Kensington Palace. The entire privy council assembled when she was barely out of her nightdress. Lively, intelligent, curious and just 4ft 11in tall, Victoria was infatuated with Melbourne. The handsome widower appointed himself her informal secretary, meeting her twice a day and dining with her three times a week. As his biographer, David Cecil, wrote, Victoria was 'emotionally at the schoolgirl stage, looking less for a lover than for a hero'. Melbourne was perfectly cast, initiating his receptive pupil into the mysteries of the constitution, then steering her into a happy marriage to the dashing German, Prince Albert of Saxe-Coburg. He explained that protocol required her to propose to him.

As some hoped and others feared, the advent of reform only meant pressure for more. In 1838 a group of radicals published a people's charter, going beyond the Reform Act and demanding equal electoral districts, universal male suffrage, a secret ballot, annual parliaments and paid MPs. Though the 'Chartists' staged mass rallies and were, to some, a proto-revolutionary working-class force, their leaders and parliamentary supporters saw Chartism as within the spirit of the 1832 act. In the tension between violent and 'constitutional' change, the latter won. Nor were the Chartists alone on the radical wing of Whiggism. The 1841 election returned the Tories under Peel, who called himself, with a touch of irony, a 'Conservative'. This serious-minded son of a cotton merchant regarded industrial progress, overseas trade and political reform as part and parcel of a new Toryism. His much-publicised 1834 manifesto to his electors in Tamworth declared his party had to 'reform to survive' and 'review all institutions, civil and ecclesiastical'. Peel, more than any leader, took an essentially reactionary parliamentary interest and made it fit eventually to govern a modern nation state.

The Industrial Revolution had by now moved far beyond the eighteenth-century centres of textile manufacture, associated with access to coal, iron ore and the fast-flowing water power of the Cotswolds and Pennine fringes. Transport was the key. When railways began to supplant canals as freight routes in the 1830s, an integrated manufacturing base spread across the midlands and the north. In the 1840s 'railway mania' saw thousands of miles of track laid, and where labourers built railways they stayed to staff the factories. Birmingham could be reached from London in a morning. Most of the country soon lay open to daily deliveries of goods and mail. While the living conditions of this new working class could be dreadful, an essentially agrarian population was released from bondage to the land into relative prosperity.

The significance of this economic and social revolution was reflected in what became Peel's ruling obsession: free trade. Manufacturing required foreign outlets, just as it required cheap imports of raw materials and cheap food for its labour force. Tariffs were the enemy of imports and exports. In this great cause Peel was joined by two radical industrialists, Richard Cobden and John Bright, who founded an Anti-Corn Law League to campaign for cheap food. *The Economist* was first published to aid the campaign in 1843. Cobden was anything but a Tory, indeed a pacifist and fierce opponent of aristocracy. But in free trade, urban radicalism found joint cause with capitalism. Only some Chartists protested that the doctrine would oppress the poor with lower wages.

In 1845 the supply and price of food became critical with the failure of the Irish potato crop and the return of a horror most thought gone from the British Isles: famine. By the end of the decade a million Irish had fled to America, often herded into lethal 'coffin ships', rife with disease and starvation. Some of these vessels were so under-supplied that they lost a third of their passengers each crossing, the bodies tossed overboard to the sharks. The only immediate solution was to cut the price of bread by repealing the tax on imported wheat. With the help of Whigs and radicals, in 1846 Peel won repeal of the 1815 taxes on corn. Though the effect was not immediate, average bread prices fell by almost half over the next thirty years.

The impact of Corn Law repeal on the Tory party and its agricultural interest was immediate. Peel's policy might have been sound economically and shrewd in allying Toryism to the new commercial interest, but party traditionalists were outraged. He was ferociously denounced by a young firebrand, Benjamin Disraeli, who characterised Peel's action as 'the wilful destruction of a great party by its leader'. In the summer of 1846, with the Tories split for and against repeal and in disarray, Peel lost office and the Whigs returned to power under Lord John Russell, yielding two decades of Whig ascendancy.

The impression left by the mid-years of the nineteenth century is of a nation in a ferment of progressive change, commercial, cultural, spiritual and architectural, not unlike 'Walpole's peace' of a century before. While Europe's 'year of revolutions', 1848, saw monarchies toppled in France, Austria, Italy and Poland, the nearest England came to political unrest was a damp Chartist rally on Kennington Common, which culminated in a humble petition being sent to parliament in three taxis, and then rejected. Across town in the British Museum, Karl Marx was composing his communist manifesto unmolested, while in the House of Commons MPs were passing a public health act.

The queen and her husband enjoyed a public matrimonial bliss, moving between Windsor, Balmoral and their favourite country seat of Osborne on the Isle of Wight. The contrast with the dissolute Hanoverians was serene. At Osborne Albert constructed a Swiss cottage, where the children were trained to keep house and garden like a normal family. Swiss cottages blossomed across Britain. London's suburbs sprawled with stucco terraces, where the profiteers of empire rubbed shoulders with continental aristocrats and intellectuals fleeing the turmoils of Europe. In 1851 a Great Exhibition in Hyde Park, organised by Prince Albert, promoted Britain not as a rural idyll but as a confident industrial and trading power. Such a new Britain was reflected in the nation's intellectual life. The novelist Anthony Trollope described the hidebound emotions of a plutocratic politics, but in terms sympathetic to ecclesiastical and political reform.

Charles Dickens saw change differently, championing the needs of those as yet untouched by reform. He spoke at public meetings and donated his profits to hostels for the homeless. The political philosopher, John Stuart Mill, charted the shifting boundary between the state and personal freedom in *On Liberty* (1859), warning against 'the tyranny of the majority' and stressing the need for active participation in a democracy: 'A person may cause evil to others not only by his actions but by his inaction.' Even the Church of England was roused from its Georgian torpor by an evangelical movement emanating from Oxford and Cambridge. This led to a burst of church-building not seen since the fifteenth century, with steeples in stern gothic stone rising over rows of classical villas. By the end of the decade their pulpits were lashed by Darwin's challenge to religious dogma, *On the Origin of Species* (1859). His application of scientific inquiry to the natural world mirrored that of mechanical discovery in industry. Even the arts turned controversial, as Pugin and Ruskin protested the ugliness of the new England, and preached a return to the values and the craftsmanship of the Middle Ages. Britain surged forward on a wave of creative argument.

Though Russell was prime minister, the period was dominated politically by the remarkable figure of Palmerston, foreign secretary throughout the 1830s and again from 1846 to 1851. During that time he wielded power from the Foreign Office while rarely consulting his colleagues. Long considered the progenitor of overseas 'liberal interventionism' Palmerston told the House of Commons in a five-hour speech in 1848 that 'the real policy of England … is to be the champion of justice and right, pursuing that course with moderation and prudence, not becoming the Quixote of the world, but giving the weight of her moral sanction and support wherever she thinks that justice is'. In 1850 he sent the navy to attack Athens in defence of an injury done to a Gibraltarian, Don Pacifico, claiming that 'the watchful eye and the strong arm of England' should always protect its citizens, as in the days of ancient Rome. While Palmerston supported revolutionary causes on the continent and was adept as what was termed 'gunboat diplomacy', he kept Britain apart from European squabbles, concentrating, like Chatham, on the Royal Navy and the security of empire. Such was his patriotism that when a Frenchman thought to compliment him by saying that if he were not a Frenchman he would wish to be an Englishman, Palmerston replied, 'If I were not an Englishman I should wish to be an Englishman.'

Palmerston was no team player and his policy was too personal for his colleagues to tolerate. He was moved to the Home Office in 1852, where for two years he engaged in a furious burst of reform. He further limited factory hours for children and promoted vaccination, clean air, prison reform and reformatories for child criminals. He was also able to avoid direct implication in the unpopular Crimean war, begun in 1853, though he argued for a strong line to be taken on behalf of Turkey in curbing Russia's expansion. The outcome of the war for Britain was trivial, marked chiefly by a *Times* campaign for army reform and by improvements to nursing, thanks to Florence Nightingale. The fiasco of the charge of the Light Brigade was turned to glory by the poet Tennyson, but the holding of an inquiry into the government's conduct of the war so humiliated the Whig prime minister, Lord Aberdeen, that he felt obliged to resign. In 1855 Palmerston took his place, after the queen had asked virtually all his colleagues to form a government and they had refused. Victoria disliked him intensely, seeing him rightly as a relentless libertine but wrongly as an unprincipled rogue.

Palmerston's brand of patrician Whiggism drew on the radical legacy of Burke and Fox through Grey, Melbourne, Russell and the generation of 1832. In 1859 he was accordingly present at a gathering in a St James's club where a group of Whigs, Peelites and Radicals decided to become the Liberals. The dominant figure present was the young chancellor of the exchequer, William Gladstone, high-minded son of a Liverpool merchant. He had been a Peelite Tory, at first opposing the 1832 Reform Act and defending slavery, but he now displayed the fervour of a convert. He had served as chancellor from 1852 to 1855 and now returned to the post for seven years (1859–66) during which time he increased income tax and halted government borrowing. In peacetime, he asserted, 'nothing but dire necessity should induce us to borrow'. Building on Peel's free-trade policy, he cut the number of duties from 419 to 48, ending those on newsprint as 'a tax on knowledge'. The lowering of food prices saw him celebrated as 'hero of the working man's breakfast'.

Though a strong slavery abolitionist, Palmerston took the Confederate side in the American civil war of 1861–5, largely from an aversion to anti-British feeling rife in the northern states and from a concern for the South's cotton exports. Gladstone also supported the South. But support did not extend to war. Palmerston died in office in 1865 after two decades in which Britain had enjoyed peace and prosperity. He was replaced by the elderly Russell, radical proposer of the original 1832 act and now obsessed with carrying it forward. Political reform returned to centre stage, spurred, as at the start of the century, by reform overseas, by Garibaldi in Italy and Lincoln in America. In 1866 Russell introduced a franchise bill to parliament along Chartist lines, seeking equal constituencies and enfranchising all adult males with skilled jobs and a settled home. The effect would be to double the electorate to roughly two million, and, through voter registration, make it correspondingly harder, or more expensive, to manipulate votes. This in turn would reduce landed patronage and strengthen the role of party organisations. Consent would begin to escape the grip of local oligarchs and come within reach of a wider public.

The bill proved too much for the Commons to swallow and Russell and his government resigned, giving way to the Tories under Lord Derby, with Disraeli as leader in the Commons. In London there was an eruption of the same reform marches as had been seen in the 1830s. A protest rally in Hyde Park was so big the police needed the help of soldiers to disperse it. The Tories panicked and, in August 1867, hurriedly passed what was essentially Russell's old bill. Now it was Disraeli's turn to be accused (by Robert Cecil, the future Lord Salisbury) of 'a political betrayal which has no parallel in our parliamentary annals', almost the same words as Disraeli had used of Peel. But if Disraeli thought he had outflanked the Liberals and would be thanked by the new electorate at the polls, he was wrong. At the first post-reform election in 1868, his Tories were rejected and Gladstone was voted into office. The stage was set for a clash of titans.

Gladstone and Disraeli

~

1868 – 1901

COMETH THE HOUR, cometh not one man but two. Britain's leaders seemed to take the stage as either giants or dwarfs. Between the Pitts, Peels, Melbournes and Palmerstons were quieter men, mostly peers with civic titles such as Liverpool, Derby and Aberdeen. They seldom brought ambition to office, rather an inherited sense of duty, as if their task was to let the nation rest awhile. The two men who now stepped forward were not in this mould. Neither Gladstone nor Disraeli was from the English ruling class, but they had little else in common, their contrasting personalities generating one of the great feuds of English history.

Disraeli was the dandified son of a non-observant Jew, who baptised him an Anglican at the age of twelve. Trained in the law, his oratorical brilliance eased him up what he called the 'greasy pole'. He first opposed the political reforms of Grey, Peel and Russell, then adopted and exploited them for personal and party gain. An accomplished novelist, his charm was overwhelming and his idealism empty, purporting airily 'to marry the two nations' of Britain's rich and poor. Though a practising Anglican, Disraeli was often the butt of anti-Semitic comment, which he would handle with robust humour. Abused as a Jew by a fellow MP, he replied, 'I am a Jew, and when the ancestors of the Right Honourable Gentleman were brutal savages in an unknown island, mine were priests in the Temple of Solomon.'

Gladstone could not have been more different. His intellect was forged on the Bible and the classics, from which he could quote copiously. His air of ethical superiority infuriated Disraeli, who commented that 'posterity will do justice to that unprincipled maniac'. Gladstone retorted that Disraeli 'demoralised public opinion, bargained with diseased appetites, stimulated passions, prejudices and selfish desires'. He was angry when, after Prince Albert's untimely death in 1861, Disraeli ingratiated himself with the grief-stricken Victoria, with oleaginous references to 'my most beloved sovereign'. Victoria said that Gladstone always left her convinced he was the wisest person in the world while Disraeli convinced her that she was. She made no attempt to hide her preference. Gladstone, she said, 'speaks to me as if I was a public meeting'.

Gladstone described his first ministry, which began in 1868, as 'the finest instrument of government that ever were constructed'. As had happened in 1832, the new MPs honoured their newly enfranchised electors with a burst of reforming legislation. First came education. In a maxim that summed up the age, the chancellor of the exchequer, Robert Lowe, declared, 'We must educate our masters.' The church, which had long enjoyed a monopoly of elementary schools, was confronted with a proposal that all schools should become secular. In the event, the Education Act of 1870 introduced 'board schools' only where church schools were thought inadequate, largely in the poorer parts of cities. The red-brick Dutch gables of the new schools rose with confidence over urban terraced housing, as cathedrals once had over medieval hovels. But the divisive legacy of 'church schools' continued to hover over English education, and does to this day.

The 1860s saw Britain at its zenith both at home and abroad. The railways had reached every corner of the land and shipping reached every continent of the world. Although traditional farming was ailing in competition with free trade in food, manufacturing was as yet unchallenged by the emerging strength of German and American industry. In local government, the municipal reforms of the 1830s had matured into a muscular civic enterprise. The population of Birmingham rose from 70,000 at the start of the century to 350,000 by 1870 and Manchester, Liverpool, Leeds, Sheffield and Newcastle saw similar growth. These were mighty cities, with town halls, hotels, railway stations and art galleries as grand as any in Europe. Municipal innovation was led by Birmingham's Liberal mayor Joseph Chamberlain, elected in 1873, who left the city, it was said, 'parked, paved, assized, marketed, gas & watered and *improved*'. He happily called such improvement socialism. At the same time Angela Burdett-Coutts and Octavia Hill championed the housing of the urban poor. Spurred by the work of the American philanthropist George Peabody, they sought to replace slums with flats for the 'deserving poor' by convincing potential developers that a reasonable profit could be had from a fair rent, a principle dubbed 'five-per-cent philanthropy'.

Gladstone's government was no less reform-minded. The civil service was to be recruited not by patronage but by examination. The purchase of army commissions was banned. The universities were thrown open to all beliefs. Dons were allowed to marry and Oxford's northern suburbs blossomed with lofty gothic houses for their families. The formation of a Trades Union Congress led in 1871 to legal unions, though they were sorely restricted by a ban on picketing. In 1872 came an act introducing the secret ballot at elections. This proved too much for the elderly Russell, who warned that it would lead dangerously 'from household to universal suffrage'. The Whigs, with a long-standing terror of 'democracy', could no longer keep up with the Liberals.

Abroad, Gladstone continued to follow Palmerston's cautious imperialism and aversion to European entanglements. Just as Britain had held aloof from the revolutionary movements of the

1840s, so now it held aloof from the emergence of a Germany united under Bismarck, and from the horrors of the 1870 siege of Paris. Ireland, however, was not so easily ignored. Famine and emigration to America had devastated the population. While England's population soared, Ireland's plummeted, from eight million, or a third of the total for the British Isles, to half that figure in two decades. Ireland was an oppressed country, owned by alien English landlords, dictated to by a foreign government and forced to practise an ostracised religion. But as long as the House of Lords, with a strong Anglican and Anglo-Irish interest, remained rigidly against reform, Gladstone could do little to ease Ireland's plight, though he did succeed in disestablishing the Irish Anglican church, and passed a series of Irish land acts extending tenant security.

After six years of office, Gladstone's cabinet was tired. Disraeli derided it as 'a range of exhausted volcanoes – not a flame flickers on a single pallid crest'. At the election in 1874, though the Liberals polled the most votes, they failed to win a majority of seats, and the Tories returned with the sixty-nine-year-old Disraeli as prime minister. He had read the message of long years of opposition, that an expanding electorate expected progressive reform. He repealed Gladstone's picketing ban, a labour leader responding that the Tories had 'done more for the working classes in five years than the Liberals have in fifty'. Disraeli also passed a public housing act, an education act, a health act and a factory act. Where he parted company with the Liberals was in foreign policy. Disraeli hoped to resume where Chatham had ceased. In 1875, he sought to protect Britain's route to the east by purchasing almost half the shares in the new Suez Canal Company. The following year he delighted Victoria by declaring her Empress of India (which, to her fury, Gladstone opposed). Yet imperialism was a two-edged sword. Disraeli encouraged Turkey to halt Russian expansion into the Crimea and Caucasus, and even mooted a repeat of the Crimean war.

The nation's patriotic juices were stirred and the new music halls chanted, 'We don't want to fight but by jingo if we do, / We've got the ships, we've got the men, we've got the money too.' Such sentiments became known as jingoism.

Gladstone tarred Disraeli with provoking 'Turkish atrocities' against Bulgarian Christians. He declared that 'there is not a cannibal in the South Sea Islands whose indignation would not arise and over-boil at the recital of what has been done'. Disraeli retorted that the worst Bulgarian atrocity was Gladstone himself. Gladstone's next move in opposition was Britain's first modern electioneering campaign, a tour of his new Midlothian constituency in 1879. Until then mass rallies had usually been associated with Methodism rather than politics. Gladstone addressed huge meetings, often standing on the rear platform of a railway carriage and using 'barkers' to relay his words to the fringes of his audience. His speeches accused Disraeli of 'a narrow, restless, blustering and self-assertive foreign policy, appealing to self-love and pride'. They were distributed in advance to the press, a practice Disraeli (and Victoria) deplored as 'unconstitutional'.

The Liberals under Gladstone stormed back to power in 1880 and Disraeli retired to his country seat of Hughenden outside Beaconsfield, where he died a year later. He was an opportunist who had mastered the political art of charm. He had an instinct for the public mood and could play on it, as he played on the queen, with uplifting terminology. While as a young man he had destroyed Peel, he inherited his mantle as champion of progressive Toryism at a time when most European conservatives were monarchist and reactionary. As such his role in liberalising English politics was crucial. As the franchise expanded over the course of his career, he read it correctly: Conservatism should change or die. In the next half century, it was ironically the Liberals who ignored that message.

Gladstone was now the Grand Old Man. His 1880 cabinet was a strange concoction of elderly peers, bereft of ideas on how to counter the first depression of an increasingly global economy. Railways were driving across the prairies of the New World and steam ships were pushing down the cost of transport. In 1882 the first refrigerated cargo vessel, the *Dunedin*, docked in London, causing a sensation at Smithfield market with its frozen New Zealand lamb. In twenty years the price of importing grain into Britain fell 90 per cent. The impact on Britain's already struggling farmers was devastating. Agriculture could no longer expect protection from parliament.

The third of the century's great reform acts, in 1884, extended voting to all male householders, doubling the electorate to over five million and embracing miners, mill-workers and farm labourers. This extension of the franchise was sufficient to see the emergence of public opinion as a political force. It was fuelled by the rise of a mass-market press, with over a dozen daily newspaper titles in London and a hundred in England as a whole. The 1880s also saw the formation of an organised 'left', a term derived from the seating plan in the old French assembly. The research-based Fabian Society was founded by Sidney and Beatrice Webb and George Bernard Shaw in 1884. It espoused the maxim of the Roman general Fabius, that 'for the right moment you must wait', to make it the despair of more revolutionary contemporaries. The Fabians were committed to 'permeating' the Liberal party.

Disraeli's overseas adventures returned to plague Gladstone. When Anglo-Egyptian forces had to be evacuated from the Sudan in 1885, he was driven by a 'jingoist' press to give the task to the charismatic General Charles Gordon, who had had a tumultuous send-off at Charing Cross station. Gordon played to the public gallery by disobeying orders and refusing to abandon Khartoum. When the town was overrun by Mahdist dervishes, Gordon was killed and Gladstone blamed for not supporting him. A storm of abuse turned GOM into MOG, or Murderer of Gordon. In June 1885 Gladstone felt obliged to resign, giving way to a brief caretaker government under the new Tory leader, the Marquess of Salisbury. Within a year Gladstone returned to power for a third time, but in a hung parliament where his survival depended on the votes of the Irish nationalists.

The primacy of Ireland over British politics in the nineteenth and early twentieth centuries is hard to imagine today, fusing as it did the emotions and interests of anti-Catholicism, landlordism and colonialism. These factors were not trivial. Had it not been for the potato famine, Irish votes could by the end of the century have been a third of the British total and Irish MPs might have held a regular balance of power in the Commons. As it was, the Irish Parliamentary Party, sitting as a group, was led by the irascible Charles Stewart Parnell, an Irish landowner and a radical with intelligence and charisma. Gladstone called him 'the most remarkable man I ever met'. Parnell insisted that a new, largely autonomous, Irish state be created and that it include the north-east province of Ulster, where most people were Protestant and unionist. This was opposed by the Tories and by a body of Liberal Unionists led by Chamberlain, now an MP and in the cabinet as president of the Local Government Board. Ireland was to be the last redoubt of blind reaction in British politics.

Seeking home rule for Ireland was to be Gladstone's last throw. He introduced a bill in April 1886 in a three-and-a-half-hour speech that was, to many, a peak of Commons oratory. It was to no avail. The bill was lost and Chamberlain resigned from the government, taking his Unionists with him and forcing Gladstone's resignation. At another general election in 1886, a coalition of Conservatives and Chamberlain Liberal Unionists took power under Salisbury. This led to an intriguing repeat of the fusion of conservative and reform Toryism seen previously in the time of Liverpool–Peel and Derby–Disraeli. In the Commons the flamboyant Chamberlain, white orchid in his buttonhole, would preach 'municipal socialism' and progress, while in the Lords, Salisbury instructed his ministers 'to work at less speed and lower temperature than our opponents'. In 1888 the county government of England and Wales was brought in line with that of the towns, with magistrates and vestries replaced by sixty-two county councils. The following year the London County Council was born.

The 1892 election returned Gladstone to power for a fourth time, now aged eighty-two, partly deaf and with failing sight, but with a voice as unfaltering as ever. The queen was appalled at 'this vast empire' being 'entrusted to the shaking hand of an old, wild and incomprehensible man'. The election was notable for the arrival of the first independent Labour MPs, the Scots miner Keir Hardie, John Burns from Battersea and Havelock Wilson from Middlesbrough. Hardie was returned for the London seat of West Ham and arrived at parliament in a tweed suit and deerstalker hat with attendant brass band. A year later he became leader of the Independent Labour Party, subject to an annual conference of local branches and an avowedly socialist agenda of public ownership. Gladstone himself had eyes and ears only for Ireland and home rule. Parnell had died in 1891, at the age of forty-five, having negotiated the details of a renewed home-rule bill with Gladstone in opposition, but losing power within his own Irish Parliamentary Party after a chaotic divorce case involving his mistress, Kitty O'Shea. The issue divided the IPP just when the Irish needed to stay united. Gladstone's new bill passed the Commons but failed in the Lords by 419 votes to just 41, an unprecedented assertion of hereditary might against the will of the electorate. Gladstone resigned, issuing a final warning that the conflict with the Lords over Ireland 'must go forward to an issue'.

Four years later Gladstone was dead. His career had traversed the spectrum of politics, from conservative Toryism to Liberal reform. He had grown up in the pomp of the Regency. He opposed the 1832 Reform Act, yet became the master exploiter of the forces unleashed by that act. His period at the Treasury in the 1850s and 1860s combined fiscal rectitude with improving the condition of the people. His later years were overshadowed by Ireland, but he was not the first or last English leader to suffer from that quarter. His body was conveyed to Westminster Abbey by underground train in the grandest funeral London had seen since Wellington's.

An election in 1895 brought the return of Salisbury, whose obsession with caution matched Gladstone's with Ireland. When Germany was building a battle fleet and moving, with Italy and Belgium, towards an African empire, Salisbury was unconcerned, adopting a policy of 'splendid isolation'. It meant no more than 'drifting lazily downstream, occasionally putting out a boat-hook to avoid collision'. It was in Britain's interest, he said, 'that as little as possible happen'. Of intervening in the domestic affairs of foreign states, he remarked, 'There is no practice which the experience of nations more uniformly condemns and none which governments more consistently pursue.'

The obligations of empire could not so casually be ignored. The prime minister of the Cape province, the diamond tycoon Cecil Rhodes, was dreaming of a British imperium stretching from the Cape to the Nile. In the way stood the independent state of Transvaal, won by the Boers in 1881 in a war with the British and now overwhelmed by the Rand gold rush. In 1895 Rhodes backed a reckless raid by a Dr Jameson to re-assert British control of the Rand. The raid was a failure, but the financial and imperial motivation behind it yielded a military confrontation and eventual Boer attack on the colonial town of Mafeking. Kimberley and Ladysmith were besieged and Natal was threatened. British public opinion, at first jingoistic, was shocked at the inefficiency of the army against the Boer guerillas.

In 1899 the government despatched its most distinguished general, Lord Kitchener, fresh from avenging Gordon's death at the battle of Omdurman, to contain the Boer advance. The war dragged on into 1902, aggravated by Kitchener's innovation of 'concentration camps' to prevent Boer families from sustaining their soldiers in the field. News of disease and death in the camps revolted world opinion. The eventual British victory brought Transvaal into the empire, but with promises of amnesty, autonomy and compensation for Boer families. The war was an example of what became a series of such conflicts in distant lands, as antibodies to the British empire began to emerge and its costs imposed themselves on the mother country, costs that seemed without any balancing benefits.

The Britain that saw in the twentieth century had changed in a hundred years more drastically than in any preceding century. Mass migration from country to town had seen the population of Britain and Ireland quadruple to forty million. Changes in lifestyle were even more dramatic. In 1800 the majority of people lived in rural cottages or hovels. They lived off their land, or from produce sold in neighbouring market towns. They lacked running water or sewerage, public education, health, a postal service or rapid transport. Heat came from open fires and light from candles. The largest settlements were still the old cathedral cities. Life in most of England would have seemed little changed to a time traveller from 1700 or even 1600.

By 1900 that England had been replaced by a new one that would, to a surprising extent, be recognisable today. Houses other than for the poorest were built of brick and stone, attached to a modern infrastructure of paved streets, water mains and sewers. Those occupied by the middle and more prosperous working class had gas and some even had electricity. On the table were daily newspapers and food from all over the world. Roads were surfaced with tarmac and cars were appearing on them, their speed restricted to twelve miles an hour (but no longer requiring a red flag to be carried in front of them). In 1900 traffic on the London to Brighton road was estimated at 1,200 vehicles an hour. Trains ran everywhere, including underground in London on electrified rails, with journey times that would compare with today's. Most communities had access to free or cheap schools and hospitals. The dark, satanic mills of the early Victorian age were giving way to clean factories. This England was a land of optimism and novelty, and unmistakably what we would term modern.

On 22 January 1901 Queen Victoria died. She had embodied constitutional decorum for two-thirds of a century. With her German husband and nine children, many married into European royal families, she displayed domesticity and cosmopolitanism that ran as threads through the upheavals of the times. After Albert's death, she had plunged into what seemed eternal mourning, dressing in black and keeping his portrait on his pillow next to hers. Her gloom was deepened by the immoral and extravagant behaviour of her son, Edward Prince of Wales, whom she regarded as a throwback to the Prince Regent. For many years she would not even allow him sight of state papers. All this was despite the pleading of ministers that she show herself more to her people. Yet to most Britons Victoria offered what they had long most craved in a monarch, stability and continuity.

The Edwardians

~

1901 – 1914

THE VICEROY OF INDIA, the most splendid proconsul on the face
of the earth, celebrated the coronation of Edward VII (1901 – 10)
with belated extravagance. In 1903 Lord Curzon summoned
the princely rulers of a realm that stretched from Afghanistan
to the Chinese border to a dusty plain outside India's planned
new capital at Delhi. Here they rode past caparisoned tents on
gold-encrusted elephants, escorted by armies of retainers. The
jewellery worn at the final banquet was said to be the greatest
display of precious stones in history. As a magnanimous gesture,
Curzon remitted interest on loans to famine-hit states. He then
sent Colonel Francis Younghusband to invade Tibet.

The empire of which India was the prize exhibit embraced
a fifth of the land area of the globe. Its population was 400
million, of which three-quarters were Indians, under the aegis
of the world's largest navy. British manufactures and British
commerce were ubiquitous. Eighty per cent of world trade was
carried in British ships. British cities were the most prosperous
in Europe, their ever expanding suburbs untroubled by threat
of invasion. Country houses were the most lavish and their art
collections the most treasured. Confidence was reflected in the
music of Elgar, the poetry of Kipling, the classicism of Lutyens
and the flamboyant portraits of John Singer Sargent.

This apparent supremacy was being challenged. Industrial
competition was growing on the continent and in America,

drawing on a global market in raw materials and on new reserves of skilled labour. Technical education and innovation in France and Germany were overtaking Britain's. Three emergent twentieth-century industries – cars, aviation and the cinema – were being led from across the Atlantic, while King Edward's two first motor vehicles were a German Mercedes and a French Renault. Nor was empire proving cheap. In the first decade of the new century, education took just 10 per cent of public spending while imperial defence took 55 per cent. Russia, America, France, Germany and Belgium all had imperial ambitions, with Germany building a navy specifically to rival Britain's. Against this background Britain reached an 'entente cordiale' with France in 1904. This was assisted by the personal diplomacy of King Edward, a fluent and engaging French speaker who, against his mother's expectation, proved a conscientious and popular monarch. In 1907 the entente was extended to embrace Russia, forming an alliance whose objective was, to all who cared to notice, the containment of Germany.

In 1902 Salisbury had handed the government to his languid nephew, Arthur Balfour, rather than his natural successor, Joseph Chamberlain. As the dominant personality in the cabinet, Chamberlain stayed as colonial secretary, treating his desk as de facto hub of empire, but he resigned a year later to concentrate on his enduring obsession to end free trade and build a tariff wall round the empire. In a stark admission that Britain's manufacturers were losing their competitive edge, Chamberlain sought a return to protection, for both foodstuffs and industrial products. He was messianic in his demand: 'Sugar is gone; silk has gone; iron is threatened; wool is threatened; cotton will go! How long are you going to stand it?' He was supported by many in business and agriculture, but the threat of more costly food, 'the smaller loaf', was opposed by the Liberals. The Tories were split, as they were sixty years before on the same subject under Peel. Balfour struggled to hold his party together and attempted to cover his flank with Irish MPs by passing yet another Irish land act in 1903 permitting Irish tenants to buy their farms. But at the next election in 1906, the Liberals won their greatest ever victory, with 400 MPs under a radical-minded Scot, the elderly Henry Campbell-Bannerman. The Tories were reduced to just 157. Some twenty-nine members were elected under the banner of the Labour Representation Committee, many of them through an electoral pact with the Liberals. They soon formed themselves into a parliamentary Labour Party.

After only two years in office Campbell-Bannerman resigned because of ill health, giving way to Henry Asquith, a mild-mannered lawyer noted for penning copious love letters to his close friend Venetia Stanley during cabinet meetings. The letters were virtual cabinet minutes and became important historical documents. Asquith's government ranked with Grey's of 1832 and Gladstone's of 1868 among great reforming administrations. It included the radical aristocrat, Lord Haldane, as war secretary, a young ex-Tory Winston Churchill at trade and an extrovert Welsh orator with a mane of black hair named David Lloyd George at the Treasury.

This last post was crucial. Under Gladstone in the 1860s, the Treasury had come to embody stern rectitude in the guardianship of the nation's finances. In the hands of Lloyd George, the first chancellor unmistakably of the left, the Treasury became a tool of creative policy. For five years measures that laid the foundation of the welfare state cascaded from the cabinet. Lloyd George and his colleagues introduced an old-age pension of five shillings for all over seventy, free school meals and school clinics. He fought for better conditions in workhouses, for labour exchanges and for maintenance for divorced mothers. Trade unions were liberated from suits for damages following strikes in a significant concession to the new Labour Party. On defence Lloyd George sought to cut 'the gigantic expenditure on armaments built up by the recklessness of our predecessors', reducing the planned six new Dreadnought battleships to four. Here at least he met his match in a press campaign led by the navy's charismatic admiral, Jacky Fisher. With a public demanding 'We want eight, and we won't wait,' Lloyd George had to capitulate, and the first Dreadnought was built in just four months.

All this was expensive. In the 1909 'people's budget', income tax rose to one shilling and twopence in the pound, with an extra sixpence on incomes over £5,000. There was also a land tax, a petrol tax and duties on tobacco and alcohol. Lloyd George delighted in the howls of complaint from the rich, glorying in 'dishing the dukes'. Indeed, 'duke' was his favourite epithet of abuse; he complained that each fully equipped duke cost more to run than two battleships. But while the budget passed the Commons, the Tory majority in the Lords ignored the convention not to oppose finance bills. What Lloyd George dismissed as 'a body of five hundred men chosen at random from among the unemployed' rejected the budget as nakedly political. This forced Asquith to call an election specifically on the budget in January 1910. He was returned as leader of a minority government, reliant on the backing of eighty-two Irish and forty MPs now specifically designated Labour.

The Lords now let the budget pass, but with Irish MPs holding the balance of power a confrontation on home rule was clearly imminent. Gladstone's prediction that the conflict with the Lords 'must go forward to an issue' was at hand. Asquith proposed a parliament bill that would limit the delaying power of the Lords to three parliamentary sessions, which the Lords duly rejected. At this moment the king died. His funeral, embracing Victoria's now extended family across Europe, was described by the historian Barbara Tuchman as 'the greatest assemblage of royalty and rank ever gathered in one place and, of its kind, the last'. Many of those present were soon to be at war with each other.

Asquith now had to seek a guarantee from the new and uncertain king, George V (1910–36) that, in the event of the parliament bill being reintroduced, he would assent to the creation of enough Liberal peers to ensure its passage, possibly as many as 250. After much argument among his highly partisan, mostly Tory advisers, the king agreed, but only with the proviso that a second election be held specifically on the bill. This took place in December 1910 and Asquith was returned, but again dependent on Irish votes. The Lords capitulated. The king had done the duty of a democratic monarch, guarding the Commons against aristocracy and chaos.

New forces were now coming into play. A strengthened labour movement flexed its muscles with a surge of industrial action. In 1911 the seamen, dockers and railwaymen all stopped work in disruptive and mostly successful disputes. Lloyd George responded with limited health and compulsory unemployment insurance for those in prominent industries. Female muscles, too, were in evidence. Militant suffragettes, led by Emmeline Pankhurst, smashed their way into parliament and Downing Street, their numbers swelling the population of Holloway women's prison in London. Emily Davison threw herself under the king's horse as it ran in the Derby, an incident captured on an early film.

National pride was sorely dented when in April 1912 the *Titanic*, the embodiment of Britain's commercial pride and at the time the largest ship ever built, hit an iceberg on its maiden voyage and sank with the loss of 1,517 lives. Far to the south in Antarctica, Captain Scott had been beaten to the Pole by a Norwegian, Amundsen, freezing to death in the effort. Scott's colleague, Captain Oates, felt unable to walk on and sacrificed himself to save his companions. His last remark lives on in legend: 'I am just going outside and may be some time.' As with the charge of the Light Brigade, British failure was recast as epic heroism.

In 1912 Ireland played what should have been its final hand. The political aspirations of the Welsh and the Scots had been met, for the time being, by their MPs at Westminster, but most Irish were unequivocal. They wanted to rule themselves. Since Asquith's government depended on Irish MPs, this could not long be ignored. A new home rule bill was passed by the Commons, but with the Lords opposed, the new Parliament Act required that its enactment be delayed until 1914. Desperate opposition was mounted by an Irish-born lawyer, Sir Edward Carson, under the slogan 'Ulster will fight and Ulster will be right'. Carson planned an 80,000-strong militia, and began buying arms in Germany. British officers at the Curragh, an army base outside Dublin, resigned their commissions in his support in March 1914. The effect was to leave home rule hamstrung on the question of whether Ulster should be partitioned, and perhaps for how long. The act became law in 1914 but its implementation was suspended pending resolution of Ulster's status.

Although there were many intimations of the coming war, few predicted the catalyst. As A. J. P. Taylor wrote, 'Nowhere was there a conscious determination to provoke a war. Statesmen miscalculated ... and became prisoners of their own weapons. Great armies, accumulated to provide security and preserve peace, carried the nations to war by their own weight.' The catalyst came in June 1914 when a Serbian nationalist, Gavrilo Princip, assassinated the heir to the Austro-Hungarian throne in Sarajevo, triggering the sequence of alliances built up across Europe over the previous decade. Austria felt obliged to mount a punitive expedition against Serbia, and began shelling its capital, Belgrade. Russia mobilised in support of the Serbian Slavs, thus activating Austria's alliance with Germany. Then, in turn, Germany's expansionist kaiser, Wilhelm II, seized his moment to pre-empt the 1907 entente between France, Russia and Britain. He declared war against Russia on 1 August, and against France two days later. Germany promptly invaded Belgium in accordance with a plan by the kaiser's former chief of staff, Count von Schlieffen, to deliver a swift attack on

France before Russia could mobilise or Britain could move an army across the Channel.

What became known as the Great War is often characterised as a morass of unnecessary slaughter, a war of 'lions led by donkeys'. In some respects it was, but its goal was little different from the wars fought by Marlborough in the eighteenth century and Wellington in the nineteenth. For Britain the objective was to protect the country from a commercial blockade, and to resist the emergence of a continental power strong enough to threaten one.

Allied to this was the threat from an expansionist Germany to the global British empire. The status of the Low Countries was particularly critical to Britain. London had been party to the creation of Belgium in 1831 and had guaranteed its neutrality. It now faced the prospect of an aggressive German navy in control of the North Sea and Channel ports and able to block Britain's imports and exports. To Asquith's cabinet this was unacceptable. When the kaiser's forces breached Belgian neutrality on 4 August, Britain responded by declaring war on Germany. A force of 130,000 soldiers crossed the Channel to confront a European enemy on territory fought over by Britons throughout history. A century of careful British detachment from the conflicts of continental Europe was abruptly at an end. The foreign secretary, Sir Edward Grey, told his staff, 'The lights are going out all over Europe; we shall not see them lit again in our lifetime.'

The First World War

~

1914 - 1918

THE FIRST WAVE OF British forces to disembark on the shores of Europe faced overwhelming odds. The Kaiser's Schlieffen plan assumed that a million German troops could reach Paris in six weeks. They would be supported by a network of railway lines across the Rhine, while similar lines fed a smaller force into Poland to resist any Russian advance. The plan began well. British and French armies fell back from the Belgian town of Mons and German units were within two days' march of Paris before they were halted at the River Marne north of the city. By then the French cabinet had declared, 'We will obtain victory in the end' and fled with its staff and papers to Bordeaux. In one of the unsung achievements of the war, an immense French and British effort pushed the Germans back east to a line running from Flanders down through Rheims and Verdun to the Swiss border. Here stalemate ensued.

For three years the western front did not move more than fifteen miles back or forward while the pounding was relentless. Artillery bombardments smashed water courses and turned battlefields to mud. Soldiers retreated into trenches, behind barbed wire and machine-gun nests. For the first time in war poison gas was deployed, though its impact was more debilitating than lethal. Pending the deployment of tanks and aircraft, the technology of war made attack even harder than defence.

The British commander, Field Marshal Sir John French, predicted that the campaign to drive the Germany army out of Belgium would be over by Christmas. His boss, the war minister Lord Kitchener, disagreed and the conflict soon expanded into a war of empires. By September the cabinet was demanding half a million new recruits for the army, to swell its ranks to over a million. Recruitment was aided by strongly pro-war public opinion and by Kitchener's advertising posters, in which he looked into the nation's eye and declared 'Your Country Needs You'.

Away from Europe, a force eventually comprising 250,000 British and empire troops, among them T. E. Lawrence 'of Arabia', was sent to fight Germany's Turkish allies in Mesopotamia and Palestine. This was reinforced by a British government decision, with Churchill as navy minister, to open a new front against Turkey in the eastern Mediterranean with an attack on the Dardanelles. A landing at Gallipoli by British, Australian and New Zealand (Anzac) forces in April 1915 was pinned down by Turks under German officers, and spent nine months trying to break out from its beach-head. The operation was eventually aborted in a humiliating withdrawal, leading to Churchill's resignation. By the end of 1915, inertia on the western front led to French's removal and the appointment of Sir Douglas Haig as commander in the field. The cabinet decided on the first conscription of able-bodied males in British history.

In May 1916 came the long-awaited battle of the Dreadnoughts. A British victory at sea was crucial if Germany were to be prevented from subjecting Britain to a full blockade. Fought in fog and darkness in twenty-four hours off Denmark, the battle of Jutland was the last great contest of warships manoeuvring as fleets. In all, 250 ships took part. At the end, British losses were greater – seven ships and 6,900 men – but the German fleet was forced back to port, and thereafter had to rely on U-boats to fight the sea war. These submarines were highly effective, sinking 100 merchant ships a month into 1917. Lloyd George eventually overruled a Royal Navy reluctant to risk its precious warships and insisted on convoys of mixed naval and merchant vessels. The result was an immediate reduction in sinkings and soaring U-boat losses. War also came to the air, with the arrival of German Zeppelins to bomb London and east-coast towns. They initially terrified a civilian population, which had seen nothing like them. The Kaiser forbade attacks on the capital west of the docks, fearing to endanger his relations, the king and queen.

The war soon led to tensions on the home front. Food prices rose sharply, giving rise to protests in Hyde Park. Women entered the labour force in large numbers, with five million eventually working in public transport, the civil service, agriculture and munitions, further reinforcing their claim to the vote. The government was reluctant to extend conscription to Ireland. With home rule in abeyance, Irish nationalists exploited the distraction of war as their ancestors had down the centuries. At Easter 1916 a group of rebels seized the General Post Office in Dublin and declared a republic. After much damage to property, including reckless shelling by a British gunboat, the revolt was suppressed and its leaders executed. But independence had been declared. There was unlikely to be any going back.

At the front the new commander, Haig, staged what was billed as his 'big push' on the Somme in the summer of 1916. Despite five days of artillery pounding, the first day of the advance on 1 July left 19,000 British dead, massacred by machine gunners on the barbed wire of German trench defences. It was the biggest ever loss by a British army in a day. Such was the carnage that the Germans allowed stretcher bearers passage to gather the killed and wounded from no-man's-land. Over the next six months 420,000 British and empire troops were to be killed or wounded on the Somme, to gain an average of two miles of ground. The battle saw the first deployment of battle tanks, so named for their disguise as water-carriers. They were too few in number to be effective. The outcome of the Somme offensive was a government crisis. Asquith took some responsibility for Haig's strategy and was toppled in a political coup in December, manipulated by Lloyd George and friends among the press barons. Lloyd George became prime minister and replaced the twenty-strong war cabinet with an inner group of five. Convinced that ministers were showing excessive deference to the generals, he also established a cabinet secretariat under Maurice Hankey, which was to survive the peace and develop into the modern cabinet office.

The year 1917 saw the French under intense pressure around Verdun, suffering periodic mutinies and crises in command. Haig attempted yet another push on the Flanders front in the summer, but this led only to the renewed horrors of Passchendaele, with 240,000 British and empire casualties and a new stalemate. Haig's strategy was becoming increasingly controversial, criticised as wasteful, heartless and ineffective. Yet a war of attrition seemed unavoidable, given the resources available.

The position worsened with developments far from the western front. The February and October revolutions against the Russian tsar broke the spirit of the Russian army and relieved Germany of the need to fight on two fronts, enabling it to move large numbers of troops to the west. This advantage was balanced by an ostensibly reckless German decision to target foreign shipping in the Atlantic, including neutral Americans. President Woodrow Wilson, re-elected as the man who 'kept us out of the war', quickly changed his tune and engaged, vowing to make the world 'safe for democracy'. In Britain Lloyd George greeted the news of America's entry by saying, 'America has at one bound become a world power.'

American reinforcements were a long time coming. Though the first troops arrived in June 1917 it was not until May 1918 that they appeared in force, eventually numbering a million soldiers, as many as the British. Their arrival was pre-empted by a German spring offensive, bolstered by some seventy divisions freed from the Russian front. The German commander, Ludendorff, was able to put three million troops into battle. He employed a new tactic using spotter planes to direct sudden bombardments followed by massed attacks at points of perceived weakness. The result was that in March the British line in Flanders was penetrated by as much as forty miles. German soldiers were again within reach of Paris. Britain frantically built tanks, backed by 'tank bonds' that raised £138 million in a single week. But the allies were shaken by the German advance. There were complaints that the Americans were battle-shy and Haig accused the French commander, Marshal Pétain, of being 'in a blue funk'. The reverses put Haig's position under threat. Lloyd George's usual command of the Commons weakened, as voices began to question his conduct of the war, including from the man whose own conduct he had undermined, Asquith.

By July 1918 the French with American support at last halted the Germans along the line of the Marne. The allies then staged a counter-attack through Amiens, supported by 420 tanks and squadrons of aircraft, breaking through the new German line. This proved crucial. Soon allied troops were streaming across open country. In the north, Haig was finally able to take the initiative in what was called the 'hundred days offensive', a victory that remained overshadowed by earlier failures. The combined battles soon became a rout, and the Germans pleaded for an armistice to avert invasion and surrender. On the eleventh hour of the eleventh day of the eleventh month the guns fell silent. Bells were rung across Britain and the day was forever commemorated as Armistice Day. It was popularly dubbed Poppy Day after the flowers that were seen to grow over the trenches, as if watered by the blood of the fallen.

Epitaphs on the First World War were mixed. It had defeated Germany and supposedly ended its dream of European supremacy. As with Napoleon a century before, Britain had helped Europe avert a threat from one nation to dominate others. Whether that threat was extensive and whether it seriously endangered Britain was debatable, but it was averted. The price was high in both monetary and political terms: a national debt of £40 million in 1914 ballooned to £360 million. Though Britain emerged from the war with its empire intact and its influence expanded across the Middle East, its primacy would soon be usurped by an America awakened to global potency. British military deaths totalled 700,000, or one in twelve of mobilised males, a huge figure though a small proportion of some ten million who were lost on all sides. Officers suffered proportionally more than their men, being expected to lead them 'over the top', 25 per cent meeting their deaths.

No war since the Middle Ages had come so close to home and hearth. German planes had flown over English towns, evoking the potential threat of bombardment with gas as well as explosives. Many landed estates were devastated by death duties and loss of staff, who either died or moved to other employment. Conscription had driven all classes and professions to war, including writers and artists who produced work of peculiar intensity. The horror of the trenches was recalled in poetry by Rupert Brooke, Siegfried Sassoon and Wilfred Owen, and in paintings by Paul Nash, William Orpen and C. R. W. Nevinson. The Macedonian front was depicted in Stanley Spencer's evocation of tedium and suffering in his murals at Burghclere in Hampshire.

The First World War was a powerful nationalising venture, taking men and women from villages and towns that most had never left before and bringing them into contact with new accents and strange places. Men fought for Britain under one government, which was freed by the concept of 'total war' to impose unprecedented taxes and powers of regulation, conscription and censorship throughout the land. What was described by H. G. Wells as 'the war to end all wars' resulted in a closer relationship between citizens and government. This was reflected in a wider franchise. In 1918 all men over twenty-one and women over thirty were granted the vote, in thanks from Lloyd George for the war effort. Women in particular were now freer to earn their own living and participate in politics. A people that had long deferred to its leaders in matters of war or peace was at last in a position to make such decisions for itself.

The Locust Years

~

1918 - 1939

BRITAIN IN 1918 WAS A BRUISED, expectant land. Those who had given their all in war believed that national security overseas should breed social security at home. British citizens wanted protection not just against foreign enemies but against want, illness, unemployment and even the unfair distribution of income. This sense of insecurity was increased when, at the very moment peace was declared, the world was hit by an influenza pandemic. In 1918 and 1919 some 228,000 deaths were recorded in Britain alone, heavily concentrated among the young. With returning imperial troops spreading the disease to their native lands, the worldwide death toll was reputedly fifty million, making it the greatest human disaster in recorded history, worse even than the Black Death.

A month after the armistice Lloyd George held an election, the first to include women. He exploited his status as war leader and argued for a continued coalition with the Tories to aid reconstruction. Given the antagonism towards him of Asquith and roughly half the Liberal MPs, he colluded with the Conservatives not to put up candidates against supportive Liberals. These unchallenged candidates were sent a letter signed by Lloyd George and the Conservative leader Andrew Bonar Law. The letters were derided by Asquith as 'coupons', causing the 1918 poll to be dubbed the 'coupon election'. The coalition won overwhelmingly, though its 478 MPs were mostly

Conservatives. Asquith's Liberals joined Labour in opposition, but the Liberal party would never again be regarded as a plausible home for the working class. That mantle passed to Labour, dismissed by Lloyd George as 'the extreme, pacifist, Bolshevist group'.

The election was dominated by anti-German hysteria, with calls to 'hang the Kaiser' and 'squeeze the German lemon till the pips squeak'. *The Times* refused to discuss the possible consequences of bankrupting Germany, merely demanding that 'we present the bill'. The 1919 Versailles treaty ignored pleas for caution in treating the defeated enemy from Lloyd George and the young economist J. M. Keynes, and sought the most humiliating way of punishing the Germans. This meant the allied occupation of the Rhineland and heavy financial reparations. Versailles meant that Germany's first taste of democracy was one of unsupportable debt, a predicament that was to give Hitler's re-founded National Socialist party an easy ride to power after 1925.

Lloyd George described Versailles as 'wild men screaming through keyholes'. Back home he reigned supreme. He was the first prime minister to govern in what approached a presidential style. He retained his wartime secretariat under Hankey and his outer office of aides in the Downing Street 'garden room'. His Welsh intonation elevated his oratory, said Harold Nicolson, 'to the class of Cromwell and Chatham'. In war he had bullied and cajoled the government machine to get things done. Now he did the same in peace. The government passed a housing act to subsidise 'homes fit for heroes' and required children to stay in school until aged fourteen. War mobilisation had doubled trade union membership and the government faced strikes by police, miners, railwaymen and even soldiers. Where they were in the public sector, the government usually capitulated.

Meanwhile across the Irish Sea, Churchill wearily remarked, 'As the deluge subsides and the waters fall short, we see the dreary steeples of Fermanagh and Tyrone emerging once again.' While Ulster Protestants continued to balk at home rule, at least without partition, Irish nationalists won almost all southern Irish seats at the 1918 election and, the following January, set up their own independent parliament in Dublin, the Dáil Éireann. This body, under the charismatic leadership of Michael Collins, declared open war on the British state. Ireland at the time was still ruled and policed by the mostly Protestant British. Terrorist outrages by the IRA were met with equal brutality by 'Black and Tan' police auxiliaries, many of them soldiers disbanded from the western front. Ireland was plunged into a guerrilla war, culminating in undisciplined soldiers burning villages and, in December 1920, the entire centre of Cork. Even under Lloyd George, British policy in Ireland was repressive and counter-productive. A Labour party report in early 1921 warned that 'there are things [in Ireland] being done in the name of Britain which must make her name stink in the eyes of the world'. Eventually the Government of Ireland Act of 1920 led to a treaty negotiated by Lloyd George in 1921, providing for an Irish Free State, with a separate assembly for Ulster's six counties. The first independent Irish elections were held in 1922.

Lloyd George's coalition soon ran out of political capital. His financing of his private office through the sale of honours had become a scandal (£15,000 for a knighthood, £50,000 for a peerage). The prime minister's womanising was common knowledge, giving rise to the popular song 'Lloyd George Knew My Father', with variations. The coalition's stock fell. The economy entered a new recession in 1920. By 1921 the Treasury was overwhelmed by the burden of the government's social programme and the cost of servicing war debts. The 'Geddes axe', named after Sir Eric Geddes, a coalition minister, proposed cuts in public spending across the board, from defence to schools, and even cuts in the pay of policemen and teachers.

British politics were now complicated by the shifting tectonic plates of the British left, as the Labour vote grew and the Liberals declined and fractured. The Tories were almost always the largest party, but faced the necessity of coalition with one or other of Labour or the Liberals. In 1922 the Lloyd George coalition was increasingly irksome to most Tory backbenchers and, in October that year, a large group of them met at the Carlton Club in St James's and decided to withdraw their support from it. A midland MP, Stanley Baldwin, said he would 'go into the wilderness' if the party continued to back a prime minister who was rarely seen in the Commons and who ruled by a personal 'kitchen cabinet'. Lloyd George was, said Baldwin, 'that terrible thing, a dynamic force'. The prompt collapse of the coalition precipitated a general election that year, which the Tories won with an overall majority. In celebration, Tory backbenchers thereafter called themselves the 1922 Committee. The Liberals remained divided and Labour took the position of official opposition. The 'Welsh wizard' was no more. Lloyd George could take credit as a principal founder of the welfare state and for his role in winning the war, but he had split his party, and done so not, like Peel or Gladstone, on a matter of principle but to hold on to personal power. Faced with the challenge of adapting Liberalism to embrace organised labour, he suffered a failure of political imagination. He condemned his party to the political wilderness for the rest of the century.

Baldwin, the new Tory prime minister, was perfectly cast as reassuring contrast, the archetypal safe pair of hands, a pipe-smoking countryman, sensible, moderate and conciliatory. When trouble beckoned, he was said to retreat to his room with a crossword until it blew over. Yet as soon as he took office, Baldwin was seized by a conviction, borrowed from Joseph Chamberlain, that the recovery of the British economy needed tariffs. This was so drastic a change in policy that, with Liberals and Labour opposed, he felt he should call an early election

on the issue. In this he miscalculated. The 1923 election was
fought over 'food taxes' and the Tories lost ground. They were
still the largest party but in a minority, with Labour in second
place. Asquith, now again official Liberal leader, argued that
the electorate had voted overwhelmingly against tariffs and,
since Labour was the largest anti-tariff party, it should form a
government, with his support.

In January 1924 Ramsay MacDonald was duly sworn in as
the first Labour prime minister. The arrival of Labour in power,
within living memory of working-class enfranchisement,
was considered sensational. Many on the right declared it
would mean the Russians would take over, property would be
confiscated, marriage banned and free love licensed. Some fled to
sybaritic lifestyles in Kenya and Rhodesia in preference. When
MacDonald took his senior ministers to the palace, the press
debated whether they should wear top hats, bow, kiss hands and
appoint hereditary peers. (The question of peers was resolved by
appointing only those with no male heirs.) As the new ministers
awaited the king's presence, one of them, J. R. Clynes, reflected
on 'MacDonald, the starveling clerk, Thomas, the engine driver,
Henderson, the foundry labourer, and Clynes, the mill-hand, all
to this pinnacle!' MacDonald took easily to the Buckinghamshire
mansion of Chequers, recently donated by the Lee family as a
place of 'rest and recreation for prime ministers for ever'. He
was soon accused of the occupational hazard of Labour leaders,
falling under the spell of office and being embraced by high
society, so-called 'champagne socialism'.

MacDonald's government was not a success. He relied on the
government's minority status to curb the socialist inclination
of some of his colleagues, but his every move was treated
with suspicion by the Tories and a mostly Tory press. When
the government withdrew the prosecution of a communist
newspaper for incitement, it was accused of being under the
influence of revolutionary groups and lost a vote of confidence.

MacDonald felt he should call what was the fourth election in six years. The cause of the left was not aided by events in Russia, which still cast a shadow over British politics. The opposition, eager to exploit any 'red scare', seized on what turned out to be a forged letter from a Soviet leader, Grigory Zinoviev, advocating 'a successful rising in the working districts of England' and bringing 'the ideas of Lenin to Britain and the colonies'. Baldwin skilfully used the new medium of radio to promise 'sane, commonsense government' and not 'revolutionary theories and hare-brained schemes'. Labour was bundled out of office with 419 Tory MPs to Labour's 151. The Liberals managed to win just forty seats.

Baldwin spoke for a nation that craved a return to pre-war normality. As the peacetime economy began to recover, the benefits of modernisation that had been enjoyed by only the richer Edwardians spread to a wider middle class. The position of women changed radically. A post-war shortage of men demanded a new self-reliance, while the growth of retail and clerical employment offered young women a new urban independence. The apostle of 'family planning', Marie Stopes, preached to a generation with access to the sexual liberation of contraception. Registered divorces increased from 823 in 1910 to 4,522 in 1928. The consumer economy boomed. The number of cars on the roads of Britain was doubling each year. Home ownership rose from 10 per cent in 1910 to a third by the end of the thirties, far ahead of anywhere else in Europe. The resulting low-density housing estates spread in 'ribbon development' across suburban England. A mere 20 per cent of English people now lived in something that could be called the countryside.

In government the spirit of Lord Salisbury returned. The Conservatives' policy of promising 'tranquillity and freedom from adventures and commitments both at home and abroad', never again to be 'the policeman of the world', was popular. The Locarno summit conference in October 1925 saw the war combatants affirm their everlasting respect for peace and for each other's borders. So enthusiastic was the Foreign Office with 'the spirit of Locarno' that it named its chief reception room after it. Britons yearned to put the trumpets and drums of battle behind them. Even the British empire was amended. In 1926 an imperial conference fashioned a new entity from the old self-governing dominions of Canada, Australia, New Zealand and South Africa, giving it the Cromwellian name 'Commonwealth'. It did not embrace non-white colonies.

In 1924 Baldwin brought Churchill back to the cabinet as a Liberal-turned-Tory chancellor of the exchequer. Churchill then made a mistake that was to hover over his career like Gallipoli, fixing the pound sterling against a price in gold at a rate considered far too high. Britain's coal exports were instantly rendered uncompetitive on world markets, leading to a cut in mining output and thus in wages. In May 1926 the TUC called on all unions to back the miners in Britain's first and only general strike. The stoppage was near universal across key industries and briefly evoked a wartime spirit among the public. Churchill edited a government newspaper and the brigade of guards escorted food from the docks. Oxford undergraduates had fun driving buses. But opinion was divided, with even the usually conservative king being heard to say of the strikers, 'Try living on their wages before you judge them.'

The cabinet struggled to mediate between the intransigent parties. One minister remarked that the miners' leaders 'might be thought the stupidest men in England, if we had not had frequent occasion to meet the mine owners'. Baldwin was in his element as peacemaker. Despite his reputed remark that a cabinet should never push its nose 'dead against the pope or the National Union of Mineworkers', he succeeded in isolating the coal industry following a commission of inquiry, and the TUC agreed to end the strike after just nine days, though the miners fought on alone and unsuccessfully. The strike took on legendary status as an example of working-class solidarity, though the union's sense of betrayal at the way it ended also showed the limitations on its power. Baldwin's lack of triumphalism afterwards, indeed his consoling personality, was critical throughout. He was always affable, not least to new Labour MPs, and later supported their demand that unions should be able to levy their members to finance their party. With Neville Chamberlain as minister for health, welfare and local government, the Tories remained in the liberal tradition of Peel, Disraeli and Neville's father, Joseph. The old poor law guardians were wound up and elected county and borough councils made responsible for clinics and the relief of poverty.

Despite Baldwin's personal popularity, the Tories lost the 1929 election, possibly as a result of finally extending the vote to the last disenfranchised adults, women in their twenties, the so-called 'flapper vote' (after a free-hanging dress much in fashion). In another hung parliament the Liberals decided to put Labour and Ramsay MacDonald back in office. The new team had no time to prove itself. Within weeks, on 24 October, a bubble in US bond prices burst, leading to a crash not only on Wall Street but on all western stock markets. Guided by Keynes, the Labour cabinet proposed an immediate programme of public works, but this met with implacable opposition from the new chancellor, Philip Snowden. He demanded curbs rather than increases in public spending.

This familiar conflict yielded economic and political turmoil. Between the 1929 crash and the end of 1930, registered unemployed rose from one million to two and a half million and continued upwards. The following year banks failed across Europe, leading to German hyperinflation and financial collapse. By August 1931 Snowden's May Committee had out-axed Geddes, proposing £24 million in new taxes and £96 million of spending cuts, of which £66 million would come direct from unemployment relief, the so-called dole. Ministers exhibited every sign of panic. They rushed back from holiday, bank rate soared and gold sales emptied the vaults of the Bank of England, which unhelpfully warned that 'national bankruptcy is near'. The press carried such headlines as 'A Matter of Hours'. The relationship between publicity and confidence was as yet little understood.

Few Labour ministers could stomach Snowden's cuts and the cabinet resigned. But when MacDonald took his resignation to the palace, he returned to tell his stunned colleagues that he and not Baldwin had been asked to head a national coalition with the Tories. He would seek 'a doctor's mandate' from the voters to push through the cuts. MacDonald amazed even the loyal Snowden by telling him, 'Tomorrow every duchess in London will be wanting to kiss me.' On radio he declared, 'I have changed none of my ideals. I have a national duty.' In October 1931 a new election gave MacDonald his mandate, but only thirteen Labour MPs stayed loyal to him and he depended on 473 'national Conservatives'. As with Lloyd George in 1918, ambition had made him a prisoner of the Tories.

Politics was becoming increasingly polarised, driven by a highly partisan press committed to specific parties. Beaverbrook's *Daily Express* and Rothermere's *Daily Mail* were Tory, the *News Chronicle* Liberal and the *Daily Herald* and *Daily Mirror* Labour. Socialism at the time played on continued guilt about the losses of the Great War and the continued poverty of the depression, driven by a mix of pacifism and mild communism. J. B. Priestley made his *English Journey* round the poorer parts of England in 1933. It was followed by the Jarrow 'crusade' of October 1936, in which 200 unemployed walked from Tyneside to London, fêted by the public along the way. George Orwell made more sedate encounters in his documentary account of *The Road to Wigan Pier*.

Some on the left turned to a glamorous labour minister, Oswald Mosley, who resigned over Snowden's cuts to form a 'new party', initially of Keynesian socialists. After a visit to Benito Mussolini in Italy in 1931, Mosley turned his party into the British Union of Fascists. At a time when democratic governments were failing across Europe, the appeal to 'vitality and manhood' and to modern dictators who, people said of Mussolini, 'made the trains run on time' carried some appeal. Had Mosley not lapsed into un-British uniforms, rallies and black-shirted thuggery, he would have been a considerable leader. As it was, while other nations responded to economic depression with Roosevelt's New Deal, Stalin's five-year-plans and the fascism of Mussolini and Hitler, Britain took comfort in a Scottish clerk and a West Midlands businessman. MacDonald and Baldwin implemented Snowden's plan, devalued the pound, raised income tax and cut the dole.

With recovery from recession, 1930s Britain resumed the economic progress of the mid-twenties. Exotic art deco factories appeared along London's Western Avenue, making consumer goods such as Hoover vacuum cleaners, Gillette safety razors and Firestone car tyres. Woolworth's proliferated in every high street. The previously private British Broadcasting Company was nationalised under charter in 1927. Its director, an austere Scot named John Reith, established a tradition of independence which has held, against many odds, ever since. By 1932 England and Wales had ten million radio listeners and two million telephone subscribers. Britain's answer to America's Model T Ford, the Austin 7, appeared in 1922 and was reduced in price in the 1930s to £125. By the end of the decade there were three million cars on the roads. Super-cinemas with names such as Roxy, Regal, Odeon and Gaumont towered over their communities, offering the escapism of Valentino, Douglas Fairbanks and Mary Pickford. American jazz became a craze.

Thus blessed, the British public took the pacifism of the previous decade to new lengths. In 1935 the biggest ever private referendum, the 'peace ballot', registered eleven million votes in support of the weak-kneed League of Nations and a prohibition on world arms manufacture. At the general election that year, at which MacDonald lost his seat, Baldwin returned as prime minister having been forced to promise, even to his own Conservative voters, that 'there will be no great armaments'. Ministers were acutely aware that Germany, under Hitler as chancellor from 1933, was not the reliable ally of Locarno and was rearming rapidly, but public opinion at the time was uninformed and naive about events both in Soviet Russia and, with less excuse, in Germany. In 1936 it also had another matter on its mind. The death of George V led to his being succeeded by the forty-one-year-old Edward VIII. The new king liked dancing and informality and took a keen interest in public life, famously saying on a visit to the poor of south Wales that 'something must be done'. But he was in love with a married woman, Wallis Simpson, whom he wanted to marry. Despite a clamp on publicity, rumour was rife and the king was eventually told by Baldwin that he would have to choose between Mrs Simpson and the crown. He said, 'In the choice of a queen, the voice of the people must be heard.' While the monarchy no longer carried political weight and Edward enjoyed some public support, the exemplary role a king must play in public life was felt to make his relationship with Simpson unacceptable. In an emotional broadcast on 11 December 1936, he chose Mrs Simpson and abdicated. He was succeeded by his brother, 'shy Bertie', as George VI (1936–52), father of the present queen.

In 1937 an exhausted Baldwin gave way to Neville Chamberlain as prime minister. As chancellor for six years, Chamberlain had steered the country safely out of depression and taken forward the welfare state. But he lacked warmth or a human touch in public, and was abused variously as 'a pinhead' and 'weaned on a pickle'. Nor had he and Baldwin, despite fast growing German belligerence, been able to sell the need for rearmament to the public. However, from 1938 Spitfire fighters went into mass production, new factories were opened and air-raid shelters planned for civil defence. When in September 1938 Hitler indicated his intentions to occupy the Czech Sudetenland in defiance of Versailles, Chamberlain travelled to parley with him in Munich. The nation was on tenterhooks, fearing war.

Chamberlain's arrival back at Heston airport, waving a paper 'symbolic of the desire of our two peoples never to go to war with one another again', was greeted with wild enthusiasm. He told a crowd later that he had brought 'peace with honour. I believe it is peace for our time.' Speaking on the radio, he added that it was 'horrible, fantastic and incredible ... that we should be digging trenches and trying on gas masks here because of a quarrel in a faraway country between people of whom we know nothing'. Churchill, now on the backbenches, was a relatively lone voice for openly opposing Germany, later calling these the 'years that the locust hath eaten'. But when he described Munich in the Commons as 'a total and unmitigated defeat', he was howled down. Whatever hindsight may suggest, British public opinion was massively relieved by Munich.

History was not kind to Chamberlain, seeing him as the principal appeaser of Hitler's Germany, though recent historians have been less harsh. Public opinion and most of the press were strongly for accommodating European dictators. They remained averse to a return to war, grasping at anything that might fuel their optimism. In addition this was the first generation of British politicians to govern under the aegis of a universal franchise and to feel bound by what they perceived as public opinion. The concept of consent to rule had finally asserted itself, and ironically done so against the security of the state. Chamberlain and his colleagues were also trapped by their military advisers. They had been rearming since the mid-thirties, but when the prime minister left for Munich, he was warned by the chiefs of staff that they were unready for any war with Hitler. Britain would be overwhelmed by a German attack and Chamberlain

had to buy time. He bought just six months. In March 1939
Hitler broke his promise to Chamberlain and occupied Prague.
In August he signed the Molotov-Ribbentrop non-aggression
pact with Stalin and, on 1 September, launched his 'blitzkrieg'
on Poland. The invasion breached allied guarantees of Polish
sovereignty and Chamberlain was forced to announce, two days
later, that Britain was at war with Germany. An army of British
soldiers crossed the Channel, as they had in 1914 and so often
before. This time they returned, at first, defeated.

The Second World War

~

1939 – 1945

THE SECOND WORLD WAR began as a classic contest between nations, waged by two authoritarian states, Germany and Japan, in pursuit of what Hitler called *Lebensraum*, 'space to live'. Probably nothing could have been done in the Europe of the 1930s to stop Hitler's invasion of Poland or Czechoslovakia, since no nation was prepared to contemplate a main-force attack on Germany. But the repetition of 1914 was uncanny when Germany struck east and west. As Scandinavia began to fall in the spring of 1940 and the scope of Hitler's ambition became plain, the political decks were cleared. Chamberlain resigned a defeated man in May 1940 and was replaced by the person who, throughout the decade, had predicted just this outcome of appeasing Hitler. Churchill's first speech to parliament as prime minister offered 'nothing but blood, toil, tears and sweat'.

German tank corps moved across the continent with unprecedented speed. By 19 May armoured columns had swept aside French positions and were racing towards Paris. To the north the British Expeditionary Force that had arrived eight months earlier was ordered to retreat to Dunkirk, where it had to be lifted from the beaches by a hastily assembled force of Royal Navy ships, with an attendant armada of 'little ships' that became the stuff of legend. Between 27 May and 4 June, 338,000 men were evacuated, 120,000 of them French, and only Hitler's order to 'leave Dunkirk to the Luftwaffe' averted the catastrophe of mass imprisonment. Virtually all the allied materiel was left behind. A British army had been soundly defeated, though as with so many British defeats, from the Crimea to Gallipoli, 'the Dunkirk spirit' was spun as a triumph of British fortitude in adversity.

Britain for the moment stood alone. Eastern Europe, Scandinavia and the Low Countries were in Hitler's grasp. Half of France was occupied and the other half was under the compliant regime of Marshal Pétain. Germany had treaties covering its flanks with the Soviet Union, the Mediterranean and Spain. In the east Hitler's ally, Japan, had already embarked on a war of imperial expansion, soon humiliating the British empire by overrunning Hong Kong and Burma and threatening Singapore and India. British invincibility was at an end. The nation faced the loss of all that Chatham, Pitt and Palmerston had secured and faced, for the second time in thirty years, the threat of a maritime blockade by Germany.

Churchill's response was a series of speeches that rank with the greatest in English history. Delivered to the House of Commons or on radio, they avoided false optimism and cliché, and used reportage and realism in a thrilling call to arms. On 4 June 1940, after Dunkirk, Churchill pledged, 'We shall defend our island, whatever the cost may be. We shall fight on the beaches. We shall fight on the landing grounds. We shall fight in the fields and in the streets. We shall fight in the hills. We shall never surrender.' On 18 June he declared, 'Let us therefore brace ourselves to our duties, and so bear ourselves that, if the British Empire and its Commonwealth last for a thousand years, men will still say, "This was their finest hour."'

America, as at the start of the First World War, held itself aloof, despite Churchill's constant pleas for help. Isolationism in Washington was strong, as was a considerable spirit of appeasement towards Germany. Yet Hitler calculated that, were America to enter the war, it would need Britain as a launch pad, a Britain that was now his one implacable foe in Europe. He needed to neutralise that option. During the summer, German-occupied ports along the North Sea and the Channel coasts filled with troops and landing craft in preparation for an invasion, code-named Operation Sealion. Despite the chiefs of staff's reservations in 1938, Britain's defences were considerable. They comprised a land army of two million men, a territorial Home Guard, and the largest navy in the world, as yet undeployed in Scapa Flow. Any German invasion fleet would be highly vulnerable to British air and sea power. The German Luftwaffe therefore had to put Britain's south-eastern air defences out of action.

What Churchill referred to as 'the battle of Britain' from July to October 1940 saw dog fights between English fighters and German bombers and their escorts, wheeling in the skies over Sussex and Kent. From below they seemed like gladiators in the Colosseum. The contest was resolved in Britain's favour, largely because German pilots were operating far from base. During the height of the battle five German planes were being lost to one British. The significance of the contest in averting invasion is much debated, given that the British fleet was still unused. The fact is that in September Hitler decided he could not risk an opposed Channel crossing and aborted Operation Sealion, much as Napoleon had aborted his invasion after Trafalgar. Like the French emperor, he directed his attention eastwards and gave England over to his bombers. Of the Royal Air Force Churchill declared that 'never in the field of human conflict was so much owed by so many to so few'.

The 'blitz' of civilian targets in Britain began in late 1940, probably in retaliation for the RAF's earlier attacks on civilian targets in Berlin. This mutual destruction of Europe's cities led to one of the war's most ghoulish strategies, the belief that the aerial terror bombing of civilian houses could destroy an enemy's will to fight. Britain also bombed such historic towns as Lübeck and Rostock to 'break enemy morale', leading the Germans to retaliate against York, Exeter and Bath, the so-called Baedeker raids of spring 1942. These attacks were followed towards the war's end by V1 and V2 rockets, developed by the Germans solely for terror purposes, landing across southern England at random and without warning. The loss of cultural monuments and even entire cities, along with tens of thousands of non-combatant lives, was militarily trivial. Yet the concept behind such air aggression survived for the rest of the century and beyond, revived by George Bush's 'shock and awe' attack on Baghdad in 2003.

Since British air superiority limited German bombing to night-time raids, city dwellers learned to sleep in shelters and underground railway stations, more than eighty of which were converted into hostels with bunks and primitive latrines, depicted in their eerie nightlights by the artist Henry Moore. Drifting through them would be songs recorded by the 'forces' sweetheart' Vera Lynn, such as 'The White Cliffs of Dover', 'There'll Always Be an England' and 'A Nightingale Sang in Berkeley Square'. Though much propaganda surrounded the 'blitz spirit' during what was a traumatic and panic-stricken time for many people, there was certainly camaraderie in adversity as both the Nazis and the government were cursed with equal vigour. King George and his wife Elizabeth became symbols of resistance when, rather than flee London, they were filmed viewing bomb damage at Buckingham Palace. Churchill was likewise a stalwart of 'London can take it', pictured in his signature boiler suit in his command centre under Whitehall.

The blitz diminished in intensity in the spring of 1941 but there was little other good news. German forces were advancing south and east. In May 1941 they captured Crete, forcing the British garrison to flee to Egypt, where another British army, the Eighth, was retreating before Rommel's Afrika Korps. Paranoia was widespread and censorship almost comical. Posters went up warning that 'dangerous talk costs lives'. The U-boat menace to supplies of food by sea meant extensive rationing, covering not just food but fuel, clothing, paper and building materials. Fish and chips remained off ration, after lobbying by the fishing industry to keep the trawlers at sea.

Civil servants struggled to run what amounted to a siege economy. Inevitably they became figures of ridicule. They made up slogans such as 'make do and mend' and wrote recipes using tinned fish, carrots for cake and egg-free apple crumble. They even dictated fashion under the 'Utility' trademark. Ladies' dresses were to be straight and boxy, with a maximum of two pockets and five buttons. Frills on knickers were banned. Ankle socks replaced stockings, which were imitated with eyebrow pencil lines drawn on the backs of gravy browning stained legs. Men's suits had to be single breasted and with no turn-ups. Some 2,000 'British restaurants' were set up, with three courses for ninepence. The comedy radio show *It's That Man Again* lampooned an official whose catch-line was, 'I've hundreds of irritating restrictions to impose on you.' He was one wartime character who never demobilised.

By mid-1941 there was still no allied army with a foothold on the continent. Hitler was approaching absolute dominance of mainland Europe and Britain's ability to continue the war was in real doubt. The diaries of Lord Alanbrooke, Churchill's military chief of staff, indicate the stresses on him at the time, with the two men in tempestuous rows, shouting and thumping tables. 'He hates me. I can see hatred looking from his eyes,' Churchill would say of Alanbrooke, who would respond, 'Hate him? I don't hate him. I love him. But ...' They stayed together, a partnership of extremes through most of the war, Alanbrooke's cerebral clarity balancing Churchill's bombastic leadership, both equally crucial to the outcome.

Churchill had to get American help. He secured a wartime loan agreement, Lend-Lease, from the American president

Franklin Roosevelt, though Congress remained neutral, in no mood for another rescue expedition to Europe and insisting that Britain pay full price for its supplies. Hitler then made a decision that was to cost him the war. Eager to secure the resources of Ukraine and the Baku oilfields and always suspicious of communists, he reneged on the Molotov-Ribbentrop pact and declared war on the Soviet Union.

In June 1941 Hitler's Operation Barbarossa against Russia saw the largest military operation in history, involving four and a half million troops and consuming Germany's resources for the rest of the conflict. Shortly afterwards, in December 1941, Japan made an equally reckless decision, to pre-empt potential American opposition to its imperial sweep across south-east Asia by bombing the US fleet in Pearl Harbor, Hawaii. The two leading axis powers had thus pitted themselves against the only nations capable of defeating them: Russia and America. A Japanese admiral was heard to say after Pearl Harbor, 'We have won a great victory and thereby lost the war.' With America roused to fury, Roosevelt declared war on Japan and Germany declared war on America. From this point on, only one outcome to the conflict was conceivable.

The fiercest fighting on land was taking place in north Africa. It was not until November 1942 that Rommel's British opponent, the testy and egotistical General Montgomery, was able to give Churchill the victory he craved. After long pounding and with superior numbers, code-breaking and air support, a British army defeated Rommel at El Alamein and prevented the imminent fall of Egypt. With the arrival of the Americans in the Mediterranean in November, Germany's Afrika Korps was forced to surrender. Coming after the fall to Japan of Singapore and the apparent demise of the British empire in the east, Churchill was relieved. Victory in Africa was 'not even the beginning of the end, but it is perhaps the end of the beginning'. The allies were now able to contemplate an invasion of continental Europe, though this did not begin until July 1943, with landings in Sicily and a long fight up the spine of Italy. By then the Soviets had defeated Hitler at Stalingrad and Germany's eastward advance was broken.

Allied naval and air commanders had by now scored successes against the Germans, aided by the fast-developing science of sonar, radar and the Enigma code-breaking computer. By the summer of 1944 Rome had fallen and the allies felt strong enough to open a western front in France. This involved what seemed interminable delays as southern England became a giant launch pad, with complex diversionary exercises intended to deceive German intelligence as to an invasion route. Operation Overlord, 'the longest day' on 6 June 1944, saw the arrival on the Normandy beaches of the greatest amphibious force in history, over 5,000 ships and 160,000 troops. The Germans fought a fierce rearguard action, retreating across France to make a stand at the German border. Their counter-attack, the battle of the Bulge, in the Belgian Ardennes at the turn of 1945, caught allied forces off guard and briefly boosted German morale. But the allied advance was relentless.

When Soviet troops reached Berlin first, they found that Hitler had committed suicide. On 4 May the surviving German generals surrendered to Montgomery at Luneburg Heath, and the war in Europe was over. Four days later Britain was able to celebrate Victory-in-Europe day. Churches and pubs filled to overflowing. Bunting for flags was declared off-ration. The royal family appeared continually at the balcony of Buckingham Palace and Churchill did likewise in Whitehall, serenaded with 'For He's a Jolly Good Fellow' by Ernest Bevin, one of the Labour ministers in the wartime coalition. All past and potential differences were put aside in an overwhelming sense of relief. Another three months were needed to defeat Japan in the Far East, where British and Gurkha troops had had to fight a fierce year-long campaign to drive the Japanese from the Burmese jungle. Victory was not achieved until the explosion on 6 and 9 August of two atom bombs on the cities of Hiroshima and Nagasaki.

By then the war had devastated half the globe, killing an estimated twenty million soldiers and forty million civilians, the highest death toll of any conflict in human history. The subsequent discovery of German concentration camps for Jews and other minorities shocked the world, as did revelations of Russian gulags and stories told by surviving British inmates of the Japanese camps. Instant histories, not least Churchill's own, depicted the war as Britain isolated and alone against the might of Germany. This was true only for a period in 1941-2, when little fighting was done. By the time of the Yalta conference in February 1945 it was Roosevelt and Stalin who divided the world. The empires of Germany, France and Italy lay in ruins, and America was adamant that Britain's too should be dismantled. The child had usurped the parent. To America, Europe's imperialism lay at the root of the two great cataclysms of the twentieth century. It was time for empires to end, or at least empires of the old variety.

Compared with the global total, British losses were comparatively modest. Some 375,000 service personnel were killed, just over half the number lost in the First World War, and 60,000 civilians had died in air raids. Two per cent of total war deaths were British, against 65 per cent that were Russian. But the impact on the nation domestically was traumatic. The extent of the blitz had the effect of melding a home front more closely than had been the case in 1914. The resulting extension of the powers of the state had led to conscription and rationing that affected every household. Careers were disrupted, families and neighbourhoods broken. Except at the front, women came to be treated as equals in national adversity.

It had been a war of a united nation, in which the word Britain was at last noticeably used more often than England.

Victory had come at a price that now had to be met. The empire could no longer be defended. The liberties of individual citizens would have to be wrested back from a jealous state, whose servants felt that they, and their regulations, had won the war. The contest was now over who would win the peace.

The Welfare State

~

1945 - 1979

WITH THE ENDING OF THE WAR in Europe, normal political service resumed. Churchill's coalition government dissolved and an immediate general election was held on 5 July, even as fighting continued in the Far East. It was as if a nation starved of democracy since 1935 could wait no longer. The campaign brought to the surface tensions long repressed, an exasperation with wartime conditions and a desire for something new. Former coalition partners fell into mutual antipathy. Churchill used the word 'Gestapo' of Labour's socialist proposals. The Labour politician Aneurin Bevan spoke of his 'deep, burning hatred for the Tory party ... So far as I am concerned they are lower than vermin.' The outcome was unequivocal, the first overall Labour victory in history, with 393 MPs. The Liberals were all but wiped out, winning just twelve seats. Churchill was shattered by his rejection. Like his ancestor Marlborough, he was left reflecting that success in war rarely evokes gratitude from the English people. After his hour of victory, he was unceremoniously shunted aside.

The new government was infused with a spirit of optimistic euphoria. It was led by Labour's coalition leader Clement Attlee, a quiet, modest man with, said Churchill bitterly, 'much to be modest about'. He drove himself and his wife in a small car, walked to parliament and crossed the park to his club for lunch. Attlee was perfectly cast to captain a crew whose wayward and contrasting egos might have sent their ship swiftly on to the rocks. They included the plain-speaking union leader Ernest Bevin at the Foreign Office, the tempestuous Aneurin Bevan at health and Herbert Morrison as deputy prime minister. Though many had worked together in the wartime coalition, they were not the best of friends. On hearing Morrison described as 'his own worst enemy' Bevin replied, 'Not as long as there's still breath in my body, he ain't.'

Labour struggled to keep alive the wartime spirit of emergency, claiming that the command economy that had won the war should be retained 'to win the peace'. Far more even than in the First World War, state control extended to every aspect of the social and economic life of the nation. This control was harnessed by Labour to the ambitions of utopian socialism. Already in the darkest days of 1942, the Beveridge report had proposed a new welfare state, taking responsibility for every citizen 'from the cradle to the grave'. A white paper in 1944 also asserted that in future it would be the job of government to maintain a high and stable level of employment, the apotheosis of a centrally planned economy. The 1944 Butler Education Act nationalised every state school in the country. Adopting the latest educational science, it ordained a national test at the age of eleven which would allocate children irrespective of class to one of three types of school: grammar, technical or 'secondary modern'. These measures, it is worth noting, had been a product not of socialism but of a Conservative-led government under Churchill.

The 1946 National Insurance Act did not beat about the bush. It implemented almost all the proposals of the Beveridge report, including child allowances, national assistance and even funeral grants. Within a year, nationalisation was extended to what Labour called 'the commanding heights' of the economy, the Bank of England, the coal mines, railways, aviation and road haulage, and later to gas, electricity and steel. In most of these cases the change meant little more than the Treasury purchasing shares in industries already placed under state regulation during the war. The chief beneficiaries were shareholders. There would also be ten national parks, the first four covering the Lakes, the Peak District, Snowdonia and Dartmoor.

In 1948 came Bevan's National Health Service Act, with a free general practitioner and hospital service for all. Opposition from the medical profession was overcome, said Bevan, only when 'I stuffed their mouths with gold'. The expectation was that charitable hospitals and public utilities would, like schools, transfer to local authorities. In part through Bevan's dislike of Morrison, a champion of localism, the cabinet opted for a centralised health service. Bevan said that 'if a bedpan lands on the floor in the hospital in Tredegar, it should be clanging in Whitehall'. This principle gave birth to a national health service that rivalled the Red Army in size. The age had come to pass where 'the gentleman in Whitehall knows best'. The trouble with the NHS over the next half century was that the gentleman kept changing his mind.

Once the post-war euphoria had passed, Britain seemed to relapse into exhaustion. The urban landscape was bleak. Its skies were grey with fog, buildings dark with soot and streets gap-toothed with bomb sites. To the dislocation of war was added the upheaval of soldiers returning, often to broken homes, a baby boom and rising crime. The 1947 divorce rate was ten times the pre-war level. As if to escape, no fewer than 50,000 British women married American servicemen. On one east–west crossing in February 1946 the *Queen Mary* carried 344 emigrating brides with 116 babies. The return traffic began only with the arrival of the *Empire Windrush* in 1948, carrying a party of 492 Jamaicans answering an advertisement for jobs in London.

Drabness was made more depressing by continued rationing, extended to include bread, which had not been rationed even in the war. Every village had its black market and its 'spiv', claiming access to secret supplies. There was a craving for style. Dior's 1947 'New Look' in Paris, with voluminous flared skirts, was not permitted in London until clothes rationing ended in 1949. The housing shortage was acute, with thousands of bombed-out families still living in hostels and shelters, and even in parts of the London Underground. Rather than let the private sector cope, the government offered temporary prefabricated houses made in old aircraft factories. These 'prefabs' proved twice as expensive as houses built traditionally in the private sector. The programme was soon abandoned, but some prefabs were still standing, treasured and even 'listed' as historic buildings, at the start of the twenty-first century.

Ministers were more susceptible to the blandishments of modern architects, eager to turn their backs on the shattered inner cities and dream of 'new Jerusalems' in the fields beyond. A New Towns Act in 1946 proposed twenty settlements at various locations, including Crawley, Stevenage, Redditch, Runcorn and Peterlee. Based on the pre-war garden city movement, they were noble in their intention of providing overspill houses for those living in cities but ignored the communalism of city centres. The dislocation of moving 'out of town' yielded the syndrome of 'new-town blues'. Stevenage was dubbed Silkingrad, after the minister of housing, Lewis Silkin.

The winter of 1946 added nature to the country's woes with some of the lowest temperatures on record. Mines froze solid and factories closed for want of power. The public had to queue for both bread and coal, in a sullen submissiveness reflecting refugee scenes on the continent of Europe. In January 1947 the meat ration was cut to less than its wartime level. For many, peace was like war without the killing. In 1947 the pressure finally told on the cabinet. Attlee, under attack from a hostile Tory press, faced two plots to replace him with Ernest Bevin, in which he was saved by Bevin refusing to cooperate.

How far the economies of Europe depended on the $13 billion in American Marshall Aid, announced in 1947, is nowadays regarded as moot. Britain received £700 million in the first year, but it all went towards maintaining a high level of defence spending, very much at America's bidding. Churchill, the arch anti-appeaser, was now warning all who cared to listen that 'an iron curtain has descended across the continent' dividing free Europe from the Soviet Union and its communist satellites. In 1945 Britain joined the New York-based United Nations, successor body to the abortive League of Nations. In 1949 this was followed by a more robust alliance with other western states in the North Atlantic Treaty Organisation, intended as a bulwark against Soviet expansionism and, as a catchphrase went, 'to keep the Germans down, the Americans in and the Russians out'. Britain's loss of world power status had gathered pace. The cabinet in 1947 declared that India should be given its independence at once, on the advice of the last viceroy, Lord Mountbatten. The result of the precipitate partition of the country into India and Pakistan was disastrous massacres across the religious divide. In 1948, Britain also withdrew its authority, mandated by the old League of Nations, from the now partitioned Palestine. This too descended into war The implication was clear. Britain's overseas policy would change its focus under America's aegis from preserving an empire to deterring communism.

Labour narrowly won the February 1950 election. On 25 June that year communist North Korea invaded the south, precipitating the first conflict of what came to be known as the cold war. Britain was still spending a higher proportion of its wealth on defence than ever before in peacetime. To pay for a British contingent to serve alongside the Americans in Korea, the government raised health charges, leading Bevan and other left-wingers to resign. Conscripted young men who thought they had escaped war suddenly found themselves shipped to the

Far East, for an ineptly fought conflict resolved by partition. It was the experience of Korea, above all, that kept Britain out of Vietnam two decades later.

Labour's swansong was an eccentric 'tonic to the nation', a re-enactment of the Great Exhibition of 1851 on the south bank of the Thames. The Festival of Britain's Dome of Discovery and pavilions to industry and the arts were intended as a colourful modernist break with the grimness of the past. Despite incessant rain over the summer, the festival was judged a success. At a second election in the autumn of that year, the Tories won a majority and Churchill returned to power at the age of seventy-six. His first act was to order the Festival of Britain demolished, apart from the Royal Festival Hall. The new government's slogan of 'a bonfire of controls' was meant to free people from Labour's post-war regimentation and bureaucracy, but the Tories did not reverse the welfare state or nationalisation. For the moment the welfare consensus of the past half century held good, dubbed Butskellism after two contemporary politicians of the centre-left and centre-right, Hugh Gaitskell and R. A. Butler.

Britain in the fifties was struggling to regard itself as still the world's leading nation. Children read magazines on 'how we won the war' and gazed at maps that depicted much of the world as in the red of empire. Britain flew the first passenger jet in service, the Comet, in 1952, and tested Europe's first atom bomb. Everest was conquered by members of a team led by Sir John Hunt on 29 May 1953, four days before the coronation of the new queen, Elizabeth II. The two events combined in an evocative morale booster. The coronation was the first national event shown on television, amid a pageantry and excitement compared with the crowning of Victoria.

No sooner had the new queen taken office than she saw her empire start to disintegrate. In colonial Kenya and Cyprus, British forces were deployed against violent uprisings, delaying an independence that was already planned for Ghana sometime after 1956. That same year, Churchill's successor as prime minister, Anthony Eden, threw the country back into imperial mode. He reacted to Egypt's nationalisation of the Suez Canal Company by colluding with Israel and France in a full-frontal invasion, landing at Port Said and attempting to occupy the Canal Zone. Pressure from an openly angry Washington, eager for good relations with Egypt's President Nasser, included the extraordinary threat, for an ally, of economic and oil sanctions against Britain. Facing a run on the pound, Eden capitulated and ordered a withdrawal. Though Suez was supported by a jingoist British public, the outcome was humiliating. It was the final signal that Britain's status as a world power was over. Washington now called the shots.

Eden resigned soon after Suez and was succeeded by Harold Macmillan, another elderly survivor of the First World War, whose ironic nickname became 'Supermac'. The Tories reverted to their traditional prudence, even aloofness, from world affairs. In 1957 they declined to sign the Treaty of Rome which established a 'Common Market' of the principal post-war states of Europe. Macmillan insisted on keeping Britain an independent nuclear power, with its implied 'seat at the top table'. Anti-nuclear protesters banded together in a Campaign for Nuclear Disarmament, formed in 1958, marching to London from the atomic research plant at Aldermaston in what became an annual festival of protest. Changes of a more refined nature came with the queen announcing that debutantes would no longer be 'presented' each year at Buckingham Palace.

Macmillan retained power at the 1959 election, re-elected by a public who, he had declared two years earlier, had 'never had it so good'. But self-doubt soon set in. In 1962 an American statesman, Dean Acheson, mused that 'Britain has lost an empire and has not yet found a role', a pointed reference to the country's continued detachment from Europe. In the same year the first curbs on immigration from the non-white

Commonwealth came into force. Racial conflict was seen in immigrant areas, notably in the Notting Hill race riots of 1958. Immigrant labour was to prove crucial in staffing the textile industry and in health and transport, but it was decided that this particular legacy of empire had to stop. The home secretary, R. A. Butler, pointed out that 'a sizeable part of the entire population of the earth is at present legally entitled to come and stay in this already densely populated country'. The Commonwealth Immigrants Act did considerable damage to Britain's liberal reputation but had little long-term effect, the foreign-born element of Britain's population growing from 5 per cent in 1962 to almost 10 per cent by the end of the century.

By the early sixties, like many parties long in office, the Tories were losing their touch. In 1963 they decided after all to join the Common Market, but were vetoed by the French president Charles de Gaulle, a 'non' he repeated in 1967. Macmillan's government was distracted by espionage and sex scandals, culminating in the spectacular revelation that the war minister, John Profumo, was sharing the services of a prostitute with a Russian military attaché. The affair was manna to the nation's new satire industry, which recalled the savagery of the Regency caricaturists James Gillray and George Cruikshank. *Private Eye* magazine was first published in 1961 and the often savage television show *That Was the Week that Was* began in 1962. They spelled the beginning of the end for the more staid humour of *Punch*.

Labour's new leader, Harold Wilson, was quick to capitalise on the mood of the 'swinging sixties'. He invigorated his party to harness the 'white heat' of technological change and reasserted the power of government to plan the economy into reconstruction. He scraped to victory at the 1964 election, enjoying the same novelty appeal as the Liberals in 1906 and Labour in 1945. Wilson was a determined modernist. The government amended Butler's selective Education Act and encouraged 'comprehensive' secondary education. It presided over a major programme of social reform largely championed by a liberal home secretary, Roy Jenkins, including the abolition of capital punishment and the liberalisation of laws on divorce, abortion and homosexuality. In 1970 it introduced the Equal Pay Act, stipulating that women be paid the same rate as men for equal work, setting in train what was to prove a long campaign to reduce social inequality. The government even abolished the archaic authority of the lord chamberlain to censor theatres. The dubious outcome was a rash of onstage swearing and an unexciting display of nudity in the London musical *Hair*. British fashion and popular music was in the ascendant worldwide, though Wilson was much ridiculed for capitalising on 'Beatlemania' by awarding the pop group MBEs in 1965.

The Labour government was less successful in its hope that more thorough economic planning could modernise an uncompetitive British industry. It failed in two crucial respects, in not reforming the City's money market and in not securing labour flexibility through trade-union reform, trammelled as the party was by its need for union money and votes. In 1967 Wilson had to resort to devaluation to protect Britain's balance of payments, pleading desperately, 'It does not mean that the pound in your pocket has been devalued.' Devaluation demoralised the government and instigated a decade of drift and defeatism in economic policy.

England's old bugbear, Ireland, remained an incurable sore. In Ulster, the 1920s partition had ossified into partisan Protestant ascendancy. By 1968 a Catholic civil-rights movement had been taken over by the IRA, initiating what became twenty years of sustained, low-intensity warfare with the British army. By 1970 the province was in armed chaos and the IRA was exporting its bombing campaign to the streets of London. Try as it might, the government could find no way through another Irish morass, any more than it had done under Cromwell, William of Orange or Lloyd George. It would spend another thirty years in the search.

Others saw the fabric of Britain facing a different threat. Over the course of the 1960s, the Labour government had withdrawn from old imperial bases east of Suez, including Malaya, Singapore and finally Aden in 1967. This marked what was thought to be the end of Britain's role as a global power. But empire was not so easily discarded. In 1968 the government decided it should admit 50,000 dependants of existing Commonwealth immigrants, admitted prior to the 1962 restrictions, despite a poll suggesting 74 per cent of the public was opposed. A messianic Tory orator, Enoch Powell, called the decision 'mad, literally mad' and spoke wildly of his vision of Britain's streets like 'the River Tiber foaming with much blood'. This demagoguery, combined with Powell's equally fierce opposition to Europe, was too much for his Conservative colleagues and his expulsion from the party front bench led him to find common cause with Ulster's embattled Protestants.

In 1970 the Tories returned to power under a downbeat former chief whip, Edward Heath. Economic management was now the central theme of British politics, in particular the balance of power between government and organised labour. Heath signalled a break with the post-war consensus by declaring he would liberate markets and deregulate the public and private sectors, energised by the 'cold bath' of finally taking Britain into the European Common Market. This last he achieved in 1973, reviving a debate among the British people over their relations with Europe that stretched back to the Hundred Years War. If the bath began cold it soon turned hot. The Heath government seemed besieged by ill fortune. The Treasury had to implement the previous government's unpopular decision to decimalise the currency, doing away with much-loved (but inconvenient) twelve pennies to the shilling and twenty shillings to the pound. A civil rights march in Londonderry was suppressed by paratroops shooting dead thirteen unarmed protesters in what was dubbed Bloody Sunday. A soaring world oil price also stoked inflation and led to running battles with the unions. Heath had to perform an embarrassing U-turn to rescue Rolls-Royce and other 'lame duck' industries, and was then hit by a miners' strike.

The cabinet responded in line with the usual custom of governments throughout the century. Faced with trouble it opted for more control. A complex statutory incomes policy was imposed on public and private sectors, undermining Heath's free-market convictions and leading to further unrest, most seriously in energy supply. In December 1973 a wartime spirit returned with a three-day week in industry, long queues to buy petrol and selective power cuts. Drivers in London experienced the eerie sensation of passing from areas with blazing street lights to areas of total darkness, with much ironic comment that traffic flowed more freely in the latter. In desperation, the miners were conceded a 35 per cent pay rise, ensuring the demise of half their industry in the next decade.

Britain in the 1970s experienced what seemed a public collapse in self-confidence. A once all-powerful government has lost the ability to command the state. The visual scars of war had for the most part been eradicated from city streets, but what replaced them was hardly more appealing. Modern architecture reflected the loss of a sense of style. The comprehensive clearance of much of central Birmingham, Manchester and Liverpool removed familiar landmarks and replaced them with a blighted townscape of concrete and tarmac. The so-called 'new brutalism' of tower blocks, shopping centres and deck-access housing estates looked drab. London was narrowly saved from a 'motorway box' cutting round its centre, that would have run just north of Regent's Park, and from the demolition of much of Whitehall. While many war-ravaged cities in western

Europe were meticulously reconstructing their pre-war centres, British architects were more eager to mimic the clear-and-build modernism of the communist bloc.

A dejected Heath sought an early election in February 1974, on the issue of 'Who governs Britain?' After a bitter campaign, the electorate replied, 'Not you.' A Labour government was returned twice that year, first with a hung parliament and then with a narrow majority, but had nothing new to offer beyond increasing the top rate of income tax to 83 per cent, plus 15 per cent on dividends, the highest peacetime rate ever. The economic situation was dire. The government was consuming almost half the national product. Inflation was running at almost 30 per cent a year with growth moribund, a phenomenon known as stagflation. Whatever welfare consensus had applied since 1945, the economy had lost the means to pay for it. Foreign commentators talked of the 'British disease' and the nation as 'the sick man of Europe'. In 1976 Wilson handed 10 Downing Street to his old colleague, the ebullient James Callaghan, the only man to have held the offices of home secretary, foreign secretary, chancellor and prime minister. He told Wilson gloomily, 'When I am shaving in the morning I say to myself, if I were a young man, I would emigrate.' He admitted he did not know to where.

Although North Sea oil started to be piped ashore from 1975, the profit from it made insufficient impact on government revenues to rescue the Treasury from its plight. In 1976 the chancellor Denis Healey was forced to go cap in hand to the International Monetary Fund for a £2.3 billion bail-out, in return for which he had to impose some £3 billion in cuts to planned public spending. Callaghan himself underwent a Damascene conversion to industrial discipline. He was appalled by the behaviour of his old allies, the trade unions, asking his cabinet, 'What do you say about the thuggish act of a walkout, without notice, from a children's hospital?' He warned his 1976 party conference against the nostrums of the 1940s, of a world, 'where full employment would be guaranteed at the stroke of a chancellor's pen ... I tell you in all candour that that option no longer exists.' The long optimism of the twentieth-century corporate state, from Attlee's command economy to Wilson's planning regime, had run out of answers. It was the monetary crisis of 1976, rather than the later advent of Thatcherism, that marked the end of the post-war consensus. Government could command welfare, but it could not command the economy to pay for it. The economy was not an army at war.

Callaghan was talking to the deaf. Like Heath he was beset by a trade unionism boosted by public sector growth to an unprecedented twelve million members. But it now entered its death throes as a political force. A strike-bound 'winter of discontent' in 1978–9, came close to being a public-sector general strike. Frozen rubbish piled up in the streets and there were improbable reports of bodies lying unburied. At one point the prime minister reportedly told the union leaders, 'We are abject before you.' In March 1979 Callaghan lost his slender majority on a motion of no confidence when Scottish MPs rebelled against his refusal to grant them a measure of devolution. The cover of *The Economist* portrayed him festooned in Scots, Welsh and Irish regalia in his attempt to retain office. He proved another English ruler toppled by the Celtic fringe. His true foe was a withdrawal of public faith in the government's capacity to run the state apparatus created over the past half century.

Four years earlier, in 1975, the Tories' convoluted leadership-election process had produced a surprise successor to Heath, the forty-nine-year-old Margaret Thatcher. The Oxford-educated daughter of a Grantham grocer was never, as she liked to suggest, a poor state-school girl held back by male chauvinism. She had risen rapidly through a party eager to advance talented women. Sitting as education secretary in Heath's cabinet, she had watched its ignominious U-turns and was convinced they should never be repeated. She now said of socialism, 'No theory of government was ever given a fairer test or a more prolonged experiment. It was a miserable failure.' Kipling's line was always on her lips: 'We have had no end of a lesson; it will do us no end of good.' On 3 May 1979, Britain elected its first woman prime minister to Downing Street. She would put Kipling to the test.

Thatcherism

~

1979 - 1990

THATCHER WAS AN UNKNOWN quantity. Her own party considered her an outsider, even part of a 'peasants' revolt' against Heath, who would soon be replaced by a more plausible leader. She had a brittle personality and seemed over-groomed, over-assertive and 'suburban', an image relieved by her husband, Denis, a study in hen-pecked golf-club joviality, who was even the subject of a musical comedy, *Anyone for Denis?* It was reported that not one of Thatcher's former cabinet colleagues voted for her.

The new government took over from a punch-drunk administration running a punch-drunk country. For all her right-wing instincts, Thatcher came to office with an empty manifesto and just two beliefs, that the curse of the British economy lay in restrictive trade practices of every sort, and an overdependence by everyone on the state. She maintained that Heath, Wilson and Callaghan had failed to tackle them through a lack of will. 'We voted not for her convictions but for her conviction,' said one colleague. On the steps of Downing Street she quoted St Francis, 'Where there is discord, may we bring harmony.' She did not mean it. With inflation at 22 per cent the new chancellor, Sir Geoffrey Howe, proved as severe as Snowden in 1931. His 1979 budget reduced the top rate of income tax from 83 per cent to 60 per cent and, while protecting welfare payments, cut back public spending at a time of rapid inflation. Support for the government plummeted to near 20 per cent. Thatcher was adamant that she would not relent, even as unemployment rose past two million. As she said over and again, 'There is no alternative.' In truth she was echoing Callaghan in 1976.

The national mood was briefly relieved by the 'wedding of the century' in July 1981, between the Prince of Wales and Lady Diana Spencer. It was an occasion of extraordinary celebration and public happiness. Britons were able to reflect that they could still do some things well. London hosted 600,000 spectators and the event was broadcast worldwide to an audience claimed to be over 500 million. The rejoicing was punctured when London, Liverpool and other city centres were hit by the worst urban riots in living memory, caused by a cocktail of racial tension, unemployment and poor policing. The appearance was of Thatcher's draconian policy not only failing but leading to acute social discord. In a letter to *The Times*, 364 economists pleaded with her to change course.

Luck then played Thatcher two cards. Labour's choice of an elderly left-winger, Michael Foot, as leader to follow Callaghan precipitated the departure of a 'gang of four' Labour luminaries to form a new centre-left party, the Social Democrats. It briefly did for Labour what Lloyd George had done for the Liberals, splitting it to the advantage of the Tories. For part of 1981–2 the new party was ahead of Labour in the opinion polls and its leader, Roy Jenkins, was much tipped as the most likely successor to Thatcher as prime minister.

More surprising help came from overseas. Apart from a belligerent speech in opposition which, to her delight, led Moscow to dub her 'the iron lady', Thatcher was unobtrusive in foreign affairs. Soon after taking office she had sent her foreign secretary, Lord Carrington, to negotiate a final chapter of empire, the dismantling of Ian Smith's rebel regime in Rhodesia and the creation of Zimbabwe. Similar negotiations began over the transfer of the British colony of Hong Kong to Chinese sovereignty. The defence secretary, John Nott, used the opportunity to end the 'out of area' reach of the Royal Navy, timed for mid-1982. This passed unnoticed, except by the military junta in Argentina, which had long claimed sovereignty over a British-held island colony in the south Atlantic, the Falklands. In April 1982 Buenos Aires sent an overnight naval expedition to seize them. However illegal the act, the Argentinians had good reason to think there would be no military response.

The seizure of the islands left Britain stunned, so much so that, lacking party and domestic support, Thatcher faced imminent resignation. With both her foreign secretary and defence chief abroad, she gambled on personally despatching a naval task force to recapture the islands. It was a highly risky venture in which Thatcher could rely only on a close friendship forged with the new American president, Ronald Reagan. Though he was reluctant to commit US forces, he gave substantial material and intelligence support, and secretly kept a carrier in readiness. Two months later, following the loss of six ships and 255 British servicemen, the islands were recaptured.

Never did democracy so reward military victory. An inquiry by Lord Franks into the original invasion tactfully whitewashed Thatcher's negligence in leaving the islands unguarded in the first place. She received a ten-point poll surge and global celebrity, courted alike by Reagan and his Soviet counterpart Mikhail Gorbachev. Not since Churchill had a British prime minister enjoyed such widespread renown. Thatcher revelled in it, cloaking herself in the rhetoric of world leadership. She lectured the Soviets on ending communism and white South Africans on ending apartheid. She fought increasingly shrill battles with the emerging socialism, as she saw it, of the European Union and behaved tactlessly but effectively at its interminable summit meetings. She commented, 'We have not successfully rolled back the frontiers of the state in Britain, only to see them reimposed ... [by] a European super-state exercising a new dominance from Brussels.' In 1984 Thatcher won Britain a rebate on its excessive contribution to the EU.

In 1983 the Tories won their biggest post-war election victory, emboldening their leader to embark on a 'Thatcherism' which, as yet, had barely begun. She first had to survive an assassination attempt by the IRA in October 1984, when a bomb exploded in the middle of the night during her party conference in the Grand Hotel, Brighton. Five people died but Thatcher boldly refused to abandon the conference, merely asking Marks and Spencer to open early so affected delegates could have their clothes replaced. It was a remarkable performance, but after Brighton she retreated behind a security wall that distanced her from her colleagues and the public. She herself merely said it made her more determined to press on with reform.

The government was already in open conflict with the coal miners who, under Arthur Scargill, were striking against the planned closure of twenty uneconomic pits and the consequent loss of 20,000 jobs. Though new laws banned 'flying pickets' travelling to strike sites and required ballots in a form that Scargill had refused to implement, the dispute took on the character of a working-class last stand. One confrontation at a South Yorkshire coking plant, the 'battle of Orgreave', saw police and strikers fighting each other medieval style, with sticks and stones and on horseback. The strike continued with mounting bitterness until it collapsed in March 1985. Widespread pit closures followed. Other battles with organised labour followed, notably at the News International printing plant at Wapping in east London. As traditional industries continued to decline, jobs boomed in the more competitive service sector. The power of the unions was waning and by the mid-eighties Thatcher's medicine at last appeared to be working.

On what was supposedly her flagship policy of privatisation, Thatcher was more tentative, not least because she was aware of the political price she was already paying for the severity of the first three budgets of the 1980s. In local government she ordered the private tendering of services such as refuse collection, and demanded that tenants be given the 'right to buy' their council accommodation. She capped local government spending more tightly than anywhere else in Europe, and in 1985 abolished London's strategic government, the Greater London Council, then in the left-wing hands of Ken Livingstone. Yet Thatcher balked at the privatisation of the coal mines, the railways or the Post Office, all of which she regarded as 'national'. Her identification with the nation was reflected in her referring to Britoil as 'my oil' and quarrelling with the European Union over 'my money'. Though in most respects a Peelite, Thatcher was also deft at playing Disraeli.

The 1983 replacement of Howe at the Treasury by Nigel Lawson, a former financial journalist and vigorous free-marketeer, saw privatisation come alive. The list of those coming forward for sale showed how far the post-war consensus had extended nationalisation across almost every sector of the economy. It included car makers, train builders, oil companies, airlines, airports, ferries, seaports, computer manufacturers, telephones, steel, gas and electricity. Activities which, until the war, had been firmly in the private sector were steadily sold back to it. Then in 1986 Lawson moved into the hitherto sacrosanct territory of financial services. The City of London 'big bang' on 27 October admitted foreign firms into the most jealously guarded of markets, merchant banking, and permitted building societies to compete as well. Barriers came down and caution went to the winds. Fuelled by the flotation of privatised utilities, the City economy boomed, until a year later on Black Monday in October 1987, the markets crashed. This coincided, ominously to some, with the biggest storm in living memory, with winds of 120 mph and forests felled across south-east England. The City recovered quicker than the trees, and within ten years London rivalled New York as capital of world finance. But the economy acquired a dependence on financial services which, two decades later, was to cost it dear.

By now 'Thatcher's Britain' had taken on a distinctive character. The country had recovered from the trauma of the seventies and was inching its way back up the league table of European prosperity. Most people were richer, including those on state benefits, though much media attention was paid to the spending on cars and houses of 'yuppies' (young urban professionals). The first generation of graduates from the rapidly growing new universities, as many women as men, were fighting for jobs. The millionaire market trader and the upwardly mobile working-class 'Essex man' were satirised in Caryl Churchill's 1987 play *Serious Money*. There was a harder edge to the London theatre, the buildings of London's Canary Wharf and such 'shoulder-pad' television imports as *Dallas* and *Dynasty*. London was getting more like New York. If the sixties had been herbivorous and the seventies carnivorous, the eighties were indiscriminately omnivorous.

Despite her image for ruthlessness, Thatcher proved closer to what she regarded as the notorious consensus than many supposed. She found it hard to curb welfare spending, which continued to rise throughout the eighties. Expenditure increased even on housing subsidies, for which she felt particular distaste, unless they took the form of mortgage subsidies for home-buyers. One right-winger, Nicholas Ridley, even dismissed the 1983 government as 'Thatcher's wasted years'. Certainly it was not until after her third election victory in 1987 that she felt strong enough to attack Whitehall departments with the same vigour she had shown towards local government and the state trading sector. Even here she backed away from privatising the NHS, while at education her changes were centralising rather than privatising. She introduced England's first ever national curriculum for schools, built round a 'core' of English, science and technology, and demoting history and geography. Changes in the running of universities ended an autonomy dating back to the Middle Ages. The education secretary, Kenneth Baker, in his 1988 white paper declared that they should come 'closer to the world of business'. It was 1940s central planning revived. The arm's-length University Grants Committee was abolished and academic assessment came directly under Whitehall, with scholars 'scored' by books published and papers written.

Thatcher's stamina was extraordinary. She would stay up late over a whisky and rise early after little more than four hours' sleep, to be groomed by her hairdresser as she listened to the farming news. A private secretary would be present to convey her regular outbursts against 'over-subsidised farmers' to the duty clerk at the agriculture ministry. By the end of the decade, however, she was visibly tiring. She gloried in the fall of the Berlin wall in November 1989, feeling it vindicated a lifetime's strident anti-communism. But she was out of touch with the mood of the time in strongly opposing the reunification of Germany. In dealing with colleagues, her egocentric and hectoring style made her difficult to work with and she retreated, like so many long in office, into a Downing Street cabal.

Thatcher's last year in office saw her authority disintegrate. In her 1987 manifesto she had promised to replace local property taxes, then known as the rates, with a 'community charge'. In reality this was the first poll tax since the time of John of Gaunt, and was popularly known as such. It was imposed in Scotland in 1989 and was so unpopular that Tory support collapsed north of the border. The English tax began in 1990 and was met with a serious riot in Trafalgar Square in March. By the year's end default orders had been imposed on 2.8 million non-payers. Tory MPs were close to despair over the tax's impact on their re-election prospects. To this strain was added the defection of

Thatcher's two most loyal lieutenants, Lawson and Howe, as chancellor and foreign secretary respectively. Both had wanted Britain to join the new European exchange rate mechanism (ERM), precursor to a common European currency. The issue did not seem crucial at the time, but cabinet relations were so bad that both men resigned within a year, in 1989 and 1990, leaving Thatcher politically exposed. In a devastating resignation speech on 13 November 1990 Howe spoke of his colleagues negotiating in Europe and finding that, 'the moment the first balls are bowled, their bats have been broken before the game by the team captain'.

Tension rose swiftly. Taking his cue from Howe, Michael Heseltine, a long-standing critic of Thatcher's dictatorial style, challenged her to a leadership contest. Though she won the first ballot, her majority was insufficient to avert a second round in which the bottom candidates stood down. In this round it seemed likely that she would lose. On 22 November she called her cabinet colleagues into her room one by one for advice. Each recommended that she resign rather than risk defeat by Heseltine, a leader few of them would welcome. She was shattered. The occasion was to be called the 'Downing Street defenestration'. To the surprise of the country and the amazement of the outside world, Thatcher did indeed resign. At a final question time that afternoon in the House of Commons, the Labour leader Neil Kinnock tried lamely to attack her. She later remarked how thankful she was to be freed to attack him and all her critics in return, 'or I might have cried'. She concluded to laughter, 'I am beginning to enjoy this.'

Margaret Thatcher's leadership both succeeded and foundered on the nature of her personality. She came to epitomise the Tories as hard-faced and class-biased, dubbed by their enemies the 'nasty' party. One of her more challenged remarks was 'there is no such thing as society'. While Thatcher's command of the cabinet and the Commons was masterful, her judgment degenerated the further it went from Westminster. It was particularly weak where politics has its ultimate bite, among the small platoons of Little England. She all but dismantled the Tory machine in the big cities, if not the shires, and devastated her party workers with the poll tax. Nor could she handle others who had assailed England's rulers throughout history, leaders on the Celtic fringe and on the continent of Europe. To them, as to much of working-class England, Thatcherism's legacy was shuttered steelworks, silent pits and cold glass towers rising over London's City and docklands, housing financiers with sky-high bonuses.

Thatcher was a ruler in Norman rather than Saxon style, a centralist and certainly no apostle of devolution or laissez faire. She believed in the power of the state, and in her elective right to wield it. While she disposed of much of the old public trading sector, what remained in government ownership was concentrated under ever tighter personal and Treasury control. Local democracy, responsible for 85 per cent of political participation in Britain, was emasculated. The relative independence of the courts, the universities, the education and health authorities and the police was weakened by a raft of legislation transferring policy over them to Whitehall. Thatcher's state was a London-based governing machine with statutes stuffed with 'Henry VIII' clauses, allowing ministers to make discretionary decisions without recourse to parliament.

For all that, Thatcher's achievement was extraordinary. She was the first British leader in half a century to attain the status of a world figure. Britain in the seventies had been the sick man of Europe, writhing in self-doubt and uncertainty, its capital city challenged as the commercial centre of Europe by Frankfurt and Brussels. Thatcher put an end to this. She reasserted the concept of 'governability', in abeyance since Heath, and revived the so-called Victorian values of authority, hard work and moral behaviour, lurching into what was called the 'nanny state' with a rapid extension of health and safety regulation. Yet Thatcher presided over an increasingly permissive and undeferential society. Whatever she might have wished, there was no reversal of the social revolution of the 1960s and 1970s. There was no going back on reforms to divorce or abortion. Most striking, Thatcher acknowledged the public's acceptance of homosexuality, one of the most momentous changes in social mores during her tenure.

By the 1990s foreign governments were lining Whitehall to seek advice on the 'Thatcher way'. Germans, French, Mexicans, Brazilians, even Americans had had strike-bound 'winters of discontent' as they emerged from their version of the post-war welfare consensus. Everywhere faith in the potency of democratic government to order the political economy was failing as public sectors seemed to expand beyond the capacity of economies to sustain them. Thatcher was seen as restoring control, albeit by asserting renewed central authority. She cut Britain's inflation rate from 22 per cent to 4 per cent and reduced the government's take from the domestic product from 43 to 36.5 per cent. She put the economy back on the road to growth through a prescription of balanced budgets and privatisation. It had been tough, and Thatcher was admired but rarely loved as a popular leader. But by 1990 she had delivered a prosperity that had eluded her predecessors for a third of a century.

Thatcher's Children

~

1990 – 2011

THE MAN WHO EMERGED as prime minister from the bloodstained chambers of Downing Street in November 1990 was Thatcher's most loyal aide, John Major. He had been chosen by his colleagues, so they said, 'to give Thatcherism a human face'. A kindly man behind a grey, much-satirised, exterior, he had an unusual past for a Tory politician, the son of a circus artiste in Brixton and without a university education. Major was seen as the safe pair of hands, the perfect 'club hon sec' and custodian of Thatcherism's Indian summer.

The new prime minister set about his task quietly. He brought back Thatcher's nemesis, Michael Heseltine, as his deputy and abandoned the poll tax. He stayed close to America in finishing the first Gulf war, expelling Iraq from Kuwait, and he negotiated a British 'opt-out' at the Maastricht talks on the future of Europe. This kept Britain out of the new euro currency zone and avoided restrictions on social and employment law. In 1992 Major led the Tories to an election victory that defied the opinion polls and stunned Labour. He won the highest popular vote in history, the only party leader to top fourteen million, though with a Commons majority of only twenty-one seats. The new government pushed ahead with privatisation, going where even Thatcher had feared to tread, selling water, coal and the railways and turning to private finance for new roads, schools and hospitals. Over all this Major sought to extend the comfort blanket of a 'citizens charter', the kind of vague 'contract' between governors and governed that appealed to turn-of-the-millennium politicians.

Major was unable to capitalise on his 1992 success. Despite Thatcher's misgivings, Britain had joined the European exchange rate mechanism (ERM) in 1990 and now found itself trapped in a mild recession and a run on the pound. On 'Black Wednesday', 16 September 1992, there was a classic sterling crisis and Britain withdrew from the ERM. Though the resulting devaluation proved beneficial, vindicating Thatcher's opposition to any sort of regulated exchange rate, the event was seen as humiliating. Major was now constantly at odds with his right wing over Europe and made unnecessary enemies in Scotland and Wales by rejecting all requests for devolved powers from Westminster. The Tories fell ten points behind Labour and did not recover.

More dramatic was the impact of the 1992 election on Labour. With John Smith at the helm it threw itself into the arms of a charismatic young MP, Tony Blair. He and an uncharismatic Scot, Gordon Brown, founded what was called the 'new Labour project', aiming to restructure the Labour movement from top to bottom. What began as a ginger group became a revolution when Blair won the party leadership following Smith's sudden death in 1994. At each party conference the project pushed changes to the constitution, emasculating union power, neutering the all-powerful national executive, replacing the old union block-voting system with one-member, one-vote for most internal elections, and depriving the annual conference of its traditional role in writing the manifesto. A mass movement whose character had remained little changed since the party's inception almost a hundred years before was turned, almost overnight, into a machine for winning elections under an all-powerful leader. The reinvention of Labour was astonishing. A history of feuding, bad-tempered meetings and splits evaporated as Labour became more like the American Democratic party that Blair and Brown had carefully studied.

Between 1994 and 1997 Blair and Brown, together with a political aide Peter Mandelson and a tabloid journalist turned 'spin doctor' Alastair Campbell, effected a second transformation. They reassured the public that Labour policy would not unpick those elements of Thatcherism that had proved popular. Blair refused to pledge a repeal of Thatcher's anti-union laws or her privatisation programme. Though once a member of CND, he was now in favour of Britain maintaining both a stock of nuclear weapons and a pro-American foreign policy. Brown vigorously endorsed 'prudence' in public finance, while promising no increase in income tax should Labour be elected. As a symbolic gesture, Blair and Brown removed the historic 'clause four' ambition of the party constitution printed on every membership card: 'To secure for the workers by hand or by brain the full fruits of their industry ... upon the basis of the common ownership of the means of production, distribution and exchange.' Just as John Major had been eager to distance the Tory party from the more brutal extremes of Thatcherism, so Blair distanced Labour from its socialist past and led it along a 'third way', one of the many catchphrases that adorned his programme. Both sides were fighting to capture the centre ground, and Blair was winning. In 1995, as he rode the crest of an opinion-poll wave, Blair scoffed at the embattled Major: 'I lead my party. He follows his.' The traditional ethos of left and right had been reversed.

The 1990s had seen Thatcherism bed down. The economy was substantially deindustrialised, relying for its wealth on financial services, information technology, tourism, culture and leisure. The soaring architecture of London's rebuilt docklands was devoted to finance and financiers. While the centres of English provincial cities continued to languish far behind those in the rest of Europe, largely through central government curbs on local enterprise, a countryside long protected by tight planning laws saw rapid development. The MII corridor in Cambridgeshire, the east midlands and the Severn valley sprouted housing estates and distribution sheds that consumed annually a land area the size of Bristol.

Agriculture showed resilience, largely underpinned by entrenched European farm subsidies. But rural Britain found new users. Walking, cycling, camping, even surfing, surged in popularity. National Trust membership rose from two million in 1990 to nearer three million by the end of the decade. The Glastonbury music festival attracted over 100,000 visitors a year. After the Kyoto protocol on climate change was adopted in 1997, politics acquired a 'green' tinge, with environmental activism calling on the nation to restrict greenhouse gases. From the mid-1990s the internet's world wide web began to penetrate every household, transforming daily communication and information retrieval. People could work from home, and economic activity develop in more distant parts of the country.

Labour's victory over the Tories in 1997 was crushing. An unprecedented 419 Labour MPs subjected the Tories to their worst defeat since 1906. Blair's campaign was unprecedented in its glitz, set to the pop anthem 'Things Can Only Get Better'. With his wife Cherie he entered office in May in an overtly presidential style. Parties crowded the Downing Street calendar under the rubric 'cool Britannia'. Peerages were showered on so-called Labour 'luvvies', from the arts and show business. Downing Street was the new Camelot. Ramsay MacDonald's champagne socialism was rebranded for the age of celebrity.

Presentation came to rule Blair's office. His closest Downing Street relationship was with his press secretary, Campbell, whose strong personality dominated the cabinet. Government seemed reduced to a succession of initiatives, each subjected to the test of, 'How will it run in tomorrow's *Daily Mail*?' The prime minister's style was described as Napoleonic or 'sofa government'. The veteran Labour MP Tam Dalyell compared it to the court of Louis XVI.

The Blair style found early expression in August 1997 on the death in a Paris car crash of Diana, divorced wife of the Prince of Wales. An extraordinary outburst of public grief was enhanced by a media 'narrative' of youthful innocence ostracised by a stuffy establishment. The royal family, no fans of Diana, were forced by public opinion to return to London from Scotland and join in a public mourning. A mountain of plastic-wrapped flowers grew outside Diana's home at Kensington Palace. Blair eulogised 'the people's princess' and her brother's hardly veiled attack on her critics was applauded at her funeral.

Blair acted with despatch on one matter that had vexed his predecessors. Legislation was introduced to set up elected assemblies in Scotland, Wales and London. A Scottish parliament was in place by 1999, the first since 1707. A new Welsh assembly, the first since the Middle Ages, met the same year. Talks with republican leaders in Northern Ireland had been secretly initiated by Major, and in 1998 Blair oversaw a 'Good Friday' agreement between Protestant and Catholic parties, though the resulting power-sharing took another decade to make secure. These measures transformed the politics of the United Kingdom. A non-English discourse was noticeable in Edinburgh, Cardiff and Belfast, with separatist parties gaining ground in all three and Scottish Nationalists actually forming the government in Scotland in 2007. After a millennium of centralisation of power in London, the British Isles were at last recovering some constitutional equipoise. It was possible that the never happy union of English and Celts might relax into a looser confederation, if not a repeat of Ireland and outright partition.

Thatcherism did not end with the arrival of 'new' Labour, however adept Blair was at disguising it. Thatcher was the new prime minister's first, and very public, official guest at No. 10. At the Treasury, Brown stuck rigidly to Tory spending plans and took pride in his one innovation, allowing the Bank of England to fix interest rates. Blair respected his party's roots sufficiently to introduce a minimum wage, a Sure Start programme for poorer children and, most dramatically, an act for freedom of government information. The last reform he later regretted, so much that he 'quaked at the imbecility of it'. Other bouts of reform, aimed at the running of schools, hospitals and local government, continued the Tory policy of private sector involvement in state services. Blair was particularly eager to privatise public investment, much to the profit of City finance houses. Nor was there any reversion to localism. While welfare in most of Europe was locally administered with less need for constant reorganisation, in Britain, investment and pay levels in the welfare state continued to be dictated from the centre.

By the turn of the century there was increasing evidence that the steady advance towards 'cradle-to-grave' welfare was under strain. The Blair government struggled to offer wider choice through diversity, sub-contracting and opting-out. Payments to the private service contractor Capita rose from £112 million in 1997 to £1.4 billion in 2005. All new hospitals built under Labour were funded by private finance, to the tune of £6 billion. New secondary 'academies' – schools that had opted out of the state system and were sponsored by private backers – sprang up throughout the country. Private companies also ran prisons and supplied traffic wardens and speed cameras. Blair hoped that privatisation would break through Whitehall's inertia, complaining of 'the scars on my back' caused by trying and failing to get things done. Cabinet fell into disuse. Its secretary, Lord Butler, reported to a select committee that there had been 146 cabinet papers in 1975 and just four in 2002.

The public endorsed Blair's methods by re-electing him in 2001, following which public spending began to rise rapidly. Leadership was taking the form not of decisions made by the cabinet but of targets and league tables issued from a Cabinet Office delivery unit. One senior civil servant complained of 'a daily cannonade of orders and initiatives'. Expenditure on 'change consultants' reached £2.5 billion in 2005, by when the cost of running Whitehall was rising at three times the rate of inflation. For all this spending, polls persistently showed opinion critical of the quality of government services. YouGov regularly reported majorities claiming things had 'deteriorated under Labour'.

Like most leaders who find themselves under pressure at home, Blair retreated to the calmer shores of foreign policy. He leaned heavily on his early friendship with US president Bill Clinton and in 1998 was rewarded with a spectacular White House dinner, to which he took an entourage with 'more than a whiff of imperial progress', according to his Washington ambassador Sir Christopher Meyer. A year later in Chicago, when British forces were fighting alongside America's to drive the Serbs out of Kosovo, Blair proclaimed a 'new generation of liberal humanitarian wars', justifying Britain's intervention wherever its leaders judged that evil was being done by one country to another and even by governments to their peoples. Though little noticed at the time, the old caution that had characterised foreign policy in the nineteenth and much of the twentieth century was being abandoned, moderately by Thatcher but massively by Blair. An aide to the gung-ho new White House incumbent, the Republican George W. Bush, complained that Blair had 'sprinkled too much adrenalin on his cornflakes'.

The new interventionism went critical after 11 September 2001, with al-Qaeda's attack on the World Trade Center in Manhattan. Blair's adrenalin level appeared high as he told his party conference that 'this is the moment to seize. The kaleidoscope has been shaken ... let us reorder the world around us.' Britain joined America in a retaliatory attack on

Kabul, followed by 'mission creep' towards a long-term project in nation-building. Blair signed up unreservedly to Bush's unilaterally declared war on terror, culminating in a secret agreement at the president's Crawford ranch in April 2002, to extend the Afghan retaliation into an unprovoked attack on Iraq.

Despite reservations over the legality of the war and the dubious claim that Iraq possessed 'weapons of mass destruction', Blair saw it as a modern crusade, arm-in-arm with America against militant Islam. The decision to invade Iraq saw London's biggest ever anti-war march, of well over a million people on 15 February 2003. Britain's occupation was to last six years and cost 179 British lives. The British army withdrew in April 2009, by which time Blair had committed it to a lead role in the escalating conflict in southern Afghanistan. The 2006 British-led expedition to assert NATO control over the province of Helmand degenerated into a debacle, with the Americans having to take over operations in the province in 2010. Though Blair won a third election in 2005, it was with the lowest poll share of any government in modern times. Iraq and Afghanistan had not dusted him with the glory of war, as the Falklands had done Thatcher. On 27 June 2007, Blair resigned after ten years in office and gave way to the unopposed succession of his old friend, but increasingly fractious colleague, Gordon Brown.

Blair's government, while extending privatisation into almost all public services, had striven to soften Thatcherism's harder edges. In 2004 same-sex partnerships were recognised in law and the 2005 parliament boasted eleven openly gay MPs. Climate change moved up the agenda, at least nominally. People still greedily consumed no-frills airline tickets at '£1 plus tax' a seat, but at least some worried about their 'carbon footprint'. Even the once-doomed railway reported more passengers each year, and reached its highest loading in peacetime in 2010. The new Tory leader, David Cameron, elected in December 2005, felt compelled to take a husky safari to the shrinking Arctic and plan a wind turbine for his London home. Cars, houses and foodstuffs were advertised emphasising their green, safe or health-giving credentials.

The other side of the coin was a government increasingly intrusive and oppressive. 'Nanny state' policies were fixated on all forms of security. There were daily stories of expeditions, events, concerts banned because of 'health and safety'. Britain was credited with the most surveillance cameras and the highest spending on police and public safety in Europe. Following 9/11 and an attack by suicide bombers on London's public transport in July 2005, the Home Office introduced internment without trial, a measure unprecedented in peacetime other than in Northern Ireland. Concrete barriers were erected round public buildings. Labour's penal policy was rigorous, taking the prison population to 85,000 in 2010, its highest ever. State agencies used the war on terror to justify what was essentially a wartime model of national security. New terrorism laws were passed almost every year.

Blair had rescued his party from defeat and brought it to terms with the Thatcher revolution. He was a poacher turned gamekeeper, opposing and then adopting the policies of his radical predecessor. While he mimicked Thatcher's aggression abroad, he chose his wars unwisely. At home he lacked her ability to make the government machine jump to prime ministerial command. He was in thrall to the right-of-centre floating voters much as his Labour predecessors had been in thrall to the trade unions. Blair's 'new Labour' was in reality a marketing ploy. His instinct was to swerve trouble and survive. He had come to office full of Saxon 'communitarianism' but left it with Thatcher's Norman state intact. Indeed, it was more than intact. Government spending had risen from 36 per cent of gross domestic product when Blair took office, to 47 per cent went he left, covered by heavy borrowing.

On one matter Blair was right, his private conviction that Brown was unsuited to national leadership. His aide Campbell admitted to coining the leaked phrase that Brown was 'psychologically flawed'. The former chancellor had overseen the Treasury for almost as many years as Gladstone, but had done so in growing conflict with his prime minister. As a result control over public spending collapsed. Brown's introversion and bouts of temper were ill-suited to high office outside the Treasury's ivory tower. He was unable to work with ministers with whom he disagreed, a serious handicap in politics, and he eventually turned to his old comrade, and latterly foe, Peter Mandelson, who in 2008 was elevated to the peerage and became virtual deputy prime minister.

By then Brown's Treasury excesses had come home to roost. Early promises to bring the NHS spending up to the European average and to rebuild every secondary school in the country had resulted in spiralling upward pressure on the budget. As world stock markets crashed in the autumn of 2008, Britain was floating on a raft of debt. The much-vaunted financial services sector saw banks peculiarly exposed, as first Northern Rock, then Lloyds and RBS shuddered and fell back on the state. At the height of the crisis, Brown asked taxpayers to underpin bank rescue loans of over £500 billion. Public confidence in government was not helped when, in 2009, hundreds of MPs were revealed as having made wild and sometimes fraudulent expenses claims. Politicians joined bankers at the bottom of the table of public respect.

Brown was defeated at the polls in May 2010, his failure mitigated only by voters delivering not a Tory victory but a hung parliament. The Liberal Democrats found themselves briefly exhilarated as they replayed the 1920s and 1930s. But they were kingmakers for a day and prisoners thereafter. A long weekend of parlaying with the Tories' David Cameron led to the Liberal Democrat leader, Nick Clegg, emerging as deputy prime minister in a Tory-dominated coalition, with a formally negotiated programme and insistence that there would be a five-year parliament. This was a curious rewriting of the constitution, since any coalition is vulnerable to erosion and collapse. The new team had immediately to rescue the public finances, reprising the cuts programmes of 1921, 1931 and the 1980s with five years of reductions covering virtually every part of the public sector. The economy was now in recession. For all the rhetoric of the 1990s that 'boom and bust are over', the ghosts of Lloyd George, MacDonald and Thatcher again stalked the corridors of Westminster. Protests and strikes erupted from students, public-sector unions, the police, teachers and health workers. British public life experienced a severe bout of déjà vu.

Beyond these immediate concerns, old tensions found new expression. Government yet again professed a desire to decentralise power from London and reduce the scale and reach of the modern state, yet found it difficult to do so. England remained Europe's most centralised political economy, with little local tax discretion, little subsidiary democracy and few public institutions free of state control. Local democracy, such as it was in 2011, was desperately stretched as central government searched everywhere to save money. Similar disciplines were demanded from the devolved assemblies of Scotland, Wales and Northern Ireland. England's parliament, guardian of its freedoms for over half a millennium, was also forced, under the 2009 Lisbon treaty, to share legislative powers with states across the Channel, as the courts had to share judicial power with a European court.

In other words the pressures that had vexed England since the Middle Ages remained the same. Government struggled to govern. The people, struggling, protesting and complaining, consented. But at centre stage was still the one institution that had guarded the constitution for almost a millennium: a constitution-based parliament. There was no sign of an end to an inherited monarchy. There was no call for a directly-elected executive, or even much call for proportional representation in the House of Commons. Parlimentary arithmetic created the 2010 coalition and would determine its stability and eventual fate. As Simon de Montfort's parliament had defied Henry III, as the Long Parliament had defied Charles I and as the 1832 parliament had saved Britain from revolution, so it remained parliament that dictated the government of England.

Epilogue

~

ENGLAND HAS BEEN A SUCCESS AS A COUNTRY. It matured early into nationhood, with remarkably little bloodshed and with only two sustained civil wars in its history, in the fifteenth and seventeenth centuries. By the end of the Georgian era most of its people enjoyed a security, prosperity and civil freedom that were rare anywhere on Earth. Even today, when other nations have equalled and even overtaken it, England still regards itself as a world power, with nuclear arms and claiming status with America as global policeman. It boasts pre-eminence in education, medicine, science and literature. Its capital city, London, its countryside, heritage and artistic activity attract visitors from all over the world.

A number of factors contributed to this success. Early in the story, the fertile geography of the eastern half of the British Isles suited the Saxon agrarian settlers. The borders formed by the North Sea, the English Channel and the uplands of Wales and Scotland were seldom peaceful, but they proved effective barriers against incursion. The Viking and Norman invasions were overwhelming, but did not obliterate the Saxon English. Newcomers were assimilated and Saxon settlements, culture and language remained largely intact. From then on, as Shakespeare remarked, England's insularity served 'in the office of a wall, or as a moat defensive to a house'. It was a defence that sufficed against Philip's Armada, Napoleon's grand army and Hitler's blitzkrieg.

The crucial fact of England's history in the Middle Ages was that it fell under the sway of a Norman dynasty that could not stop fighting. War with France lasted some four hundred years, off and on, from 1066 to 1453, ending only when the Plantagenets began fighting each other even more furiously than they did the French. Yet from this tribal belligerence arose the tradition of 'consent to rule', since to pay for their wars monarchs had to raise money and this required some popular collaboration. Nothing curbed Norman autocracy as effectively as the king's need for taxes. From this arose the power of the City of London under Richard I, a codified rule of law under King John and a House of Commons in the parliaments of Henry III and Edward I. This bartering of power was absolute. Even the ruthless Edward I worried that people might take against him, and 'the aid and taxes which they had paid to us out of liberality and goodwill ... may in future become a servile obligation.' He was right.

In the sixteenth and seventeenth centuries England was blessed with monarchs, counsellors and politicians whose talents guided it through storms of revolution to a new constitutional settlement. Henry VIII's marital woes drove him to shift wealth from the church to himself, and then on to a new middle class of merchants, lawyers and state officials. With wealth, as always, went power. Henry's religious revolution was entrenched by his second daughter, Elizabeth, one of the few European rulers with an instinct for a monarchy rooted in consensual government. In the seventeenth century, a newly empowered middle class engineered a second, political revolution against the Stuarts. Parliament disposed of the divine right of kings by executing Charles I in 1649, and of the royal prerogative by welcoming William of Orange in 1688. By the start of the eighteenth century England had rid itself of medieval autocracy and turned itself into a modern state. An assembly embracing England, Wales, Scotland and later Ireland established party politics, parliamentary procedure and judicial independence in forms that are recognisable to this day.

These forms produced a stability that emboldened England's maritime prowess and allowed Chatham and his son, Pitt the

Younger, to acquire the most extensive overseas empire in the world. This empire survived the loss of the American colonies in the 1780s and also the shock of the French revolution, events that led not, as many predicted, to rebellion but to a national debate, one that culminated in the extraordinary revolution of the 1832 Reform Act. The resulting Victorian prosperity saw parliament concede an ever wider 'consent to rule', as more and more Britons were brought within the orbit of the franchise. This underpinned what was now a United Kingdom's emergence as the leading world power, blessed with natural resources, free trade, a liberal tradition and a spirit of scientific inquiry and enterprise, all seemingly without limit.

Throughout this time, the central institution of the British state, a bicameral parliament, never lost control. It was unrepresentative and always hesitant towards change, but it respected open debate and ultimately chained government to the will of the people, guiding Britain towards full democracy and a welfare state in the twentieth century. The so-called 'game-changers' of English politics may be listed as Cromwell, Walpole, Chatham, Peel, Disraeli, Gladstone and Lloyd George, but it was the collective of parliament that harnessed their talents to the service of the state. At no point in English history did extra-parliamentary action find political traction. When it did so in Ireland, the result was catastrophe. If there is any hero in this book, at least until the twentieth century, it is parliament.

At the time of Victoria's death in 1901 these achievements were coming under threat. Free trade was undermining the economic power of empire. Other nations in Europe and America were outstripping Britain in capitalist enterprise and developing their natural and human resources. The rise of a competing imperialism, notably that of Germany, cost Britain dear in two world wars, such that after the second what was left of the British empire decomposed in just two decades. Nor was it only the overseas empire that failed. The earlier English empire within the British Isles was challenged. Ireland mostly broke loose in 1921, leaving Ulster to cause England continuing anguish. Separatist revivals in Scotland and Wales led eventually to the granting of partial autonomy. While the United Kingdom as a monarchy was secure, for the first time in history its parliament was forced to surrender power, both to the Celtic regions of the British Isles and to the a new confederacy formed of the states of western Europe. The Plantagenets would have turned in their graves at such concessions.

These changes led to tensions. Post-imperial Britain had, in the words of the American Dean Acheson in 1962, 'not yet found a role' in the world. Island powers are usually ambivalent towards their adjacent continents, but Britain was neurotically so. Towards Europe it remained divided and undecided. While the empire had been discarded with relative ease, the cast of mind that created it had not. The twenty-first century saw Britain involved in successive wars of 'liberal intervention', variously claiming to champion humanitarianism, democracy, nation-building and regional stability. At times it seemed as if the Norman crusaders were back in the ascendant. Once chosen by the electorate, the executive proved adept at treating parliament not as a check on its discretion but as a rubber stamp.

Doubts also arose over the scale of that executive. Twentieth-century war had meant a rapid increase in the size and scope of the state, continuing in peacetime to meet the popular demand for welfare 'from the cradle to the grave'. By the middle of the century, Britain's health, education and social services, its public utilities and much of its industry and commerce had come under state control. This drift of authority to the centre was initially greeted with approval as part of the so-called welfare consensus, but by the 1980s the size of government and its inability to curb or reform itself led the consensus to dissolve. One response was the privatisation of much of the public sector, pursued by Tory and then Labour governments alike. But even where state activity was subcontracted to the private sector, nothing seemed able to curtail state spending. By the start of the twenty-first century, government was consuming 47 per cent of the nation's output, a peacetime record.

It is as if Britain's governors, shorn of an overseas empire, now craved a domestic one. But this new empire was as unwieldy as the old one. Economies of scale had become diseconomies. Whitehall and its agencies were unresponsive to the checks and balances of what was still an informal constitution. The tax system appeared unable to sustain an ageing population, with a soaring health and welfare bill. Government slid easily into debt. The potency of the Norman state was reborn, but this time the Saxon people who had once fought to curb its excesses were now the grateful recipient of its largesse. The electorate willed the goals of state power, but balked at supplying the means in higher taxes.

Every age has its prophets warning against Leviathan. At the start of the new century it was widely held that the state, however benign its intent, cannot continue to grow inexorably, since the economy cannot support it. Across Europe, governments were proving unable to divest themselves of power. In Greece, Ireland, Portugal and even Britain, the spending of public money had grown ever more distant from the task of earning it. Yet democracy seemed unable to discipline it. Ask politicians why they cannot show stronger leadership and they will say, because the people who elect us will not allow it. Central government, long the agent of discipline, had become an accomplice in indiscipline.

Throughout history, England's constitution has been forced to change only when its rulers have been deaf to the cries of the people, or at least to the march of events. It happened when medieval monarchs yielded to baronial and territorial power. It happened when the church yielded to Reformation and to an emerging merchant class. It happened when Stuart kings yielded to the rule of law and to the commons in parliament. In each case the monolithic tendency of the state was confronted by resurgent forces in society to which it had to give way. Even the nineteenth-century parliament, England's greatest contribution to European civilisation, had to yield to popular pressure for reform, while the roots of the welfare state emerged not from parliament but from innovative municipal corporations. Change came because the ruling elite proved sufficiently open to challenge and competition.

I regard this openness of English society as the crucial message of history. Today it is again being tested. Unless the central state shows more respect to community and territorial loyalty, it starves itself of renewal from below, of innovation, experiment and new blood. England in its most potent era, the nineteenth century, was driven by a civic provincialism far from the metropolis. People are likely to lose faith in self-government when those exercising it on their behalf grow distant and unfamiliar. This is already noticeable in declining confidence in public services and a turning to private ones, for health, education and security. Few people in England can identify or name a leader of their local community. This anonymity is depoliticising communities and entrenching social divisions in a peculiarly domestic class system. While countries such as Spain, Italy, Germany and even France have devolved power to provinces, communes and mayors, England continues to concentrate it on London, Westminster and Whitehall.

That said, the picture is not all gloomy. The professions, universities, media and the law remain strong and relatively pluralistic, buttressed by such recent innovations as the internet, freedom of information, human rights law and a new supreme court. There is also a significant exception to the centralising trend, constitutional devolution within the United Kingdom to Scotland, Wales and Northern Ireland. The boundaries set for England in the Dark Ages are gradually re-emerging from the mist of time. The accretion of central power, required by the Saxons and then the Normans to define and defend England from the ancient Britons, is being reversed. The power of London, already withdrawn from the empire overseas, is now withdrawing from the empire at home. It is possible to see the acts setting up assemblies in Edinburgh, Cardiff and Belfast as the first documents of a new constitutional settlement.

England is thus losing the will to govern the non-English peoples beyond its borders, even those elsewhere in the British Isles. There is a continuing need for institutions of a 'united kingdom', as long as the Scots, Welsh and some of the Irish want them. But the asymmetric nature of the Westminster parliament, with England's government in partial thrall to MPs from the semi-autonomous Celtic fringe, cannot be sustainable in the long term. It is a distorted democracy. Sooner or later, England will need its own assembly, either inside or outside the ambit of the Westminster parliament.

I used to regard written constitutions as a device of immature states. I have changed my mind. The incorporation of the European convention on human rights into British law has already given Britain a sizeable 'written' charter, whether or not it is later supplemented or replaced by a new bill of rights. The tradition of constitution where, in Tennyson's words, 'freedom slowly broadens down / from precedent to precedent,' is no longer sufficient to guard against elective dictatorship. Rights need writing down since they are persistently under threat, whether from surveillance technology, an obsession with imprisonment and an ever growing state discretion. The scope of local democracy needs codifying, to refresh the recruitment pool of the London establishment and refresh a public sector that now consumes a third of England's wealth. There is nothing novel in this. Such layered, subsidiary politics operated through most of English history, and still applies in the rest of Europe.

It was to these open traditions in England's history that the American revolutionaries turned for inspiration in the eighteenth century, even as they rebelled against the English crown. They mimicked the independent Tudor boroughs, counties, sheriffs and mayors, and the hallowed democracy of the town meeting. They turned to the early rule of law, to the Long Parliament, the glorious revolution and the bill of rights. The nations of the British Commonwealth, such as Canada, Australia and even sub-continental India, followed suit. They wrote down what mattered, and were guided by it in creating what are now exemplars of world democracy.

The message of history is that nations evolve most successfully when any change, social, economic or political, surges up from below. Central power corrupts those who wield it, becoming a conservative, repressive force. Those who believe in freedom and democracy must forever hold it in check. Hence Kipling's ringing words in saluting the earliest such curb, Magna Carta:

> And still when Mob or Monarch lays
> Too rude a hand on English ways,
> The whisper wakes, the shudder plays
> Across the reeds at Runnymede.
> And Thames, that knows the moods of kings,
> And crowds and priests and suchlike things,
> Rolls deep and dreadful as he brings
> Their warning down from Runnymede!

One Hundred Key Dates

~

DATES ARE THE FINGER-POSTS OF HISTORY. I regard those below as the hundred most important turning points in the national story:

1277	Edward I invades Wales and defeats Llywelyn
1295	Edward summons 'Model Parliament'
1314	Edward II defeated by Scots at Bannockburn
1327	Murder of Edward II in Berkeley Castle
1337	Start of Hundred Years War against France
1346	Edward III wins battle of Crécy
1348	Black Death kills quarter of population
1381	Richard II ends peasants' revolt
1399	Henry IV usurps Richard II
1415	Henry V wins battle of Agincourt
1431	Joan of Arc burned at stake
1453	English defeat at Castillon ends Hundred Years War
1455	Battle of St Albans begins Wars of Roses
1469	Warwick the kingmaker switches allegiance to Lancastrian Henry VI
1471	Yorkists win battle of Tewkesbury
1483	Murder of two princes in Tower of London
1485	Henry Tudor's defeat of Richard III at Bosworth ends Wars of Roses
1509	Henry VIII crowned king
1520	Henry meets Francis I at Field of Cloth of Gold
1533	Henry weds Anne Boleyn
1534	Henry's act of supremacy over English church
1536	Dissolution of monasteries begins, execution of Anne
1547	Death of Henry, Edward VI crowned
1553	Accession of Mary I, start of Counter-Reformation
1556	Cranmer burned at stake
1558	Accession of Elizabeth I restores Reformation
1588	Spanish Armada defeated
1603	Death of Elizabeth, accession of House of Stuart
1605	Guy Fawkes' gunpowder plot foiled

1628	Parliament's Petition of Right against Charles
1640	Long Parliament meets
1642	Civil War begins
1644	Defeat of Royalists at Marston Moor
1649	Execution of Charles I
1653	Cromwell named Lord Protector
1660	Restoration of Charles II
1665	Plague hits London
1666	Great Fire of London
1688	Invasion of William of Orange, Glorious Revolution
1704	Marlborough wins Battle of Blenheim
1707	Act of Union with Scotland creates Great Britain
1714	Death of Anne, Hanoverian succession
1720	South Sea bubble
1746	Battle of Culloden ends Jacobite rebellion
1759	Climax of military success in Seven Years War
1781	Cornwallis surrenders at Yorktown
1793	French revolutionaries declare war on Britain
1800	Act of Union with Ireland creates United Kingdom
1805	Nelson wins battle of Trafalgar
1807	British slave trade abolished
1815	Napoleon defeated at battle of Waterloo
1819	Peterloo massacre leads to widespread repression
1832	Great reform act
1837	Accession of Queen Victoria
1838	Publication of People's Charter
1846	Repeal of the Corn Laws
1851	The Great Exhibition in Hyde Park
1853-6	Crimean war
1867	Second Reform Act
1876	Disraeli declares Victoria empress of India
1899	Start of Boer war

1901	Death of Victoria
1909	Lloyd George's 'People's Budget'
1914–18	First World War
1920	Home rule for Ireland
1926	General strike
1929	Great crash and depression
1936	Edward VIII abdicates
1939–45	Second World War
1947	Independence of India
1948	National Health Service founded
1953	Coronation of Elizabeth II
1956	Suez crisis
1973	Britain joins Common Market
1976	Callaghan seeks IMF loan to relieve economic crisis
1979	Thatcher is Britain's first female prime minister
1981	Wedding of Prince Charles and Lady Diana Spencer
1982	Thatcher wins Falklands war
1990	Fall of Thatcher
1997	Blair elected prime minister
2003	Invasion of Iraq
2008	Global financial crisis
2010	Coalition formed under Cameron

Kings and Queens
of England from 1066

~

NORMANS	1066 – 87	William I of Normandy
	1087 – 1100	William II Rufus
	1100 – 35	Henry I
	1135 – 54	Stephen and Matilda

PLANTAGENET	1154 – 89	Henry II
	1189 – 99	Richard I
	1199 – 1216	John
	1216 – 72	Henry III
	1272 – 1307	Edward I
	1307 – 27	Edward II
	1327 – 77	Edward III
	1377 – 99	Richard II

LANCASTER	1399 – 1413	Henry IV
	1413 – 22	Henry V
	1422 – 61; 1470 – 71	Henry VI

YORK	1461 – 70; 1471 – 83	Edward IV
	1483	Edward V
	1483 – 85	Richard III

TUDOR	1485 – 1509	Henry VII
	1509 – 47	Henry VIII
	1547 – 53	Edward VI
	1553 – 58	Mary I
	1558 – 1603	Elizabeth I
STUART	1603 – 25	James I
	1625 – 49	Charles I
	1649 – 60	Interregnum
	1660 – 85	Charles II
	1685 – 88	James II
	1689 – 94	William III & Mary II
	1694 – 1702	William III
	1702 – 14	Anne
HANOVER	1714 – 27	George I
	1727 – 60	George II
	1760 – 1820	George III
	1820 – 30	George IV
	1830 – 37	William IV
	1837 – 1901	Victoria
SAXE-COBURG-GOTHA /WINDSOR	1901 – 10	Edward VII
	1910 – 36	George V
	1936	Edward VIII
	1936 – 52	George VI
	1952 – present	Elizabeth II

Prime Ministers of the United Kingdom

~

1721 – 1742	Sir Robert Walpole, Whig
1742 – 1743	Earl of Wilmington, Whig
1743 – 1754	Henry Pelham, Whig
1754 – 1756	Duke of Newcastle, Whig
1756 – 1757	Duke of Devonshire, Whig
1757 – 1762	Duke of Newcastle, Whig
1762 – 1763	Earl of Bute, Tory
1763 – 1765	George Grenville, Whig
1765 – 1766	Marquess of Rockingham, Whig
1766 – 1768	Earl of Chatham, Whig
1768 – 1770	Duke of Grafton, Whig
1770 – 1782	Lord North, Tory
1782 (MAR – JUL)	Marquess of Rockingham, Whig
1782 – 1783	Earl of Shelburne, Whig
1783 (APR – DEC)	Duke of Portland, Whig
1783 – 1801	William Pitt, Tory
1801 – 1804	Henry Addington, Tory
1804 – 1806	William Pitt, Tory
1806 – 1807	Lord Grenville, Whig
1807 – 1809	Duke of Portland, Whig
1809 – 1812	Spencer Perceval, Tory
1812 – 1827	Earl of Liverpool, Tory
1827 (APR – AUG)	George Canning, Tory
1827 – 1828	Viscount Goderich, Tory
1828 – 1830	Duke of Wellington, Tory

1830 – 1834	Earl Grey, Whig
1834 (JUL – NOV)	Lord Melbourne, Whig
1834 (NOV – DEC)	Duke of Wellington, Tory
1834 – 1835	Sir Robert Peel, Tory
1835 – 1841	Lord Melbourne, Whig
1841 – 1846	Sir Robert Peel, Tory
1846 – 1852	Lord John Russell, Liberal
1852 (FEB – DEC)	Earl of Derby, Conservative
1852 – 1855	Earl of Aberdeen, Tory
1855 – 1858	Viscount Palmerston, Liberal
1858 – 1859	Earl of Derby, Conservative
1859 – 1865	Viscount Palmerston, Liberal
1865 – 1866	Lord John Russell, Liberal
1866 – 1868	Earl of Derby, Conservative
1868 (FEB – DEC)	Benjamin Disraeli, Conservative
1868 – 1874	William Ewart Gladstone, Liberal
1874 – 1880	Benjamin Disraeli, Conservative
1880 – 1885	William Ewart Gladstone, Liberal
1885 – 1886	Marquess of Salisbury, Conservative
1886 (FEB – JUL)	William Ewart Gladstone, Liberal
1886 – 1892	Marquess of Salisbury, Conservative
1892 – 1894	William Ewart Gladstone, Liberal
1894 – 1895	Earl of Rosebery, Liberal
1895 – 1902	Marquess of Salisbury, Conservative
1902 – 1905	Arthur James Balfour, Conservative
1905 – 1908	Sir Henry Campbell-Bannerman, Liberal
1908 – 1916	H. H. Asquith, Liberal
1916 – 1922	David Lloyd George, Liberal
1922 – 1923	Andrew Bonar Law, Conservative
1923 – 1924	Stanley Baldwin, Conservative
1924 (JAN – NOV)	Ramsay MacDonald, Labour
1924 – 1929	Stanley Baldwin, Conservative
1929 – 1935	Ramsay MacDonald, Labour (from 1931 National Labour)

1935 – 1937	Stanley Baldwin, Conservative
1937 – 1940	Neville Chamberlain, Conservative
1940 – 1945	Winston Churchill, Conservative
1945 – 1951	Clement Attlee, Labour
1951 – 1955	Winston Churchill, Conservative
1955 – 1957	Anthony Eden, Conservative
1957 – 1963	Harold Macmillan, Conservative
1963 – 1964	Sir Alec Douglas-Home, Conservative
1964 – 1970	Harold Wilson, Labour
1970 – 1974	Edward Heath, Conservative
1974 – 1976	Harold Wilson, Labour
1976 – 1979	James Callaghan, Labour
1979 – 1990	Margaret Thatcher, Conservative
1990 – 1997	John Major, Conservative
1997 – 2007	Tony Blair, Labour
2007 – 2010	Gordon Brown, Labour
2010 – present	David Cameron, Conservative

Author's Note

~

IN RESEARCHING A BOOK OF THIS NATURE I inevitably encountered variations in the spelling of names and places, and in the chronology at least of early dates. I have given those most commonly accepted, including those taken from Bede and the Anglo-Saxon chronicles. A short history is chiefly reliant on secondary sources. I have mostly used the *Oxford History of England*, Churchill's monumental *History of the English-Speaking Peoples* and G. M. Trevelyan's social history series. Longman's *Chronicle of Britain* was a useful reference. I also delved into excellent general histories that have appeared recently by David Starkey, Simon Schama, Roy Strong and Rebecca Fraser.

The books I have used on specific periods are too numerous to mention. The one exception is where the story begins, in the continuing debate over the origins of the English people, admirably set out in David Miles's *The Tribes of Britain*. More idiosyncratic aids were John Vincent's *An Intelligent Person's Guide to History*, Jonathan Clark's 'counter-factual' *A World by Itself* and my old stand-by, Barbara Tuchman's *The March of Folly*. The last is a sober corrective to the entire corpus of world history.

I thank Ken Morgan, Tom Jenkins, Jeremy Black, my publisher Daniel Crewe and numerous others for reading and correcting the text in whole or part. Thanks too to Celia Mackay for the adnirable picture research. I also thank Andrew Franklin of Profile Books for the head-spinning idea of attempting to put so much information into so few words in the first place.

List of Illustrations

~

Helmet, early seventh century, found at Sutton Hoo, Suffolk. British Museum, London. Photo: akg-images

King Offa, from *The Golden Book of St Albans*, 1380. Photo: akg-images/British Library

King Ethelred the Unready, from *The Chronicle of Abingdon*, c. 1220. Photo: akg-images/British Library

William the Conqueror riding with his soldiers, from *Liber Legum Antiquorum Regum*, 1154–89. Photo: © British Library Board. All Rights Reserved/The Bridgeman Art Library

Henry I in bed with Princess Nest of Wales, manuscript illumination by French or Flemish school, c. 1315–25. Photo © British Library Board

The Murder of Thomas à Becket at Canterbury Cathedral, early fifteenth century painting by Master Francke. Kunsthalle, Hamburg. Photo: akg-images/ullstein bild

Execution of the Despensers, from *The St Alban's Chronicle*, fifteenth century. Photo: © Lambeth Palace Library, London/The Bridgeman Art Library

Peasants Revolt showing John Ball leading the rebels, from *Froissart's Chronicles*, c. 1460–80. © British Library Board. All Rights Reserved/The Bridgeman Art Library

The Battle of Agincourt, 1415, from *The Chronicle of Enguerrand de Monstrelet*, c. 1390–1453. Photo: The Art Archive/Bibliothèque Nationale, Paris

Coronation of King Henry VI of England as King of France, Paris, 16 December 1431, from *Anciennes Chroniques d'Angleterre,* French School, fifteenth century. Bibliothèque Nationale, Paris. Photo: akg-images

King Richard III, English School, fifteenth century. Photo: Private Collection/The Bridgeman Art Library

Henry VIII, c. 1516, Flemish School. The Fairhaven Collection, Angelsey Abbey. Photo: © NTPL/Derrick E. Witty

Allegorical depiction of England under the Tudor Rose, illumination, English School, 1516. Photo: akg-images/British Library

Cardinal Wolsey, after Hans Holbein the Younger. Photo: © Ipswich Borough Council Museums and Galleries, Suffolk/The Bridgeman Art Library

Sir Thomas More c.1600, after Hans Holbein the Younger. Kenwood House, London Photo: © English Heritage Photo Library/The Bridgeman Art Library

Thomas Cromwell, by Hans Holbein the Younger. Photo: IAM/akg-images

Thomas Cranmer, 1546, by Gerlach Flicke. Photo: National Portrait Gallery, London/The Bridgeman Art Library

Queen Elizabeth I being carried in Procession, c. 1601, attributed to Robert Peake. Photo: Private Collection/The Bridgeman Art Library

James I, by John de Critz the Elder, seventeenth century. Photo: Roy Miles Fine Paintings/The Bridgeman Art Library

Charles I and Henrietta Maria with their two eldest children, Prince Charles and Princess Mary, 1632, by Sir Anthony van Dyck. Photo: The Royal Collection © 2011 Her Majesty Queen Elizabeth II/The Bridgeman Art Library

Unfinished miniature of Oliver Cromwell by Samuel Cooper, c. 1657. Photo: Private Collection/The Bridgeman Art Library

Detail of William and Mary, from the ceiling of the Painted Hall, 1707–14, by Sir James Thornhill. Royal Naval College, Greenwich. Photo: James Brittain/The Bridgeman Art Library

Detail of John Churchill, Duke of
Marlborough at the Battle of Blenheim
1704, from a tapestry at Blenheim Palace,
Woodstock. Photo: © The Print Collector/
Alamy

Horace Walpole talking to the Speaker in
the House of Commons, 1730, by Sir James
Thornhill. Clandon Park, Surrey. Photo: ©
NTPL/John Hammond

William Pitt the Elder, by William Hoare,
nineteenth century. Private Collection. Photo:
© Bonhams, London/The Bridgeman Art
Library

The Death of General Wolfe, *c.* 1771, by
Benjamin West. Private Collection. Photo:
Phillips, Fine Art Auctioneers, New York/The
Bridgeman Art Library

John Wesley preaching in Old Cripplegate Church,
undated, English School. Photo: Private
Collection/The Bridgeman Art Library

Detail from *The Peterloo Massacre, 1819*, by
Richard Carlile and George Cruikshank.
Photo: Manchester Art Gallery/The
Bridgeman Art Library

Leeds from Rope Hill, *c.* 1840 by Alphonse
Douseau. Photo: © Leeds Museums and Art
Galleries/The Bridgeman Art Library

The Royal Family, 1846, by Franz
Winterhalter. Photo: The Royal Collection
© 2011 Her Majesty Queen Elizabeth II/The
Bridgeman Art Library

Keir Hardie addressing suffragettes at a free
speech meeting. Undated photo. Photo: Mary
Evans Picture Library

David Lloyd George and Winston Churchill,
1910. Photo: PA Photos

Mrs. Pankhurst arrested outside Buckingham
Palace, 21 May 1914. Photo: Topfoto

Coal miners demonstrating in Jarrow, 1936.
Photo: Topfoto

Neville Chamberlain holding the Peace
Accord, signed with Adolf Hitler, September
1938. Photo: Private Collection/The
Bridgeman Art Library

Winston Churchill mobbed by crowds after his
victory speech on V. E. Day, May 1945. Photo:
PA Photos

Elizabeth II, 1952. Photo: Mary Evans Picture
Library

Margaret Thatcher when Education Secretary,
1973. Photo: PA Photos

Marriage of Prince Charles and Lady Diana
Spencer, St Paul's Cathedral, July 1981. Photo:
Tim Graham/Getty Images

Floral tributes to Diana, Princess of Wales,
Kensington Palace, September 1997. Photo:
Fiona Hanson/PA Photos

Tony Blair and Gordon Brown, April 1997.
Photo: AFP/Getty Images

David Cameron, left, greets Nick Clegg on the
doorstep of 10 Downing Street, London, May
2010. Photo: PA Photos

Index

~

Index

Index

Index

Index